Contents

Introduction

Free web resource

Unit 9: Work based project is available for you to download from our website at www.heinemann.co.uk/vocational, click on: *Sport studies* in the subject list on the left-hand column on the page. From there click on: *Free resources* in the *Resource centre* box in the right-hand corner of the page.

Where to find Unit 9: Work based project on the Heinemann website (Note: the webpage may look slightly different from this picture.)

Introduction

The Sports Industry is a growing and varied industry which not only provides enjoyment and careers for thousands of people, but also generates millions of pounds in income for a large number of shops, clubs and other organisations. The sports industry provides many sporting activities that fill many people's leisure, or 'free' time. These vary from joining a gym to watching your local football team play in the Premier League; from taking part in a fun run to jet skiing on a local lake. Sport has many important benefits for both individuals and the country as a whole.

How to use this text book

Your BTEC First in Sport course is certificated by Edexcel, one of the country's leading awarding bodies for vocational qualifications. This student book covers the three core units, and four of the most popular specialist units of the qualification. The units covered are:

Unit 1: The Sports industry
Unit 2: Health, safety and injury
Unit 3: Preparation for sport
Unit 4: The body in sport
Unit 5: Sports leadership skills
Unit 6: The sports performer
Unit 11: Practical sport

We have also provided an additional specialist unit, Unit 9: Work based project, which is available for you to download from our website at www.heinemann.co.uk/vocational, click on: *Sport studies* in the subject list on the left-hand column on the page. From there click on: *Free resources* in the *Resource centre* box in the right-hand corner of the page.

Assessment

You will be assessed by a series of assignments. Each assignment is designed so that you can show your understanding of a number of **learning outcomes** for each unit. Each unit may be assessed by one large assignment or a series of smaller ones designed to cover certain grading points (Refer to the *Grading Criteria* for each unit in your course handbook for further guidance on these grading points). You will see that for each unit there is a pass **P**, merit **M**, and distinction **D** grade. Within each grade there are a number of criteria for which evidence is required. To gain a pass, you will need to provide sufficient evidence for each criteria

BTEC FIRST

Sport

Bob Harris, Ramela Mills, Shanon Parker-Bennett

www.heinemann.co.uk

✓ Free online support
✓ Useful weblinks
✓ 24 hour online ordering

01865 888058

Inspiring generations

Heinemann Educational Publishers
Halley Court, Jordan Hill, Oxford OX2 8EJ
Part of Harcourt Education

Heinemann is the registered trademark of
Harcourt Education Limited

First published 2004

08 07 06 05
10 9 8 7 6 5 4 3

British Library Cataloguing in Publication Data is available
from the British Library on request.

10-digit ISBN 0 435454 60 9
13-digit ISBN 978 0 435454 60 9

Edited by Frances Ridley
Designed by Artistix
Typeset by Tech-Set Ltd., Gateshead, Tyne & Wear
Original illustrations © Harcourt Education Limited, 2004
Printed in the UK by Scotprint

Acknowledgements
I would like to thank the following people and organisations for their help and advice in
helping me to contribute to this book:
- Staff at Bourne Leisure Centre and The Deepings Leisure Centre
- Matt Gill and Paul Stevenette of Peterborough City Council
- Sam Youngs of Huntingdon Swimming Club
- My children Matthew and Stephanie Harris
- My wife Sheila for her encouragement and help in times of great stress.   *Bob Harris*

No matter how long and hard it gets Kerry, Leilah and Owen always give their time to
support me, in work, sport and life. As I have developed through the last few years, so has my
other son, Chris: who has now found the route to his happiness – cooking. Always thankful
for the times that we have, good and bad – they make us strong. I would also like to thank
Steph Oatridge as a colleague, and friend, who supported me with words and plenty of fluid.
                                                                Ramela Mills

The inspiration and joy in my life – my son Joshua. My family for their continued love, support
and encouragement. Adi Whatling, Wendy Weddell and Barbara Treverton – sometimes in life
you find special friends who change your life by being a part of it. Thank you.
                                                        Shanon Parker-Bennett

The authors and publishers would like to thank the following individuals and organisations
for permission to reproduce photos in the book and the web unit (Unit 9):

Alamy pages 214 and 221; Collections page 18; Corbis pages 4, 12, 33, 54, 67, 103, 104, 120,
173, 195, 200, 230, 260, 289, 290, 307, 308 (bottom) and 34 (web unit); EmPics pages 26, 27,
70, 143, 172, 192, 197, 198, 208, 234 and 16 (web unit); Getty Images/Photodisc pages 2, 17,
44, 63, 236, 237, 273, 279 and 308 (top three); Harcourt Education/Gareth Boden page 13
(web unit); Harcourt Index pages 20 and 126; Photodisc pages 53 and 97; and Science Photo
Library pages 79, 81 and 93.

Every effort has been made to contact copyright holders of material reproduced in this book.
Any omissions will be rectified in subsequent printings if notice is given to the publishers.

in the pass grade. To gain a merit, you will need to gain not only all the pass criteria but the merit criteria as well. For a distinction grade, you will need to provide evidence for all the pass, merit and distinction criteria.

How will this book help you?

Through the text there are a number of features that are designed to encourage you to reflect on the issues raised, relate the theory to your practice and assist you to understand the relevant concepts and theories. These features are:

Think about it	questions designed to encourage refection or discussion with others
Let's do it	activities that encourage you to go out and do some research in the 'real' world of sport
Key points	a list summarising the key topics covered in that section
Case studies	examples of real scenarios to help explain a concept or help to link the theory with real practice
Assessment activities	activities designed to support achievement in relation to learning outcomes
In summary	feature summarising what you have just learnt in the unit

Many of these features will help you to compile the evidence needed for your assessments. In addition, you should try to carry out the following on a regular basis:

- watch the television and listen to the radio for items and articles on the sports industry
- read both the local and national papers
- keep a scrap book of important news stories on a range of issues connected with sport

All of this will keep you up to date with what is happening in the world of sport. This is very important as some of the grading criteria require you to complete tasks independently – this is with little or no help from your tutor or lecturer. The more aware you are of what is going on, the easier this will be for you!

What else do you need to do?

Always make sure you complete the pass criteria for each unit to ensure you succeed. Many assessment points follow on through pass, merit and distinction grades. Pass criteria generally ask you to list, define or describe. For merit, you will need to compare (what is the same and what is different?) or explain (give reasons for something). For a distinction, you will have to analyse (examine in detail the reasons for or the organisation of ...).

Finally **Good Luck!** The Sports industry is an exciting and dynamic one with a wide range of subjects and areas for you to study. We hope this student book helps you to reach great success in your course.

Bob Harris, Ramela Mills and Shanon Parker-Bennett

The sports industry

Introduction

In this chapter, you will look at the nature, organisation and funding of the sports industry. You will learn how big the sports industry is and how important it is to all of us, and to the country as a whole! You will also understand the various issues that currently affect sport and the importance of the media industry to sport in general.

How you will be assessed

This unit will be assessed by an I.V.A. (Integrated Vocational Assignment). This will be set by the awarding body of this qualification, Edexcel, marked by your tutor and then re-marked by an external moderator. You will then be awarded a number of points, depending on the grade you achieve. The points you are given for this unit are doubled, so it is very important that you make sure you cover all the content which follows and apply it to your I.V.A.

All the learning outcomes (see below) will be assessed by successfully completing the I.V.A. You will be given an assignment which will place you in a 'job related' situation and asked to complete a number of related tasks. By completing these, you will show that you understand and are aware of the four learning outcomes. Marks will be awarded for each task and a total mark for the I.V.A. will be calculated. This total mark will then give you a grade for this unit.

This section of the book provides a number of assessment activities that are designed to prepare you for your I.V.A. and which ask you to carry out tasks similar to the ones that you will need to complete in the I.V.A. unit later in the year.

After completing this unit you should be able to achieve the following learning outcomes:

1. Investigate the nature of **sport, sports participation and sports development** – why people play sport and why they do not; what is meant by sport; what is done to try to encourage as many people as possible to play, watch, coach and so on.

2. Examine the **organisation of sport** – who provides sports activities, events and equipment; how different organisations are related and work together.

3. Explore different **sources of funding** for a range of different sports, from premiership football clubs to your own local sports club.

4. Investigate **key issues and the influence of the media** on sport – for example, performance enhancing drugs, the effects of satellite television on football and racism in sport.

The Sports Industry covers a huge variety of sporting activities both professional and leisure

Sport, sports participation and sports development

Sport

The leisure industry

The sports industry is part of the overall leisure industry, which provides a wide range of products and services. Sport and other recreation activities employ 412,000 people in the UK. Can you define the word 'leisure'?

The Oxford Concise English Dictionary defines leisure as, 'Time spent in or free for relaxation or enjoyment'. How did your definition compare with this? Were there any key points that appeared?

Let's do it!

Complete the following table with some examples of leisure activities:

Active leisure activities	Passive lesiure activites
Playing golf	Reading a book

Sport and physical recreation

The Oxford Concise English Dictionary defines sport as, 'An activity involving physical exertion and skill in which an individual or team competes against another or others for entertainment'.

It is generally accepted that to be called a sport, an activity must:

- be competitive
- have rules and regulations
- require skill and fitness if the participant is to be successful.

The sports industry

The sports industry is one of the most important sectors of the leisure industry and provides a wide range of products and services including:

- sports to take part in
- sports to watch
- activities to maintain health
- sports clothing and merchandise
- sports related gambling.

It also includes the sports retail industry (for example, sports shops) and the rapidly emerging extreme sports industry. The sports industry employs a large number of people. In the year 2000 some 400,000 people were employed by the sports industry.

Think about it

In small groups, list as many types of jobs in sport as you can. Discuss your lists as a class.

Amateur and professional sport

There are many reasons for participating in sport.

The pleasure of playing (in a team or against one other person)

The opportunity to compete

Reasons for participation in sport

The satisfaction of achievement (a personal best, or the completion of a marathon, for example)

The excitement of challenge (against the clock or the elements, for example)

The thrill of winning

Think about it

In small groups, discuss the following questions:
- what is it about sport that you enjoy?
- what types of sport do you like/dislike?
- how does a player become a professional? (Do they always start as an amateur, for example?)

Sport can be played by amateurs or by professionals. Amateurs play sport for their own enjoyment and in their own free time, and are not paid for doing so. Professionals are paid to play, or have the opportunity to win money from tournaments.

Professionals can earn large sums of money. The winner of the men's singles tennis title at Wimbledon in 2003, Mark Federer of Switzerland, earned £575,000, and Michael Schumacher's contract with Ferrari is reported to be worth £1,000,000 per race! Not all professional sportsmen and women earn such huge amounts of money. A typical professional footballer in division two or three, in comparison, may earn between £500 and £600 a week.

Different types of sport

The different types of sport can be categorised as:
- **target** games such as golf and archery
- **team** games like football and netball
- **individual** sports like mountaineering and running
- **net** games such as tennis and badminton.
- **motor** sports such as Formula One and motorcycling
- **outdoor** sports such as canoeing and skiing.

Let's do it!

Can you think of any other ways of classifying sport? Draw up a table and choose ten sports. How can you define them?

Taking part in and watching sport

For some, playing sport is part of their daily lives. Professional sports people occupy this category, as well as many keen amateur players. For others, watching other people playing is their way of becoming involved in sport. Spectator sport forms a big part of the sports industry. Manchester United had an average crowd attendance at their home games for the season 2002–2003 of over 67,000. Millions more people around the world watch sporting events live on television.

The development of sports venues, leisure centres and health clubs

Why has sport become so popular and important? In the early 1960s there were very few 'sports centres'; in 1995 there were 450,000 sports centres with some 355 million admissions. To understand this growth you need to look at the benefits of sport to us as individuals and to the country as a whole. Sport is compulsory at school, so there must be some value to it!

It is generally accepted that sport is good for:

- health – it provides exercise which keeps us fit and helps us to live healthy lives
- society – it brings people together in a common cause and reduces crime and anti-social behaviour.
- the country – it earns the country a great deal of money through taxes and sports tourism, for example, Euro '96 generated £118 million from 250,000 foreign visitors. The Millennium Stadium in Wales generated, in one year, £18.5 million from just seven high profile football matches, including the F.A. Cup final and the divisional play offs.
- employment – sport provides jobs and careers. There are a wide range of courses offered by schools, colleges and universities, and qualifications that can be gained.
- character building – sport teaches us values such as teamwork and playing by the rules. These lessons are important throughout our lives.

 Key points

Sport is a major contributor to the UK economy and accounts for around 2% of G.D.P.
- The Government receives four times more money from sport through taxes than it returns through central and local government grants.
- Consumer spending on sport stood at £15.2 billion in 2000 (around 3% of G.D.P.), an increase of 70% since 1990, with 64% being spent on sports services. Spending fell by 5% in 2001 as a result of foot and mouth disease. This fall particularly affected sports related gambling, sports tourism and sports clothing, but is predicted to grow by 10% in 2002 (Sheffield Hallam University – Sport Market Forecast).
- Approximately £1.6 billion was bet on greyhound racing in 2000 – nearly 4% of the UK gambling market.
- £5bn was spent on horse betting in the UK in 2001.
- National Lottery sales are currently £4.8 billion.

When the Sports Council was formed in 1972, its aims were to encourage more people to *play* sport and more *places* to be built to play sport in. Its goal was to raise the *performance* of our best sportsmen and women so that they won more medals and championships on the world stage. In addition, in the last few years people have become much more aware of their health and fitness. As a result, there has been a huge increase in the number of fitness centres and health clubs around the country. Sales of fitness equipment and fitness videos for the home have expanded and there are huge numbers of fun runs and similar events organised every week to help and encourage people to get fit.

 Key points

There are:
- 2328 public fitness facilities
- 1943 private health clubs
- 5,839,565 public and private health and fitness members in total
- 933 clubs under development or in planning in the private sector and 641 sites in the public sector
- 3621 public sports centres.

Nobody really knows how many football or cricket pitches there are!

Sports clothing

Sport now includes much more than just 'playing or watching'. Many people like to wear sports clothing casually because it is fashionable. Sports shops sell not only 'performance' equipment that is designed to help a person play better but also 'leisure' wear, or everyday clothing.

Let's do it!

How many of the people in your class are wearing sports related clothing? Make up a table. Count how many people are wearing a particular brand or make, like Adidas or Nike. Count how many are wearing a particular 'sports' item, such as a baseball cap or sweatshirt. Ask them *why* they are wearing these items.

Extreme sports

Some people take part in particular sports and activities because they want to adopt a particular image. Others participate in a sport because it has a *cathartic* effect on them. In recent years, extreme sports, such as snow boarding, mountain biking, paragliding and so on, have become more and more popular. These sports:

- help people forget the strains and stresses of their normal life
- provide the 'adrenalin buzz' which for many is missing in today's society
- allow people to 'get back to nature' and 'feel alive'.

Assessment activity 1: Sporting activities

P In pairs, decide what the word sport means by answering the following questions:
- How would you define the term 'sport'?
- What different ways can you classify sport?
- What do you think are the factors that make an activity a sport?
- What must exist for an activity to be called a sport?

M Make a list of 10 different types of sporting activities that are available locally and nationally, and why you think they are different.

D In small groups look at the range of sporting activities you have listed and discuss if you think that any need improvements or changes, and why.

You can record your findings in writing or video your group discussion.

Participation

Getting people involved

For some people, playing sport is part of their daily life either because they are professional sportsmen or women, or because they have developed a love of sport at an early age and have retained this throughout their lives.

One of the most important factors in encouraging people to participate in sport is the range of facilities provided. Nearly every town and city has sporting facilities provided by a number of different organisations, offering opportunities to play and to watch sport both indoors and outdoors.

It is helpful to be able to place people into different groups in order to help as many as possible to participate in sport. This is so that you can identify *what* these people want to do, *why* they might want to do it and the *typical* reasons why they cannot do it at present.

These groups might include:
- teenagers
- adults

- the elderly
- families
- people from different cultural groups, such as Muslims or travellers
- the unemployed.

Think about it

Can you think of any more different groups that people could fall into?

Let's do it!

Ask your tutor to arrange a talk with a local sporting celebrity. Find out why they started playing sport, why they play sport now, and why it is important to them. If she or he is a professional sportsperson, how and why did he or she move from being an amateur to a professional?

Geographical factors

Case study: Matthew

Matthew is 15 and attends the local grammar school in the town of Bourne, in Lincolnshire. He is preparing for G.C.S.E. exams next year. Bourne has fairly good sports facilities. The school has a sports hall and playing fields and runs clubs at lunchtimes and after school. Teams from the school play matches against other local schools. In the town, there is a large leisure centre, with a leisure pool, sports hall and fitness club. The town also has a tennis club, a semi-professional football team and an outdoor swimming pool, which opens in the summer months from May to September. There are clubs for netball and rugby, keep fit classes and playing fields with football goals where people can go and have a 'kick about'. The nearest big city is Peterborough, 15 miles away. Bus services are available every 30 minutes most days.

Now answer the following questions:

1. What factors in the case study will have a **positive** effect on Matthew's participation in sport?
2. What factors do you think will have a **negative** effect?

All of these factors will affect participation:

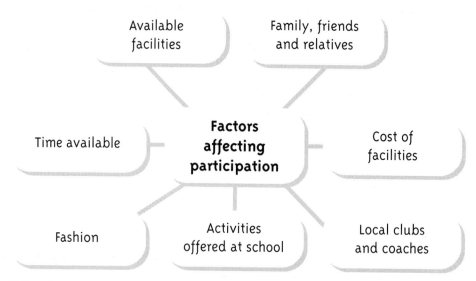

Other factors, such as race, culture and disability will also affect participation.

Where you live has an important part to play in the type of sport you might choose. It goes without saying that the UK does not produce very many top skiers, because we do not get much snow! In Switzerland and Austria, the winters are much colder, with plenty of snow on the mountains. Similarly, it would be difficult for Matthew, in the case study on page 9, to take up rock climbing, since there are no mountains in Lincolnshire!

Sports development

Providing services at a local and national level

In recent years, sports development has emerged as a means of helping to encourage more participation and provision of sport. The drive to increase participation generally comes from the Government. They regard sport as important because:

- it keeps people healthy – this means that people need to see the doctor less and so the demand on the National Health Service is reduced
- the nation looks good when it does well in a particular sport or competition, for example, the success of the England Rugby Union team in winning the World Cup in 2003
- it helps to reduce anti-social behaviour – if people have more opportunity to take part in sport, they are less likely to spend their spare time behaving in an anti-social manner, for example becoming involved in vandalism or other forms of crime.

Much of the work is carried out by:

- Regional Sport England Offices – look up the details of yours!
- the Sports Development team of your local authority
- sports development officers employed by a Governing Body of a sport

Much of the work is carried out *in partnership* – this is where two or more organisations get together and work towards one common goal. For instance, Sport England and a local authority may share the salary of a sports development officer to undertake a particular role.

Let's do it!

1. Contact your local authority leisure department and find out *how* and *why* it tries to increase sports participation.
2. Visit the Sport England website at www.heinemann.co.uk/hotlinks and learn about Active Sport, Active Schools and Active Communities.
3. Visit the website of a sport of your choice. What does the Governing Body do to increase the numbers of people playing that sport?

Target groups

There are some groups of people who, for various reasons, do not or *cannot*, take part in sport. These, in the past, have included:

- disabled people
- ethnic minorities
- mothers of young children
- the elderly
- females aged 16–25.

Other reasons might include:

- racism – people being discriminated against because of the colour of their skin

WHITE MEN STILL DOMINATE FOOTBALL

Newspapers often run stories that expose racism in sport

- poor access to facilities – the person may not have access to a car, or public transport may be infrequent or non existent.
- no facilities allowing babies and toddlers to be left in safety (if a parent has nowhere safe to leave a baby or toddler, then she or he will be unable to take part in sport themselves)
- the attitude of society – for example, society may not like the idea of women being sweaty or aggressive!

How does this image make you feel?

activities offered at the wrong time, in the wrong place or at the wrong price – because of any or all of these reasons, they may not interest the particular person at whom they are aimed.

Removing barriers

One aspect of sports development is removing barriers that prevent people taking part in sport. For example, a local council may employ a disability sports officer to develop and organise sport for those people with some form of disability, such as cerebral palsy or a sensory disability.

Case study: Matt Gill

Matt Gill is employed as a disability sports officer by the Peterborough City Council's Leisure Department. His role is to improve sporting opportunities for disabled people. His salary is funded by the Children's Fund, which obtains its funding from the National Lottery. Matt's role involves him finding out what disabled people would like to do and comparing this with what is currently available. He can then suggest what opportunities could be provided. The post Matt fills lasts for three years. At the end of this time, the results of Matt's work will be reviewed to decide if the post should remain. The council will also have to decide if they wish to fund Matt's salary themselves.

Now answer the following questions:
1. What examples are there of partnership working (two or more organisations working together towards the same aim or objective)?
2. Why does Matt concentrate on only one particular group of people?
3. Why do you think Matt's job is important to Peterborough City Council?

Another barrier is cost. Some people may not be able to afford the cost of using local facilities. Many local authorities make provision for people on low incomes by reducing the charges made at certain times.

Religion or culture could also be a barrier. Muslim women who might be interested in swimming cannot be seen by men in a swimming costume. A local pool could make provision by covering all windows to prevent other people looking in, and using only female lifeguards. There are many other ways that barriers can be removed and overcome.

Let's do it!

Contact a local leisure facility and find out how they make provision for different groups within the community. Bring the information you gather back to your group to discuss.

Influences on services and their delivery

Many factors can affect what is offered to local people and how it is delivered to customers. Some areas of the UK suffer from high social deprivation. This might mean, for example, that facilities are old and run down, or that unemployment is high amongst the local population. These areas may be eligible to receive a wide variety of funds from the Government and from Europe to assist in regeneration.

Case study: Sheffield

Sheffield was once a city world famous for steel production. A great many people were employed in the steel industry, producing a material which was sold around the world. For a variety of reasons, the steel industry collapsed and many people lost their jobs. This had serious effects on other local businesses, since those people who worked in steel now had no jobs and little money. Sport has been used as a means of bringing life back to the city of Sheffield. It is now world famous for a number of facilities including:

- Ponds Forge International Swimming Centre – this was built for the World Student Games in 1991, and now hosts many national and international competitions, not only in swimming but also in bowls and basketball.
- the new National Ice Arena
- Don Valley International Stadium – this hosts Grand Prix athletics meetings and rock concerts
- the Crucible Theatre – this is the home of the Embassy World Snooker Championship.

Now answer the following questions:
1. In what ways has sport helped the people of Sheffield?
2. How has building the large number of international standard sports facilities regenerated the area? (think about hotels, jobs etc.)
3. How will other local businesses be affected?

Other influences on sports provision

Each local authority is made up of local councillors who are elected by local people. The councillors will have their own ideas about what is important to a local area. This may or may not include sport and could affect what is provided and how.

The area in which you live is a factor. Some parts of the UK are very rural or very remote, for example, and people may live a long distance from a sports club or facility. Providers may need to go to the people instead, offering activities which may take place in village halls or community centres.

Playing, watching, coaching and officiating are all ways of encouraging people to participate in sport. Local clubs depend on volunteers who take on positions such as Manager, Treasurer or Chairperson. These people give up their time for free but might need help and guidance about what to do, and how to do it. Sport development officers might put on courses to help improve the way people run clubs or coach teams.

The sports continuum

The work of sports development is based around the 'sports continuum'. This is a model which shows the different levels at which people can participate in sport. The arrows on the diagram show how a person might progress through the various levels.

Elite

Performance

Foundation

Participation

Foundation level – learning the basic skills needed for sport, such as catching, throwing, passing and so on. This is generally covered in schools through timetabled physical education lessons.

Participation – playing a sport for enjoyment and fun, at a local club or leisure centre. Results and performance are not critical; people participate at this level to have fun, meet friends and keep fit.

Performance level – playing for a club in leagues and competitions. Players at this level train hard to improve their skills and abilities. This level includes not only local but regional competition. A player may play in a semi-professional manner and represent a district or region.

Elite level – playing at a national or international level. Players at this level are engaged full time in their sport. They may be paid for this and will receive support from a number of different organisations, sponsors and so on, to help them develop. Top sports men and women, like David Beckham and Jonny Wilkinson, are at this level.

Assessment activity 2: Participation

P What sports do *you* play and why do you play them?

M Think about all the sporting activities you do not take part in. Why don't you play these sports? List some of these sports in the table below and outline the factors that have affected your participation:

Sport	Factor	How did it affect your participation?
1		
2		
3		
4		

D Work in groups. Look at each of the categories in the table below. Try to identify why these particular groups of people may be unable to take part in sport. What could be done to help them?

Group	Reasons why they do not play sport	Suggestions for improvements or changes
Disabled people		
Ethnic minorities		
Mothers of young children		
The elderly		
Young women 16–25 years		

The organisation of sport

Sport has important benefits for both individuals and the country as a whole. The sports industry is important to the many people who work in it and to those people who use the products and services it offers. This section will look at how the industry is organised and the strengths and weaknesses of its various providers.

There are three main providers of sport in this country:

- the **public sector** – organisations such as the Government in Westminster, and local authorities who provide services to the people in their area.
- the **private sector** – organisations that are involved aim to make a profit for themselves or other people. These include private clubs providing facilities and services for the benefit of members
- the **voluntary sector** – generally, local people and organisations that provide activities for the benefit of local people, and to meet a local need. Often, these people have a common interest or skill, or feel that the activity they do is worthwhile and important. Volunteers give up their time and energy for free.

In addition, there are other organisations, both local and national, who influence and support the work of these three main providers, such as the Central Council for Physical Recreation (C.C.P.R.).

The public sector

This sector provides services to local people. These services include libraries, parks, playgrounds, sports pitches, leisure centres and swimming pools. The public sector operates at different levels. The UK Government is based in Westminster in London. Decisions of national and international significance are made here. Parish councils, on the other hand, make decisions which affect a small local village or area.

The different levels at which the public sector operates are:
- parish councils
- town councils
- district councils
- city councils
- large unitary authorities.

Facilities provided by local authorities are *for* local people. In part, they are also *paid for* by local people, through the community charge or business rates levied on each house and business in an area. In addition, a local facility will make charges for the use of its facilities and services. The charge is generally not very high, so as to encourage people to take part. Facilities may not be of the highest standards but will be more than adequate for local needs. Local authority facilities and services are discretionary. This means that a local authority does not have to provide them. There is nothing to stop your local authority closing a swimming pool or sports hall if there is a shortage of money.

Let's do it!

Find out who your local authority is and make a list of the sports facilities it provides. Obtain details of the prices it charges.

Many local facilities owned by local authorities are managed by other organisations. This is part of 'Best Value', a scheme designed to ensure that local people are getting value for money and the best provision possible from the services provided by their local council.

The public sector can provide a range of other services in relation to sport. These include:

- hiring pitches, courts and other facilities for playing sport
- providing grants and other sources of finance to local clubs and associations
- providing other sources of help, including assistance with lottery applications, raising awareness and acting as a link between national agencies, such as Sport England, and local clubs, schools and so on.

The public sector can hire courts for playing sports

Case study: Ponds Forge International Swimming Centre

Ponds Forge International Swimming Centre is owned by Sheffield International Venues Ltd. It is an internationally renowned swimming facility comprising a 50 m long by 25 m wide swimming pool, a 5.8 m square diving pool, and a separate leisure pool. The centre was built for the 1991 World Student Games, which were held in Sheffield. It has a host of special features including a movable floor to the main pool, seating for 2500 spectators, plus fitness studios, a large multi-purpose sports hall, a night club and conference facilities. The facility is used by elite performers as well as the people of Sheffield. It is open seven days a week and is run by Sheffield International Venues. You can visit their website at www.heinemann.co.uk/hotlinks to find out more. Sheffield International Venues is a private company and this has a number of benefits:

- The private sector managing agent has money to invest in new facilities – often, local authorities have more important priorities!
- The private sector often has a better understanding of business.
- Sheffield City Council – part of the public sector – does not have to provide finances for the pool or appoint staff to operate it. It can concentrate staff and resources on other, more pressing, issues.
- Sheffield City Council have a major input into the range and nature of the provision made, the pricing policy in operation and the standard of service provided. Although it does not actually manage the centre, it still has a large say in what is provided and how.
- By working in this way, Sheffield City Council benefits from a facility which helps meet their overall aims and objectives for much less money than if they ran the facility themselves.

Now answer the following questions:
1. How do you think the people of Sheffield have benefitted from the swimming centre?
2. Why do you think the private sector understands the sport business better?
3. What stops Sheffield International Venues only offering activities that make a profit?

The private sector

This sector is concerned with making a profit from the activities and services it provides. This profit is then either reinvested in the business, or is distributed to people and organisations who have invested money in the business. Some of these businesses sell shares on the stock exchange. This allows anybody, including you, to invest money in that company. If you look in the newspapers you will be able to see how well your shares are doing. The value of these shares may go up or down: if they go up, shareholders make money, if they go down, they lose money.

Private sector businesses are involved in a wide range of activities, including sports equipment and clothing, gambling, sports you pay to watch, like horse racing, and sports that you pay to take part in, like golf.

Let's do it!

Imagine you have £5000 to invest in companies involved in the sports industry. Work in groups. Look at newspapers like the *Times*, *Guardian* or *Daily Telegraph* for information on shares. Decide how your group is to spend the £5000. You could buy shares in a chain of fitness clubs, a football team or a sportswear manufacturer, for example.

Track the value of your shares for four weeks. Calculate the value of your shares at the end of this period.
1. Have you made or lost money?
2. What factors might explain the performance of the businesses you invested in?

Private sector organisations are accountable to their shareholders. These people and organisations have invested in the business and they have a large say in how the business should be run. For instance, if a Premier League football club is losing money, perhaps through failing to qualify for Europe or because of poor results, it may have to sell its star player.

Private sector organisations must be able to respond quickly to changes in demand from customers. For example, fashions in sports clothing change quickly. If a sports clothing company is not flexible enough to respond, it could lose a lot of money.

Let's do it!

Visit your local high street or look through the yellow pages. List all the shops and businesses which are related to sport. Can you organise them into groups?

Private clubs

Another type of private organisation are private clubs. These are often provided by companies for the benefit of their staff, to improve motivation and working conditions. Other private clubs are set up to meet a particular need. Such clubs include golf clubs, racket clubs or health and fitness facilities.

Many health clubs are exclusive

Facilities are often of a very high standard but membership is usually expensive. As a result, the club may only be available to those with sufficient personal wealth. Many people feel the exclusive nature of these organisations is worth the high price. Like all sports related organisations, private clubs and businesses are vulnerable to changes in the income of their customers. This is because:

- people spend their 'disposable' income on sport, in other words, the money left over after all the bills and essentials have been paid for – if the cost of the weekly shopping or the mortgage on your house goes up, you have less to spend on luxuries like sport
- fashion can affect the popularity of a club – after Christmas and before the summer holiday, people may join a fitness club to lose weight and tone up but very often they lose interest and leave soon after. Gyms and health clubs have to work hard to attract and then keep their members, so that the membership fees keep coming in!

The voluntary sector

The voluntary sector exists to meet local needs for little or no cost. These clubs are set up by people with a common interest, like a local netball team, or because a person feels that the activity is important and worthwhile. Baden Powell, for example, formed the Scout movement because he believed that gaining experience of the outdoors was invaluable to young people.

Voluntary clubs often exist on members' match fees and membership subscriptions. They are often involved in fund raising activities to keep the club going. Voluntary clubs are very important to sport in the UK. Many of our top sports men and women started out as members of local clubs and teams.

Let's do it!

Investigate local clubs and associations in your area.
1. How many are there?
2. Who do they provide for?
3. How many members do they have?

Remember to bring your findings back to your group.

The voluntary sector provides opportunities for people to play a sport they like, and also provides the volunteers that are needed for coaching, refereeing, organising and running local clubs and sports associations. It is almost impossible to calculate the value and amount of time given up by volunteers. People who cannot afford to join a private club to play tennis or squash might join a local club run by volunteers. This promotes social inclusion, ensuring all members of society have access to sporting opportunities.

The relationship between the three sectors

If you consider the three areas we have discussed, you should see that they are often related:

Public sector — local council hires out facility for club to meet in

Private sector — local sports shop sells kit and equipment to players

Voluntary sports club — people join to play, provides coaches and referees, etc.

Other agencies

There are other organisations that are involved either directly, or indirectly, in sport. Some of these are national organisations, like Sport U.K. or The British Olympic Association. Others are regional, for example a local county Football Association or Netball Association. Others are local, for example a local sports group or committee. Some are international, for example F.I.F.A., the governing body for world football.

Some organisations are sport specific. This means they are only concerned only with a particular sport. Some are involved with a specific competition, such as the Olympics. Some are concerned with sport in general. Each, however, has a specific role or aim within sport. This could be to increase participation, to get more people playing a particular sport, or to select and organise a team for a particular event.

Let's do it!

In pairs, use the Internet and your school or college library to complete the table below. Can you think of any other organisations that have a particular role to play in the organisation of sport?

Organisation	International?	National?	Regional?	Local?	What sport? (where relevant)	What does it do? (Give an example)
U.E.F.A.						
L.T.A.						
Lincolnshire F.A.						
Sport England						
C.C.P.R.						
British Sports Trust						
Sprito						
F.I.N.A.						
British Athletics						
A.E.N.A.						
R.L.S.S.						

Assessment activity 3: Private, public and voluntary sectors

P Gather together information on sports provision made by the public, private and voluntary sectors in your area.

M In small groups look at the information you have collected and compare the provision made by the three sectors.

- Ask yourselves how the provision is the same, and how it is different. For example, all three sectors might provide fitness clubs but the private sector might provide better quality facilities at a higher price.
- Now look at the range and number of facilities. Are there areas in which there is too much or too little provision? For instance, there may be a large number of golf clubs but very few indoor tennis courts.
- Present your information as a chart or display, to illustrate your group's findings.

D Think about provision in the future – what is required, and how could it be provided? For instance, if you wanted to encourage more people to swim, you would need to provide more pools and more swimming teachers. Which organisations could provide these facilities?

Sources of funding

Sport costs money! Whether you are buying a replica shirt, watching your favourite team or going for a relaxing swim, you will have to part with some cash! Where do organisations and businesses involved in the sports industry get the money they need? There are very many sources of funding available, depending on whether you are an individual sports person, a local club or association, or a large business with a new product or service to offer. This section will first consider the main available sources of funding and then look at how they apply to the main providers of sport.

Sponsorship

Sponsorship means that a business or other organisation provides money or goods in return for linking the name of the business or a particular product with an individual, team, sport or competition. Sponsorship is a very important source of funding for many sports teams and competitions. Without it, many sports would find it difficult to continue in their present form, and many competitions would struggle to continue at all. Sponsorship is becoming increasingly popular in certain sports and has a number of benefits.

Let's do it!

Complete the table below:

Sponsor	Sport	Competition	Individual
			David Beckham
Embassy Cigarettes			
		The Premiership	
	Test match cricket		
	England rugby team		
		The F.A. Cup	
	Ferrari Formula One Team		
O2 Mobile			
Telephone Network			
		The London Marathon	
Vodafone			

A good example of the link between sport and sponsorship is provided by football. In the 1970s, football was declining in popularity. The game was not as attractive to sponsors as it had once been, because its image was linked with hooliganism. Steps were taken to successfully reduce the problem of hooliganism. This, together with increased media coverage of football through radio, newspapers and terrestrial and satellite television, encouraged sponsors to invest in football once again.

Now, spectatorship and viewing figures are increasing. Potential sponsors know that many millions of people worldwide are likely to see brand names on players' shirts, for example, or Michael Schumacher's Ferrari. Current sponsorship deals are huge. The latest Sky deal to show Premiership football is worth £1 billion!

As certain sports have increased in popularity over recent years, they have attracted an increased level of sponsorship. Other sports find it difficult to attract sponsors. The media plays a key role here. Many sports, like squash for example, are not well suited to television because of the nature of the game. Others, like archery or lacrosse, are simply not very popular with the public and are rarely seen on television or in the newspapers.

Other sources of funding

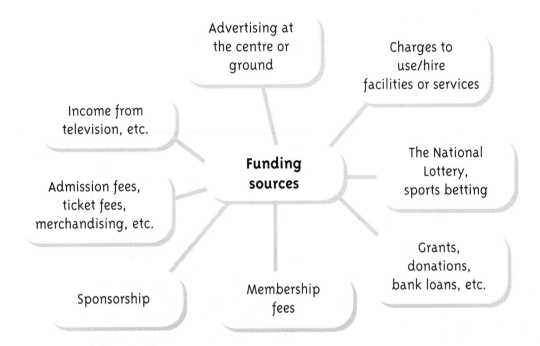

The above diagram shows the main sources of funding for sport. Each of the main providers of sport uses a different combination of these sources of income.

The public sector

Local councils or authorities have a number of sources of funding available to them, which they use to provide services and facilities for local people:

- The council tax – this is the main source of funding and refers to charges made to all local residents. The amount is based on a number of factors, including the value of the house in which you live, whether you are in work or full time education, and your age.
- Money from central government.
- Money from charges made to use local authority facilities like sports halls, swimming pools and car parks, and from selling merchandise such as squash balls or swimming goggles.
- Money borrowed from banks, for example to build new facilities.

Local authorities may also apply to the National Lottery for funds.

The private sector

National and local businesses and clubs have a number of sources of income available.

A business can raise money by selling shares on the stock exchange. This is where people and organisations, who want to make money, buy shares in other businesses in the hope and belief that the business will be successful. This can be quite risky because if the business doesn't do well the investor will lose money. A number of Premiership football clubs, such as Manchester United, Leeds United and Tottenham Hotspur, sell shares on the stock exchange.

The private sector also generates money through fees and charges made for its products and services. A replica football strip costs nearly £40, but it does not cost this much to produce; the price includes a profit for the seller. Health and fitness clubs raise money through membership fees.

Case study: Manchester United

Manchester United is the most successful Premiership football team. They have won the Premiership a record seven times, as well as winning countless other trophies. Last season, their average home attendance was over 67,000. In 2001, Manchester United generated a profit, before tax, of £21,778,000.

All Premiership sides earn money in this way, to a greater or lesser degree. Choose a Premiership football side.

Let's do it!

Write to the club chairman to ask for a copy of the annual report. In small groups, examine the information in the report. Identify the sources of income from the club, for instance, money from television, sponsorship agreements and so on.

For some clubs, the amounts of money involved are huge! Other sports are not as fortunate as football. Lack of popularity means they find it more difficult to generate income and attract sponsorship.

Let's do it!

1. Choose a sport which is less well known than football. Obtain an annual report like you did in the previous exercise, and compare the sources and amounts of funding generated.
2. What problems might this cause the sport receiving fewer funds?

The voluntary sector

This sector can find it very difficult to generate funds. Since the organisations are usually quite small, there are limits to the amounts of money they can raise. There are a variety of sources of income that voluntary sport organisations can access.

The National Lottery – this was launched in 1994 and has regular draws twice a week, on Saturday and Wednesday. People buy lottery tickets hoping to win a large cash prize for themselves and friends and family. A certain percentage of the cost of each ticket bought goes to good causes identified by the Government. It has so far contributed £1.6 billion towards the arts, heritage and sport. Organisations involved with sport can make an application to the lottery for funding to help improve facilities such as changing rooms and pitches. One difficulty is that an organisation must raise the same amount of money itself; the lottery will only 'match fund'. This can be a problem for small local organisations, such as a local netball club

Fund raising – this is often the most popular way for voluntary sports clubs to raise funds. Activities may include raffles, car boot sales, sponsored events, or entertainment such as a disco. A proposed development at the club may require a number of events and activities to raise the required sum of money.

Local authority grants – the local council may give a local club or association a sum of money to help with their activities, or they may give help in other ways, such as reduced costs for using facilities owned by the council. The local council will also help with lottery applications in some cases.

Sponsorship – another popular way for local clubs to raise money is to approach a local business for help. In this situation, the club would receive money or goods in return for promoting the business by, for instance, wearing the name of the business on their team strip.

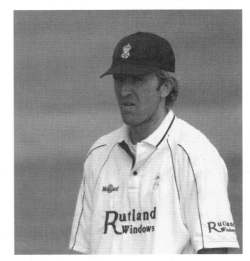

Many businesses sponsor teams to get free advertising

Sport specific funding – there are various sources of funds of this sort that a local sports club could tap into. A football team, for example, could apply for funding from the Football Association via the Football Foundation. Find out more by visiting the F.A. website at www.heinemann.co.uk/hotlinks to look at the grass roots work that is being undertaken.

Let's do it!

Visit the website of a sport other than football, and find out what help is available to develop the sport at a local level.

Membership fees – nearly all local clubs, whatever the sport, will raise income by charging a membership fee to join the club. Match fees may also apply, to help cover the cost of administration, washing kit and replacing damaged equipment, etc.

Grants and donations – a club may benefit from the generosity of local people who donate money to local good causes. This money might be left as part of a person's will. There are also funds which exist to remember a local dignitary or benefactor, to which clubs and individuals can apply for financial assistance. In some situations there are a number of criteria that must be met before an award can be made.

Think about it

Can you think of any other sources of funding that a club you play for has used?

The advantages and disadvantages of different sources of funding

Although many sponsorship deals have been very important to the continued existence of some sports and sporting competitions, it is not all good news and there is often a price to be paid. Let us look at some examples.

Moral objections – tobacco and alcohol sponsorship

Vast sums of money have been invested in sport by both the tobacco and drinks industry. Many Formula One racing teams, like Ferrari and Maclaren, have received huge sums of money from tobacco companies such as Marlborough. The Snooker World Championship is sponsored by Embassy Cigarettes. However, public opinion is changing, as is the image of certain sports. Many people believe that allowing sport to be sponsored by businesses which make money from products known to be bad for you, like smoking, is no longer acceptable. In some countries, tobacco advertising is now banned from sport. If the same ban was applied in the UK, it would have a very big effect on sport. In the short term, many sports would find it very difficult to replace these sponsorship deals. In the long term, the hope is that other, more acceptable, sponsors can be attracted to a particular sport.

Let's do it!

List the sports, teams and competitions that would be affected by a ban on tobacco and alcohol advertising. In small groups or as a class, discuss views on the topic of tobacco and alcohol advertising. How do you feel about this subject? Can you see any problems?

Dependency on a source of income

The collapse of the I.T.V. digital agreement with the Nationwide Football League caused problems for many clubs, who suddenly found that money they had already spent was now not going to be forthcoming. By being dependent on a single source of income, they found themselves at the mercy of factors outside of their control. In the same way, a local club may enter into an agreement with a local business which then fails, and can no longer provide the funding it promised.

The influence of the source of income on the sport

Some sports have changed a great deal as a result of entering into deals with other companies. Football provides a good example. In the 1970s and 1980s, football was played on Saturdays and Wednesdays. Saturday games kicked off at 3 p.m. Now, with the control that Sky television has as a result of its huge financial commitment, matches are played seven days a week at a variety of times, to suit the broadcasting schedules of Sky.

Sometimes, rules are changed to make games more 'telegenic'. For instance, cricket has seen the emergence of the 'Day-Night' game, and certain finals at the Olympics are run at times to suit American television companies. In bowls and cricket, players now wear clothing in a variety of colours instead of traditional white. How far should this be allowed to go?

Let's do it!

In small groups, discuss the effect of the media on a sport of your choice.
1. Do you think the effects have all been positive, or are there some negative effects?
2. How far should the media be allowed to change the nature of your chosen sport?

Now choose a sport that struggles to gain any significant media interest.
3. What have the effects of this been on the sport?

Assessment activity 4: Sports funding

P Make a list and describe all the sources of sport funding in the UK that you know of.

M In small groups, complete the table below for a local sports club.

Source of funding	Administration and paperwork	Amount of money available	What can money be spent on?	Any conditions attached?
The National Lottery	Large amount of paperwork required		Buildings and facilities – not kit, etc.	
Sponsorship from local company		Usually smaller amounts		Regular mention of club publicity
Fund raising			Anything	Clashes with other, similar events
Membership and match fees	Setting charges and recording payments			Different rates for unemployed, school age players, etc.
Grants and donations	Letters to be drafted and sent	Various		
Funding from a national Governing Body		Often set limits	Often decided by N.G.B.	

D Using the list you created for **P** , critically analyse the different sources of funding and what you think their effects on sport might be. Think about both the positive and negative factors.

Key issues and the influence of the media

Key issues in sport

Sport is faced with a number of key issues, some of which have been present for a long time and others which have arisen recently. As society changes, so do the expectations that people have of sport and the role it plays in peoples lives.

Accessibility

National and international success

Social inclusion

Discrimination

Disability

Key issues

Sportsmanship

Gamesmanship

Fair play

Drugs

Cost

Participation and excellence

Social inclusion

 Think about it

1. What do you think the term 'social inclusion' means? Discuss your definition with your tutor.
2. Why do you think social inclusion is important in today's society?

The society we live in today includes many different types of people: people of different ages, different ethnic backgrounds, different religious beliefs, and people who have special needs because of a physical or mental disability. In the past, little or no sports provision was made for people who were 'outside the norm'. Today, the belief is that *all* members of society should have access to the same opportunities in relation to sport. Values in our society have changed gradually over the years. For instance, in the 1968 Olympic Games, there was no track event for women over 800 metres because it was still believed in some circles that racing over longer distances might damage a woman's ability to bear children!

It is now accepted that all people have the same rights and should have the same opportunities, and this includes access to sporting opportunities and facilities. Legislation now makes discrimination on the basis of sex, ethnic background or disability against the law. Sports halls are now designed and built with the needs of the disabled in mind. Sports centres also try to encourage all members of society to use a centre, by offering the elderly, the unemployed and the under-fives a concession on the entry price. All these measures help to include everyone in the community and offer everyone the same *opportunity* to participate in sport and reach their full potential, at whatever level that may be.

Discrimination

The Oxford Concise English Dictionary defines discrimination as, 'Making an unjust distinction in the treatment of different categories of people, especially on the grounds of race, sex or age'. This is now illegal under legislation drawn up by the Government and affects all areas of life and work.

Think about it

Have a look at your college or school's equal opportunities policy. What is your school or college's position on the issue of discrimination?

Racism

In sport, there have been a number of high profile cases concerning racism in sport. For example, Emile Heskey was racially abused while playing for England against Macedonia, and the Newcastle player Lua-Lua complained that he was racially abused by opponents in a European Club Championship game. The Football Association have instigated an anti-racist campaign called 'Let's Kick It Out'. You can visit the F.A. website at www.heinemann.co.uk/hotlinks to find out more.

Racism is an important issue in sport at the moment. Racist behaviour gives sport a bad image, which has the effect of turning off both spectators and sponsors.

Sexism

This is where a person is discriminated against because of his or her gender. Usually, the discrimination is against women.

 Think about it

1. At the Wimbledon Tennis Championship in 2002, the Men's Singles winner won £525,000 while the women's prize was £486,000.

   ○ Discuss this with your group. Do you think this is fair?

   ○ One of the arguments used is that the men play five set matches while the women play only three. Should this make a difference?

2. Look at the following two images. Do they show a form of sexual discrimination?

Ageism

This is where a person is treated differently because of their age. In sport, many activities are considered to be for young people. Many older people are still fit and healthy, however, and there is no reason why they should not continue to enjoy many of the activities that younger people participate in. The population of this country is getting older as people live longer, so it makes financial sense for companies to cater for older people, too. For example, many travel companies now design holidays specifically for the older customer.

 Think about it

1. What are your local centres providing for the older customer (the 'grey market')?
2. Many leisure centres employ school pupils or college students. Why do you think this is?
3. Some employers, such as the B&Q store chain, employ older people. What do you think the benefits are of employing older personnel?

Drugs

Abuse of drugs continues to be a problem in sport

Another important issue is the use of drugs in sport. These drugs are illegal substances designed to artificially improve performance. There are many types available to sportsmen and women. Anabolic steroids help athletes to train much harder and recover more quickly. Blood doping allows the body to carry more red blood cells and thus improves its ability to carry oxygen around the body. Diuretics reduce the water content in the body, so reducing body weight.

Let's do it!

Look through the newspapers in your college or school library, and search for any articles concerned with drugs in sport.
- How is the issue reported?
- What do you think this issue does for the image of the sport?
- Do you think that drugs in sport should be allowed?

One of the factors that make an activity a sport is that it has rules and regulations. Drug taking is very often described as cheating. The Oxford Concise English Dictionary defines cheating as, 'Acting dishonestly or unfairly in order to gain an unfair advantage'. Cheating in sport might include deliberate diving in football or tampering with the ball in cricket, as well as the use of illegal substances. Part of the appeal of sport is that an individual or team wins because of superior skills, technique or tactics. If the team or individual has deliberately broken the rules, this is no longer the case.

The problem is that there is a very fine line between cheating and gamesmanship. Gamesmanship is defined in the same Dictionary as, 'The art of winning games by using various ploys and tactics to gain a psychological advantage'.

Where do we draw the line? Is 'sledging' in cricket (where fielders and bowlers make a variety of often 'unpleasant' comments to the batsmen) cheating or gamesmanship? When Dwayne Chambers deliberately takes his time when called to his starting blocks by the starter, is he using gamesmanship to unsettle his opponents? When the New Zealand rugby union team perform the 'Haka' before each game, is this a tactic designed to gain a psychological advantage?

Let's do it!

In small groups, discuss the following questions.
- What is the difference between cheating and gamesmanship?
- What are your own attitudes to cheating and drug use in sport? Does it really matter?
- How would you feel if sport allowed competitors to take drugs openly?
- Would *you* take drugs to perform better?

Developing participation and the pursuit of excellence

There are those who argue that you cannot possibly develop the very best sportsmen and women *and* develop more participation by the general public.

Let's do it!

In small groups, discuss what you think about the issue of performance versus participation.
- Can both be developed side by side?
- Should the nation concentrate on only one area?
- What problems can you see in doing this?
- List and describe ways in which more participation could be encouraged.
- What practices or policies need to be changed?
- What extra facilities or clubs should be provided?

Sport England is involved in both areas. They promote campaigns and schemes designed to encourage as many people as possible to participate in sport. At the same time, they make facilities and services available to allow the best sportsmen and women the chance to reach the very top. As a result, the country has a number of National Sports Centres, a variety of Sports Institutes and a 'World Class' programme designed to help sporting stars win gold medals and world championships. This costs a great deal of money. How do we decide if this is money well spent, when it could be used to improve schools or build new hospitals?

Since the early 1970s, there has been a vast increase in the number of sports facilities available for people to access. There are now many more swimming pools, leisure centres, outdoor pursuits centres and so on. These offer a vast range of activities and pursuits, but at a price. It is a fact of life that people earn different amounts of money and have different priorities when spending that money. Taking part in sport is an everyday occurrence for some and a luxury for others. Is this right? Should certain activities only be available to those who can afford to pay? Or should everyone have to right and opportunity to take part in whatever they want?

The media and its influence on sport

The mass media exerts an enormous influence on sport and its supporters and spectators, and can be a power for both good and bad. It can have long lasting effects on the reputation of a sport and on how the public view that sport, as well as seriously affecting the lives of those people who play sport and are in the public eye.

 newspapers and magazines

 television (both terrestrial and satellite)

The media includes:

 radio

 the Internet

 Think about it

Think of some sporting moments that have been important to you in some way, for example, your favourite team winning a game. What effect did coverage of this event have on you?

Find a report in a newspaper of a sporting story. Does the *style* of reporting have any influence on your behaviour?

In recent years, sports coverage in the newspapers has increased enormously. Sport sells newspapers – but how is sport portrayed and which sports are covered?

Newspapers fall into two main groups: tabloids and broadsheets. The tabloids, sometimes called the 'red tops', include *The Sun* and *The Daily Mirror*. They tend to be more 'sensational' in their coverage of a story, with less emphasis on facts and more on gossip and rumour. The language used is simpler, and tabloids often use headlines that deliberately attract attention.

There are many newspaper headlines exposing the misuse of drugs

The broadsheets, such as *The Times*, *The Daily Telegraph*, and *The Guardian*, are much less concerned with gossip and more concerned with reporting the facts accurately. The range of sports covered is much wider and the language used is more complex.

The media can have a huge effect on people's opinions. When David Beckham was sent off playing for England against Argentina in the 1998 World Cup, the story was headline news at home. As a result of the coverage, Beckham became Public Enemy Number 1 for some time and his reputation was tarnished. He received abuse from the terraces when playing for Manchester United the following season, all because of one silly mistake caught on television. Sportsmen and women are in the media spotlight more than ever before, and the increased pressure on sportsmen and women has seen an increase in the number taking drugs to improve their performance. Player behaviour both on and off the field is under much closer scrutiny than ever before.

Think about it

In 1995 Eric Cantona attacked a Crystal Palace fan during a mid week match. Millions of people watched this on television. What effect do you think this had on:
- the public's opinion of Eric Cantona?
- the image of football as a national sport?
- potential football sponsors?
- the behaviour of fans towards Eric Cantona in the future?

Many sports personalities are seen as much on the front pages of the papers as they are on the back pages, where sport is traditionally covered. Their private lives are regarded as public property. The public know which player is dating which pop star; which player is going to which club, and what players' latest hairstyles are.

This increase in coverage has had many effects.

- Sponsors have been attracted to a number of sports because of the amount of media coverage they receive.
- The dress and language of many people is influenced by what their sports heroes wear and say.
- The opinion of millions of people can be influenced by what they read about sport in newspapers and magazines, and what they see and hear on the television and radio.
- Sports have changed their rules and competition format to accommodate the needs of the media. Football has done this for Sky T.V., due to the amount of money the company has put into the game.
- Many sports are now seen as 'fashionable'.
- Sports that receive increased media coverage also enjoy increased numbers of players and spectators.

How have sports that have been 'overlooked' by the media been affected? Since they receive less media coverage, they struggle to generate and attract sponsorship and so find it hard to develop.

Let's do it!

Choose two different sports, a very popular sport and a 'minority' sport. Investigate the following for each sport:
- the main sponsors
- the amount of media coverage
- participation rates.
- public awareness.

Devise some simple questions about each sport and give them to fellow students to answer, for example, 'Who is the captain of the national side?'

There is no doubt that the coverage of sport by the media has greatly changed the behaviour of people when it comes to their behaviour, opinions and attitudes.

Let's do it!

Look the statements listed below. Which seem true to you? Choose at least three of the statements. In small groups, look at media sources and provide evidence to support your chosen statements. The evidence might be from a newspaper article, a television report, a website on the Internet or a radio programme.

1. Football is seen as fashionable and has greatly increased in popularity.
2. The reporting of hooliganism has led to a huge decrease in the trouble found inside football grounds.
3. Many footballers are household names and attract vast sums of money in sponsorship and endorsements.
4. Players' salaries in some sports, including football and athletics, have increased dramatically.
5. Many sports are highly dependent on the income they receive from the media, especially television.
6. Sport is 'hyped up' more than ever before and personalities are increasingly important.
7. The coverage of certain sports by the media has attracted many new sponsors, at the expense of other sports.
8. Sports competitions are increasingly affected and influenced by the needs of the media, leading to changes in rules and competition formats. How soon will it be before Wimbledon drops its 'all white' clothing rule, for example?

Think about it

Ask other students and staff in your school or college what their opinions are. You could ask them whether they feel that football players earn too much, or how much sport they watch on television, read about in the newspapers or play themselves.

Look at the changes in a sport over the last ten years. Are more people:
- playing?
- watching?
- aware of the 'star' names?

Key points

Gambling is a large part of the sports industry. In the UK:

- there are 688 bingo clubs
- there are 122 registered casinos
- there are 83,000 betting offices
- there are 255,000 fruit machines
- 4.1 million punters 'went to the dogs' in 2000, attending the 50+ greyhound racing stadia
- 5 million people spent a day at the races
- 2 million play the football pools weekly (compare this with the 25 million who attend football matches);
- gambling is most popular with people aged 25 to 54.

Employment	No. of employees
Greyhound racing	20,000
Horse racing and breeding	60,000
Casinos	12,000
Bingo clubs	c21,000
Gaming machines	c23,000

Assessment activity 6: Mass media and sport

Find out the differences between tabloid and broadsheet newspapers for yourself, by comparing how each type of paper covers the same sports story.

P Choose a current sports story. Then choose a tabloid newspaper and a broadsheet and compare how the story is covered. Look for differences in language used, how the story is approached, the headlines, and so on.

M Looking at the same papers, calculate the amount of coverage given to a range of sports. Draw up a table and list some sports. Estimate the coverage in terms of 'column inches'. What differences did you find?

D Discuss the effects of this coverage on the sport concerned. Record your findings.

In summary

In this unit you have examined a wide range of factors concerned with the sports industry, looking at:
- definitions of various terms
- the main providers of sports activities and facilities
- the importance of sport to individuals, communities and the country
- the funding of sports clubs and organisations
- the effects of the media on sport
- the key issues which currently affect sport in the UK.

CHECK WHAT YOU KNOW!

Look back through this unit to see if you can you answer the following questions:
1. What is the difference between amateur and professional sport?
2. What are the factors which have led to the growth of the sports industry?
3. Which factors can affect participation in sport?
4. What are the benefits of taking part in sport?
5. How is sports development carried out, and for what reasons?
6. What can be done to overcome barriers to participation in sport?
7. What are the three main sectors in sports provision? Give local examples of each.
8. Give the main reason why each of these three sectors makes sports provision.
9. Describe a local example of how each sector is involved in the provision of one sport of your choice.
10. Why is it important that people are encouraged to participate in sport?
11. How might you encourage groups of people to take part that traditionally do not?
12. When England won the Rugby World Cup, what resulting effects might you have expected to see locally in each of the three sectors?
13. Name three of each of the following:
    - local sports organisations
    - regional sports organisations
    - national sports organisations
    - international sports organisations.
14. Choose two contrasting sports, for example a major sport and a minor sport. Your teacher can help you to decide. Now look in both local and national newspapers. Calculate the amount of coverage each sport receives over, say, a week. How might this affect public awareness for each sport, the chances of each sport obtaining sponsorship, and the pressure on its participants.
15. Choose an issue which you feel strongly about that currently affects sport. Describe the effects you think it is having on sport and suggest ways that it could be tackled.

Health, safety and injury

Introduction

In any sporting environment, health and safety is of the utmost importance. It must be maintained in order to prevent injuries occurring to participants, visitors or staff. Sports are fun and enjoyable but participating in any sporting activity carries an element of risk.

Sports centres, leisure centres, outdoor facilities and gymnasiums all carry risks of different kinds. They may have large pieces of machinery, or there may be lots of different people of different ages using the facilities, or there may be a swimming pool. All of these have potential hazards that could cause harm to visitors, staff and customers if correct procedures of ensuring health and safety are not followed.

Anyone working in the sports industry, from management to general staff, should be aware of the issues that surround health and safety in the work place. They should be fully trained in certain aspects, for example the use of chemicals in a swimming pool. It is important to identify risk factors, look for ways to prevent or minimise the risk and take appropriate steps to avoid unsafe practice.

How you will be assessed

During this unit you will gain an understanding of health and safety issues and the risk factors that can cause sporting injuries in different sporting situations. This unit will be assessed through work that you submit, and which achieves the learning outcomes. You can choose from the following:
- a written assignment
- a video recorded presentation.

After completing this unit you should be able to achieve the following learning outcomes:
1. Investigate the **main risk factors** that can cause sporting injuries and explore ways to minimise and prevent them.
2. Examine **common sporting injuries** and basic treatment procedures.
3. Prepare a **risk assessment** for a sporting activity.

The main risk factors that can cause sporting injuries

Here are some important definitions to help you through this unit:

- **Health** – being free from illness, injury or disease and having a general sense of well being.
- **Safety** – being free from anything that could cause harm.
- **Injury** – anything that occurs or happens to an individual that causes bodily harm.
- **Hazard** – anything that can cause physical bodily harm, for example a slippery floor, fire or certain items of sports equipment, for example javelins or darts.
- **Risk** – the probability or chance of injury occurring because of a hazard. The risk could be great or small.

You can break down the main risk factors that can lead to or cause sporting injuries under the following headings:

- the participant or sporting individual
- the coach
- the environment
- other users and participants
- equipment and personal protective equipment
- lifestyle
- parental influence.

You can reduce the risk of injury by wearing protective equipment such as goggles, helmets and kneepads

Case study: Hillsborough

The Hillsborough football disaster in April 1989 claimed 96 lives and a further 170 people were injured. These people had gone to watch the F.A. cup semi final between Nottingham Forest and Liverpool at the Sheffield stadium. A gate was opened to allow a big crowd of fans into an already crowded centre section of the stadium. This resulted in fans being crushed in the entrance tunnels, on the steps and against the perimeter fencing. This was one of the worst disasters in Britain's sporting history. The organisers and promoters of the event had a duty of care to ensure that all visitors, staff and players were in a safe environment. This was obviously not the case.

Now answer the following questions:
1. Identify the injury risk factors.
2. In what ways could these have been minimised or prevented?

The participant or sporting individual

The participant or sporting individual, through their actions, can be an injury risk factor, particularly if he or she is misbehaving, has a negative attitude towards the sport or is not following the rules. The following spidergram identifies the risk factors related to the sporting individual or sports participant:

Attitude/behaviour

Over training

Not following the rules of the sport

Misuse of protective equipment

Potential risks for the participant

Lack of warm up

Technique/skill

Inappropriate clothing/footwear

Lack of cool down

Incorrect lifting and carrying procedure for specialist equipment

Physical fitness/screening

Attitude/behaviour

If you have the wrong attitude to the sport or to the coach, you are more likely not to listen, and to think that you know what is best. This could lead to you being injured through wrong practise, misuse of equipment, or performing a skill or technique incorrectly.

Think about it

Get together with two or three others in your group and discuss your own experiences of being coached. Was your coaching experience positive or negative? Identify how your coach helped you, or didn't help you, to improve.

Over training

Continuous training without adequate rest or recovery periods can place a lot of stress upon the soft tissues of the body (muscles, ligaments, tendons and joints). All these areas are prone to injury. Over training can result in an athlete injuring themselves, and will also have a profound effect on the athlete's mental state.

Technique/skill

Skill development or skills training is a very important component of a training regime and is necessary for safety in sport. If you do not develop the specific skills needed for your sport, you are more likely to become injured. Therefore skill development and training can be a means of preventing injury.

Think about it

Have you ever injured yourself because you incorrectly performed a technique or skill? Discuss your experiences with your group.

Lack of warm up

A warm up is designed to gradually increase the flow of blood around the body. This in turn increases the core temperature of the muscles and allows for freer movement at the joints. It also prepares the athlete mentally for the work ahead.

The warm up must be specific to the individual and should also be sports specific, encompassing techniques and skills to be used in the training session. The warm up should include mobility, pulse raising and stretching exercise. If you don't warm up, your muscles, ligaments and tendons are more prone to injury.

Let's do it!

In a group, discuss the different warm up and cool down exercises that you have experienced. Try to think about what each exercise is designed to do. Together, create a suitable warm up and cool down routine for an aerobics session, or other sport of your choice.

Lack of cool down

The aim of a cool down is to gradually decrease the heart rate back down to near its non-exercising state, to improve recovery time by removing the waste products from the muscle tissue, and to help reduce the pain associated with muscle soreness and stiffness. All training sessions should finish with a cool down. If you don't cool down after exercising, you are more likely to be stiff and your muscles will be sore. This will affect the range of movement at the joints, your flexibility and your performance.

Physical fitness/screening

Any sports participant must be in good health. If you are not physically fit, you may become tired and injuries may result. You may not be able to execute skills correctly because you lack the stamina to do so.

All participants in sport should undergo health screening. This may involve filling in a PARQ (Physical Activity Readiness Questionnaire), which asks questions about your health, lifestyle and medical history. This will ensure that it is safe for you to take part in physical activity.

Inappropriate clothing or footwear

All sports participants must wear the appropriate clothing for their particular sporting activity. Clothes that are too baggy can get trapped or caught in equipment. Clothes that are too tight can restrict movement. This may make it difficult for you to perform in a technically correct way, which could result in some form of injury.

Footwear is for support and protection and must be correct for the type of activity. A runner, for example, should wear specialist trainers made specifically for running. These trainers are designed to absorb impact and so reduce the risk of injury.

Inappropriate footwear could result in unnecessary stresses being placed upon the feet, ankles, legs, or even the back.

The correct clothing and footwear must be worn for all sports!

Think about it

Think of other instances where it is essential to wear the correct kit. How is the kit designed to keep you safe?

Misuse of protective equipment

A sports participant who does not use protective equipment has a greater risk of becoming injured during play. Helmets, shinpads, mouth guards and gloves are just some of the protective equipment that is used in sport.

Incorrect lifting and carrying procedure for specialist equipment

Sports participants should always be taught how to lift and carry any heavy specialist equipment. Incorrect lifting and carrying can result in injuries of the back.

Not following the rules of the sport

All sports have specific rules that need to be followed. These rules are usually set by the governing body or association for each sport – for sport participants, enjoyment and safety. Injuries and accidents can occur when sports rules are ignored.

Think about it

Think of instances in sport where rules have not been followed. The examples can be from professional televised sport or from your own experiences.

Let's do it!

Risk factor	Who might be harmed?	How might the risk affect sporting performance?	How could the risk be minimised?
Over training	The athlete	Puts stress on muscles, joints, tendsons and ligaments, resulting in a restricted range of movement, muscle soreness and stiffness, or minute tearing of the muscles. All of the above have a negative effect on performance	Devising an effective but safe training programme. Providing adequate rest periods. Sports massages to help prevent injuries or reduce the risk of injuries occurring
Lack of warm up	The athlete	Training heavily on muscles that are cold and have not been sufficiently warmed can lead to injuries, such as tears	Allow sufficient time to warm up and stretch before any type of activity begins
Misuse of protective equipment	The athlete; other participants	Not wearing protective equipment increases the risk of injury	Follow the rules for the specific sport. Wear protective equipment when necessary. The coach should check that equipment is worn/used properly

The table above shows three of the risk factors that can cause sporting injuries. Draw a similar table, and complete it for the remaining risk factors described on pages 46–48. State who might be harmed and how this might affect sporting performance, and suggest ways in which the risk could be minimised or prevented.

The coach

A sport's coach could contribute to injuries being caused by inappropriate coaching methods or even his or her desire to win at all costs. The following spidergram identifies some of the risk factors related to coaching behaviour.

Coaching styles

No knowledge of sporting tecnique

No first aid provision

The risk factors involved in coaching

Incorrect technique

Over training

Desire to win

Pushing too hard

Coaching styles

The style of coaching that the coach adopts could result in injuries occurring to the participant. For example, if you find it difficult to talk to or approach your coach, you are less likely to ask for advice or pose questions. This may lead to you learning to perform skills in a technically incorrect way, and this could result in a soft tissue injury.

Pushing too hard

If the coach pushes the participant very hard, with little time for recovery, this will make the participant more susceptible to injuries.

No knowledge of sporting activity

It is important that a coach has knowledge and experience of the sport that he or she is coaching. He or she must have tactical awareness skills, be able to analyse strategically, and be able to implement and apply the rules of the sport. The coach must also be able to plan a programme of training to match each individual's needs and abilities. If the coach has no knowledge of the sport, then he or she is more likely to teach incorrect techniques.

Incorrect technique

If the coach does not teach technically correct skills or techniques then the participant will execute those skills and techniques incorrectly. This will leave him or her more prone to injury. For example, if a karate coach is teaching a sidekick that requires specific movement at the hips, and is teaching it with no movement, then this could lead to groin injuries.

Desire to win

Coaches who just have a desire to win are probably not thinking about the stresses placed upon the athlete's body. Continuously pushing in training sessions is not the right way to get the best out of an athlete.

Over training

Continuous pushing may lead to over training. Too much training places severe stresses on the muscles and joints, which could result in muscle soreness, stiffness, minute tearing and over use injuries. If you over train you will also become fatigued, make silly mistakes and may sustain an injury as a result.

No first aid provision

Adequate first aid provision is vital. Minor injuries may become worse if immediate treatment is not to hand. A good example of this is an impact injury where swelling occurs. If no ice or ice packs are available to help reduce the swelling then it will become worse and effectively lengthen the recovery time following injury.

Let's do it!

Risk factor	Who might be harmed?	How might the risk affect sporting performance?	How could the risk be minimised?
No first aid provision	The athlete; other paticipants	Minor injuries may take longer to heal	Provide adequate first aid provision, e.g. a fully stocked first aid kit. A qualified, appointed first aider must be present at all times
No knowledge of the sporting activity	The athlete; other participants	Skills may be taught incorrectly. Rules may not conform to those laid down by the sports associations	Coach must be fully qualified to teach the sport. Coach should regularly update knowledge and take further training courses
Coaching styles	The athlete; other participants	An athlete knows his or her own body and whether or not a specific skill or drill is suitable – if the coach will not listen or the athlete is too afraid to speak, injury may result	Coach should be selective in coaching styles, depending on who he or she is training. Coach should be aware of how the different coaching styles will affect the athletes and their sporting performance. Coach should be willing to listen to the athletes he or she is training.

The table above shows three of the risk factors that can cause sporting injuries. Draw a similar table and complete for the remaining risk factors described on pages 50–51. State who will be harmed, how it will affect sporting performance and suggest ways in which the risk could be minimised or prevented.

Case study: the coach

The coach of a local athletics team usually teaches 16–18 year olds. He has been asked to cover ten sessions, coaching 8–10 year olds in high jump. He is not a high jump specialist and his knowledge is limited. His coaching style is dictatorial, and winning is his main aim.

Now answer the following questions:
1. What potential hazards and risks can you see in this scenario?
2. How might injuries occur?
3. What are the health and safety implications?

The environment

The environment can pose a risk to sports participants for example, running on a hard surface can increase the likelihood of 'shin splints'. Certain weather conditions will affect playing surfaces and can lead to injuries being sustained. The spidergram below identifies some of the environmental risk factors:

Weather conditions can seriously increase the risk of injury

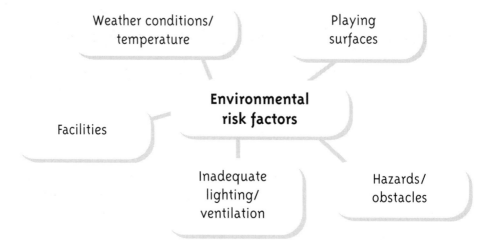

Weather conditions/ temperature

Playing surfaces

Environmental risk factors

Facilities

Inadequate lighting/ ventilation

Hazards/ obstacles

Facilities

If facilities are hired for training purposes it is the responsibility of the coach and of the owner to liaise with each other to ensure that the facilities are safe to use. Indoor facilities must be clean and well maintained. Current health and safety regulations covering the facility must be regularly checked and updated.

Weather conditions/temperature

Weather conditions can cause injuries to occur. For example, rain, snow or frost could make playing surfaces slippery, leading to falls that could result in breaks and sprains.

Extremely hot weather could lead to dehydration, so it is important that participants drink lots of fluid and wear the correct clothing, and that training time is minimised. A cap is essential to protect the head from the sun and to prevent sunstroke occurring. The sun can also cause an accident or injury to happen by temporarily blinding participants.

Playing surfaces

Playing surfaces must be correct for the sport in question. A good example is aerobics, or any type of dancing activity, which should be undertaken on a 'sprung' floor. This type of floor is designed to reduce the impact on the joints, thereby reducing any impact associated injuries. Hard surfaces can cause injuries to the soft tissues of the body, especially when you are not use to playing or training on them. If a playing surface is constantly being changed, for example from grass to concrete or wood, it is likely that this will have an effect on the legs and could induce injury.

 Think about it

In your group, discuss all the different playing surfaces you know about.
1. What experience do you have of them?
2. Have any of you been injured through playing on the wrong surface?

Hazards and obstacles

All playing or training surfaces must be free from obstacles or hazards that could cause injury. It is the coach's responsibility to check the areas before each session. He or she should also encourage the participants not to drop litter or leave things lying around that could cause harm to others. Wet floors in changing rooms are another common hazard.

Inadequate lighting and ventilation

Adequate lighting and ventilation need to be provided for any training or playing that takes place indoors. Everyone must be able to see what they are doing and be able to move around safely.

Floodlights are usually provided at specialist facilities for playing out doors. If they are not then it is important that you are aware of the time when it starts to get dark, to ensure everyone's safety.

Let's do it!

Risk factor	Who might be harmed?	How might the risk affect sporting performance?	How could the risk be minimised?
Unsafe facilities	The athlete; other participants; visitors	May be the cause of injury, e.g. old or broken tiles on a changing room floor might cause minor or serious injury to the feet	Ensure facilities are in good working order. Deal with hazards immediately to prevent injuries occurring
Hazards/ obstacles	The athlete; other participants; the coach	May be the cause of injury, e.g. broken glass on a football pitch puts players at risk of cutting themselves if they fall or slip	Conduct a risk assessment of the sporting environment before any activity, to ensure it is safe to play and free from any hazards tht could cause bodily harm
Inadequate lighting and ventilation	The athlete; other participants; the coach	May cause injury, e.g. if athletes can't see what they are doing this could lead to an accident happening	Be aware of the time when it starts to get dark and ensure that training is scheduled in daylight. If using a floodlit pitch, ensure that all floodlights are in good working order. If using indoor facilities ensure that all lighting is working and report if necessary to facilities' owner

The table above shows three of the risk factors that can cause sporting injuries. Draw a similar table and complete for the remaining risk factors described on pages 54–55. State who will be harmed and how it will affect sporting performance, and suggest ways in which the risk could be minimised or prevented.

Other users and participants

When playing sports in any environment there are often other participants, and users of the sporting facilities. Their actions and behaviour could lead to other participants being injured. The spidergram below identifies some of the risk factors related to to other participants and users:

| Attitude and behaviour | | Misuse of equipment |

Other users and participants

| Vandalism and graffiti | | Peer pressure |

Attitude and behaviour

The attitude and behaviour of other participants is very important. A small group misbehaving with equipment, for example throwing javelins when they have been told not to, can result in serious injuries occurring to others within the training environment.

Misuse of equipment

Many situations require participants to be supervised when setting up or taking down equipment, as well as when using specialist equipment. If the coach does not supervise the participants, then they could misuse the equipment.

Is playing cricket with a badminton racket and a cricket ball a safe way of using equipment?

Vandalism and graffiti

If equipment has been vandalised, this must be reported to prevent accidents occurring. If there is a fault with a trampoline, for example, or it has been vandalised, the next group of people to use it could sustain an injury.

Peer pressure

Peer pressure is another factor that could cause, or lead to, an injury in sport. If you try to train like one of your most experienced counterparts from a higher ability group, you might injure yourself. If you feel under pressure to be as good as your peers, you might over train, which can lead to over use injuries.

Equipment and personal protective equipment

Equipment that is not checked regularly or properly maintained can become a big risk factor. Most sporting associations and governing bodies specify what protective equipment must be worn during each particular sport. It is important to remember that, as well as those listed below, vandalised equipment or not wearing protective equipment at all are risks factors.

Faulty or damaged equipment

Inappropriate specialist equipment

Equipment and personal protective equipment

Faulty or damaged equipment

Equipment must be regularly checked, maintained, repaired or replaced in order to prevent injuries occurring to individuals who use it.

Inappropriate specialist equipment

Specialist equipment necessary for specific sports must be made available and be in good condition. If it is not, certain areas of the body will either not be fully protected, or not be protected at all. High-risk sports, such as contact sports, require more preventative measures.

Let's do it!

Risk factor	Who might be harmed?	How might the risk affect sporting performance?	How could the risk be minimised?
Vandalised equipment	The athlete; other participants; the coach	Damaged equipment may be unsafe to use	Ensure all equipment is put away after use. Highlight dangers in local newspapers. Install CCTV camera. Store equipment in a lockable cupboard

The table shows one of the risk factors that can cause sporting injuries. Draw a similar table and complete for the other risk factor described on page 58. State who will be harmed, how it will affect sporting performance and suggests ways in which the risk could be minimised.

Lifestyle

An athlete's lifestyle could have a bearing on his or her performance. Alcohol and drugs – too much partying – affects an athlete's ability to think logically or react quickly. The spidergram below identifies some of the injury risk factors associated with lifestyle:

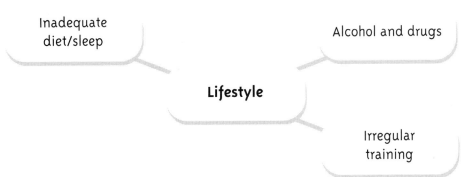

Inadequate diet/sleep

The types of food you eat will have a major bearing on your health, fitness, training and performance. If you are not eating a healthy balanced diet, or not eating much but training heavily, this will lead to light headedness, dizziness or even fainting. This is true for sleep too – too little sleep could lead to slow reactions and increase the risk of injury.

Alcohol and drugs

Training or playing when alcohol or drugs are in your system can be dangerous to yourself and other participants. Some sportspeople in the past have used alcohol as a way to calm nerves before a competition or event. Alcohol slows down reaction time and affects balance and coordination. It also affects the way in which you think about, and judge, situations and will negatively affect your athletic performance.

Drinking alcohol before or during a sporting activity is not permitted and can lead to serious accidents or injury

Irregular training

Regular guided training, together with adequate recovery and rest time, is a requirement of any sport. If you train only when you feel like it, and have no specific routine, then your body will not be trained to cope with the demands of your sport and injuries can occur as a result.

Let's do it!

Risk factor	Who might be harmed?	How might the risk affect sporting performance?	How might the risk be minimised?
Inadequate diet	The athlete	The athlete will fatigue quickly and performance will be hindered due to tiredness and low energy levels	Educate the athlete on the right and wrong foods to eat. Ensure the athlete perseveres with the new nutritional plan

The table above shows one of the risk factors that can cause sporting injuries. Draw a similar table and complete for the remaining risk factors described on page 60. State who will be harmed and how it will affect sporting performance, and suggest ways in which the risk could be minimised or prevented.

Parental influence

Some parents are very demanding, and want their child to be the best. This can create an adverse reaction in the child. The child athlete may train harder to please his or her parents, or the parents may push the child to train harder. Both these scenarios could lead to over use injuries.

Parents may push their child too hard, without realising the consequences

Assessment activity 1: Injury and risk factors

The following is a list of different sporting situations:
- a crowded ice rink
- a crowded swimming pool with one lifeguard on duty
- a fitness instructor giving an induction to a busy over-50s session at the gym
- a football match at a ground with stadium capacity of 10,000. Tickets are being sold on the gates and more people are being let inside than the stadium is designed to hold
- a circuit training class at which no PARQ is given out (Physical Activity Readiness Questionnaire).

Choose **four** different types of sporting situations from the list.

P Write a list of all of the injury and risk factors associated with each of the four sports you have chosen.

M Using your list, explain why you think each is an injury and risk factor.

D Compare and analyse the impact of injury and risk factors on successful sports performance.

Assessment activity 2: Minimising the risk of injury

Choose two of the different sporting situations from the list given above.

P What are the best methods to minimise the risk of injury occurring?

M Prepare and carry out a risk assessment for your chosen sport or activity on your own. Remember to explain the relevant laws, rules and regulations.

D Using the risk assessment you prepared in **M** . Discuss the **effect** of the relevant laws, rules and regulations in maintaining a healthy and safe working environment.

In summary

Ways to minimise the risk of injury occurring include:
- obeying the rules
- wearing the correct clothing and footwear
- warming up
- cooling down
- using appropriate training methods
- training under a qualified, knowledgeable and experienced coach
- wearing personal protective equipment
- ensuring activities are suited to age and ability levels
- following a suitable training and fitness programme
- ensuring adequate supervision
- avoiding over training
- following correct lifting and carrying procedures
- removing obstacles and hazards
- health screening
- following a good diet
- practising skills and techniques.

Warming up and cooling down are important steps for preventing injuries

You, health and safety and the law

Key legislation and regulations

When you are working in sport, it is important to be aware of the relevant laws that deal with health and safety. These laws are sensible and are there to protect you. Whether a facility or training ground is large or small, it is covered by the laws laid down by the Government in the Acts of Parliament. The coach and facilities' owner have to ensure that everyone is aware, and abides by, relevant regulations and legislations. In this way, the health, safety and welfare of athletes, staff and other participants within the working environment will be maintained.

It is also the responsibility of the facilities' owner and coach to obtain updated information on any changes in regulations. Breaking the law, by ignoring or not updating this information, could result in severe punishment. This in turn is likely to be costly to the sporting environment in a number of ways, which could include any of the following:

- closure of the sports ground/stadium or playing environment
- a bad reputation
- a hefty fine
- imprisonment
- an order to pay compensation if a preventable injury occurs.

In addition, some facilities may have voluntary codes of practice. These are rules which the organisation wants you to follow for good will and are not usually laid down by the Government. A common example of this is a sign in a swimming pool saying no running, no eating or drinking, no diving, and no splashing. These are all voluntary codes of practice and are there to ensure the safety of yourself and other users.

Health and Safety at Work Act 1974

Under the Health and Safety at Work Act 1974, all employers have a duty of care to ensure that a safe working environment is provided which is free from anything that could cause harm or cause a risk to health or life. (In this instance, the employer will be the coach and the facility provider.)

Think about it

With your group, think of some examples of risk factors within a leisure centre environment. Decide whom these risk factors might affect, for example members of staff, visitors and/or customers. Then discuss the best ways in which to minimise the risk or prevent them from occurring.

Manual Handling Operation Regulations 1992

Working in the sports industry may involve lifting and carrying heavy equipment. The Manual Handling Operations Regulations 1992 state that all employees who are involved in lifting and carrying must have sufficient training in these procedures, in order to promote safe practise and to prevent injuries occurring.

Think about it

- Think of any sporting situation where you might be required to lift something heavy.
- How can you minimise or prevent injuries occurring when you lift something heavy?

Personal Protective Equipment at Work Regulations 1992

This regulation requires all employers to provide protective clothing if necessary. For example, those involved with handling swimming pool chemicals may need to wear gloves, boots or goggles. Sports participants may also be bound by law to wear protective equipment, for example in motorbike racing.

Think about it

Think of four sports for which you are required, by its rules or regulations, to wear protective equipment.

Control of Substances Hazardous to Health Regulations 2003 (COSHH)

Under this regulation, employers must ensure that anyone who uses chemicals or substances that could cause harm to others is aware of safe practices relating to handling, use and storage.

Let's do it!

Visit a leisure centre find out:
1. about the chemicals which are used in a swimming pool
2. whether staff have to wear any protective clothing
3. whether staff have had training on how to use the chemicals.

Identify:
4. risk factors to the public (via the swimming pool) or to the staff (using chemicals)
5. the methods used to minimise any injuries or accidents occurring.

Health and Safety First Aid Regulations 1981

The key intentions of this regulation are that there must be qualified first aiders within leisure facilities, companies or any organisation. These people need to be able to take control of first aid situations and look after the first aid equipment. A fully stocked first aid kit must also be available.

Let's do it!

1. If this Act was not followed at a big athletics meet, what would the injury risk factors be?
2. Identify the best ways to minimise the risk.

Children Act 1989

Coaching young children can be very rewarding but you need to be aware of the Children Act 1989

This Act protects children and states that anyone working with children must:
- obtain clearance from the police and criminal records bureau before he or she can actually work with children
- be suitability qualified to work with children
- be trained to recognise the signs of abuse
- be trained in methods of dealing with abuse, and in reporting procedures and referral.

Let's do it!

1. A newly qualified coach, who was trained with adults, is employed to work with children. Identify the injury risk factors in this situation.
2. Identify ways to minimise or prevent injuries occurring.

Safety at Sports Grounds Act 1975

This Act is designed to protect the safety of spectators at sports events. The onus is on the organisers of the event to ensure that spectators, participants and staff are all within a safe environment. If the capacity of the stadium holds 10,000, then a safety certificate is required.

Key points

A number of factors can cause or lead to sporting injuries and injuries can happen to any part of the body through participating in sport. Coaches and organisers of events should:

- have a sports first aid or a general first aid qualification
- have a basic understanding of injuries, or the common injuries that can occur within their sports
- know methods of immediate treatment and injury management
- know when a referral to a physiotherapist or hospital is necessary.

 Think about it

Working with a partner, discuss any injuries that you have had.

- When did it occur?
- Where did it occur?
- How did it happen?
- Why did the injury occur?

Now use the knowledge you have gained from this section to answer the following questions:

1. Was there anything that could have prevented the injury from occurring?
2. Was there anything you could have done differently to minimise the risk?

Common sporting injuries

How injuries are caused

Many injuries that occur in sports are minor, such as cuts and bruises. Other injuries are more serious, and can be categorised under the following headings:

- impact or direct blow injuries
- over use injuries
- accidental injuries
- injuries caused by environmental factors
- chronic injuries.

Key points

Injuries can occur as a result of an internal force within our body, or an external force from outside our bodies.

- An example of an internal force is where extra stress is placed on muscle tissue. This might result in minute tearing of the muscle, tendons or ligaments. This is also known as an intrinisic risk factor.
- An external force could come about, for example, as a result of the environment, contact, or a tackle or blow during a game of football or rugby. This is also known as an extrinsic risk factor.

Injuries arising from an impact or direct blow

These injuries are common in the following sports:
- rugby (direct tackle)
- football (blow to the legs during a tackle)
- hockey (injuries with stick or ball)
- cricket (speed of the ball on impact with the body, for example a hard ball in the eye)
- show jumping (falling off the horse)
- running (injury as a result of the impact of the hard ground)
- golf (club or ball injuries)
- martial arts (direct blow from opponent).

Over use injuries

These injuries usually occur as a result of an excessive repetition of a specific movement or series of movements. Over use injuries are most common in the following sports:
- running (shin splints)
- racket sports (tennis elbow)
- football
- gymnastics (gymnast's back, which is caused by arching of the back
- athletics.

Accidental injuries

Accidental injuries are common in most sports and tend to happen when you least expect them. They can happen in any sporting context.

Chronic injuries

If an injured athlete returns to training before he or she is fully recovered from an injury, then this injury can develop into a chronic injury. Chronic injuries can sometimes take a long time, or be difficult, to heal.

Injuries	Intrinsic (internal)	Extrinsic (external)
Acute (traumatic injury)	Internal bruising from blow to body by racket, or kick	Blow to leg from hockey stick
Chronic (over use)	Pulled muscle; shin splints	Blisters from gripping a racket

Key points

Injuries can occur to both soft and hard tissues of the body.
- The soft tissues of the body are muscles, tendons and ligaments, cartilage and skin. Soft tissue injuries include strains, sprains and tears.
- The hard tissues of the body are bones. Hard tissue injuries include breaks, fractures and dislocations.

Injury management

Injury prevention by wearing protective gear is better than cure

All athletes should try to keep a well-balanced body. You can do this by participating in regular activity, maintaining all aspects of fitness and making sure you recover through rest and physical therapy.

Injuries during physical activity still occur, however, even if you follow the above advice. It is the responsibility of the coach and athlete to recognise that an injury has occurred and evaluate the extent of this injury. This can only happen if they have a strong background of anatomy and physiology, and hold a first aid qualification.

Once the injury has been identified, basic first aid is usually the next step:
- Assess the situation.
- Determine whether the limb can be moved.
- If the limb cannot be moved, make the injured person as comfortable as possible and then call for an ambulance.
- If the limb can be moved, follow the R.I.C.E method (see below). This is classed as one of the most important elements in injury management. It can reduce the swelling of the injured site and so help in the recovery process.

The R.I.C.E. method

The R.I.C.E method stands for **r**est, **i**ce, **c**ompression and **e**levation.

Rest

Advise the injured person to stop using the injured area immediately. He or she should avoid any weight-bearing activities (i.e. walking) and use crutches if the injury is to the lower body. If no crutches are available, help the injured person to move to an appropriate location.

Ice

Applying ice packs can to help stop or reduce internal bleeding of the injured area. Internal bleeding is due to blood vessels such as capillaries being damaged. The cold from the ice helps these small vessels to constrict, resulting in the reduction of blood flow. This stops the blood collecting around the injured site.

Use iced water in a bucket for small injuries to toes or fingers. Use ice packs for injuries to larger areas of the body. (These packs can be made from ice cubes placed in a bag.) Place the ice pack in a towel or cloth covering and then place on the skin where the injury has occurred.

Key points

- *Do not* place ice and ice packs directly on to the skin – this can cause ice burns.
- Leave the ice pack on the injury for approximately 15 minutes. Check the skin after one minute, to feel how cold it is. Ask the injured person how they are feeling and whether the ice application is painful or burning. He or she must tell you if these sensations are felt at any time.
- Allow the area to regain some heat for 15 minutes and then reapply the ice pack. This process should be continued for up to three hours after the injury has happened.
- If pain and swelling continues, refer the injured person to a medical professional.

Compression

Compression reduces the amount of swelling around an injured area. Fluid from neighbouring areas can bleed into the injured area, delaying the recovery of the damaged tissues. To compress the injured area:

- use elasticated bandages, or wrap the area with a cloth – the wrapping should be firm and include the ice pack if possible
- remove the wrapping immediately if the area becomes blue in colour, or the injured person experiences a feeling of pain, numbness or cramps – these are signs of a reduction of blood to the area, and this will also hinder recovery.

Elevation

Elevation helps to decrease swelling further. Elevate the injured part above the heart level to help with venous return. You can use pillows or solid objects to support the injured part. Make sure that the arrangement is comfortable to the injured person.

Key points

Venous return refers to the flow of blood back to the heart.

Rehabilitation

Rehabilitation of the injured part of the body usually takes place once the inflammation of an injured site has reduced considerably (between 24 and 72 hours after injury). The aim of rehabilitation is to return the injured person to the level of fitness he or she enjoyed prior to the injury. The rehabilitation phase of recovery focuses on all components of fitness, i.e. strength, flexibility and endurance. A rehabilitation programme should be designed in consultation with the athlete, and exercise goals should be set.

Key points

- Rehabilitation of the injured part should be partnered with exercising the rest of the body.
- Rehabilitation programmes should not be followed after serious injuries without clearance from doctors or consultants. Such injuries include fractures, dislocations and severe sprains.
- A first aider cannot prescribe any medical agent for any injury.

Types of injuries

There are many different types of injury that can occur as a result of sports participation. Some are more common than others and usually occur if care has not been taken to minimise the risk of injury. The spidergram below identifies some of the most common types of injury.

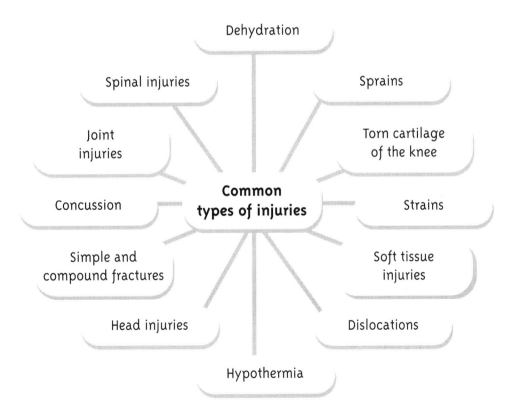

Head injuries

Causes and risk factors	Signs and symptoms	Minimising risk of injury	Treatment
Head injuries are common in sports such as football, for example when two players attempt to header a ball at the same time resulting in their heads colliding. They are also common in contact sports such as boxing, wrestling and ice hockey, or any sport where a fall could occur. Someone who has sustained a head injury may be conscious or unconscious. All injuries to the head are dangerous and require immediate treatment, especially if the athlete is unconscious	The signs and symptoms of a head injury depend on its extent but could include some or all of the following: <ul><li>blurred vision</li><li>drowsiness</li><li>nausea</li><li>different sized pupils</li><li>headache</li><li>temporary loss of memory</li><li>bleeding from the scalp</li><li>irritability</li><li>confusion</li></ul>	Wear protective headgear	Unconscious athlete: <ol><li>Ask someone to dial 999 and tell them you have an unconscious athlete with a head injury.</li><li>Place the injured person in the recovery position (see page 88) and keep a regular check on his or her breathing pattern, pulse and level of response.</li><li>If the athlete regains consciousness, keep monitoring and under no circumstance allow him or her to rejoin the sporting activity. Any athlete who has been unconscious must go to hospital.</li><li>Following medical examination, an athlete recovering from unconsciousness may be kept in for observation. This is because the first 24 hours after a head injury are critical and the symptoms can reappear. If the athlete is allowed home then a responsible person must watch the athlete, and check each hour for a response. If any of the following symptoms appear they must be reported immediately to the doctor or hospital:</li></ol> <ul><li>stiff neck</li><li>inability to move arms or legs</li><li>vomiting/nausea</li><li>blurred vision</li><li>severe headache</li><li>confusion</li><li>different sized pupils</li><li>high temperature.</li></ul>

Concussion

Concussion can be defined as a disturbance of the brain function.

Causes and risk factors	Signs and symptoms	Minimising risk of injury	Treatment
Concussion can be caused by a blow to the head, which results in a short period of unconsciousness and then a full recovery. It is most common in: ○ contact sports ○ motor cycling	○ Memory loss ○ Change in breathing rate ○ Temporary loss of consciousness ○ Loss of balance ○ Disturbed vision ○ Dilated pupils	Wear protective headgear for sports where there is a high risk of sustaining a head injury	First aid: 1. Prepare an ice pack and place on head if there is any bleeding. Leave on for 15 minutes. After five minutes check the injured area to see whether the bleeding has stopped. Ensure that there is a towel or cloth between the ice and the skin. Never place the ice directly onto the skin as this could result in ice burns. 2. Ensure that the head is higher than the heart (elevation) to reduce swelling. 3. If symptoms persist, refer the athlete to his or her doctor or hospital. 4. At home, ensure the athlete is in the care of a responsible person, who should look out for the signs and symptoms indicated on page 74 for the unconscious athlete

 Key points

Lots of active people suffer from recurring injuries. These are usually triggered if an injury was not treated previously, or if the athlete had an insufficient rest period and resumed activity without being fully recovered. You will need to refer the athlete to a physiotherapist or a doctor for further investigation.

Spinal injuries

An example of a spinal injury that could occur in sports is a stress fracture. This is when a small fracture develops after repeated stress is placed on the spine.

Causes and risk factors	Signs and symptoms	Minimising risk of injury	Treatment
A spinal stress fracture is caused by twisting or direct stress to the bone. It is common in the following: • contact sports, such as football and boxing • gymnastics	• Pain in the back or neck • Swelling and bruising • Redness and warmth • Tenderness to touch • Numbness	• Increase calcium intake • Perform strengthening exercises of surrounding muscles to help protect underlying bone	There is no first aid treatment, as the fracture is something that gradually develops. If a spinal stress fracture is suspected, refer the athlete to his or her doctor

 Key points

- Spinal injuries can be extremely dangerous. If the injured person has fallen from a horse or a motorbike, or is at the bottom of a rugby scrum and hasn't moved, then a severe spinal injury is possible. In these situations, do not move the athlete and call for appropriate help.
- If the athlete is unconscious but with a pulse, then he or she needs to be moved into the spinal injury recovery position in order to protect the airway. This is an adaptation of the normal recovery position. It is important that the head and trunk are kept aligned at all times

Let's do it!

With a partner, practise putting each other into the spinal recovery position.

Simple and compound fractures

A fracture can be defined as a crack or break in the bone or cartilage. A **simple fracture** is a clean break in a bone and is sometimes referred to a closed fracture.

A **compound fracture** is where part of the bone breaks through the skin, which causes bleeding. This is sometimes referred to as an open fracture.

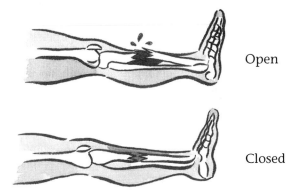

Open

Closed

Open and closed fractures

Causes and risk factors	Signs and symptoms	Minimising risk of injury	Treatment
Fractures are caused by indirect or direct forces	○ Simple fracture: pain, redness, swelling, bruising and discolouration ○ Compound fracture: bone breaking through skin, bleeding, pain, swelling, redness and bruising	Wear protective clothing if required	○ Simple fracture: support the injured part and take casualty to hospital for medical attention ○ Compound fracture: ask someone to call for medical help or telephone 999. To prevent blood loss and reduce the risk of infection, cover the site of the fracture with a sterile dressing and apply pressure to stop the bleeding (do not apply pressure over the fractured bone)

Dislocations

Dislocations usually occur at joints. They can be caused by a direct force, or by placing joints in an abnormal position. A common site of dislocation is the shoulder joint, where the upper arm bone comes away from its socket.

Causes and risk factors	Signs and symptoms	Minimising risk of injury	Treatment
Dislocations are commonly caused by a blow, for example to the shoulder. They are most common in: • contact sports • football and basketball • wrestling • falling from a horse • throwing activities in athletics, for example the javelin • weight or power lifting	• Severe pain • No movement • Visible bone deformity • Swelling • Bruising • Numbness	• Adequate warm up • Adequate strength training for the sport in question • Protective equipment • Wear strapping	First aid: • Call for a trained person if one is present, or phone 999 • Ensure the athlete is kept warm to prevent shock occurring • Immobilise neck and dislocated shoulder with padded splints or a sling • Do not attempt to reposition the dislocated bone; only a trained person should do this

 Key point

It is important to ask an injured person if they are in pain. The pain could be defined as discomfort, stress or agony resulting from the physical activity. Pain signals that something is wrong. You are not a doctor and cannot give qualified medical help. What you can do is make the injured person feel comfortable, reassure them, and send for medical help. Under no circumstance should you give any pain killers to an injured person in pain.

Joint injuries

A joint injury occurs when there is inflammation of the muscles and tendons and/or the tissue that covers bones. Tennis and golf elbow are two of the most common joint injuries.

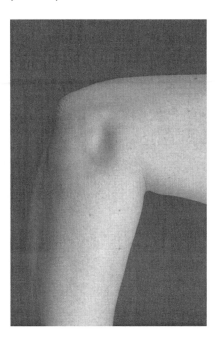

Tennis elbow

TENNIS ELBOW			
Causes and risk factors	**Signs and symptoms**	**Minimising risk of injury**	**Treatment**
Tennis elbow is caused by partial tears of the tendon and attached covering of the bone. This can occur because of: ● sudden stress on the forearm ● incorrect grip of the racket ● the wrist snapping at contact point with the ball ● incorrect technique when hitting the ball ● incorrect equipment	Pain or tenderness in the elbow, which gets worse if the arm rotates or attempts to grip an object	● Do not play racket sports for long periods of time without adequate rest periods ● Perform strengthening exercises for the forearm ● Undertake a thorough warm up and cool down ● Use strapping	First aid: Advise the athlete to rest. Tennis elbow can also respond well to heat treatments. Alternatively, refer the athlete to a doctor for a corticosteroid injection, which will reduce inflammation and relieve pain

GOLFER'S ELBOW			
Causes and risk factors	Signs and symptoms	Minimising risk of injury	Treatment
Golfer's elbow is another very common joint injury, and usually occurs during the follow through of a swing. It is caused by repeated tensions that force tears in the muscles of the wrist and forearm. This also occurs to javelin throwers after the release of the javelin. Overhead actions aggravate the elbow region	• Pain in the elbow • Possible popping and tearing sound in severe injuries • A sharp pain experienced during overhead movements • Possible tingling and numbness of the area	• Avoid repetitive prolonged training without adequate rest periods • Ensure a sufficient warm up and cool down • Wear a protective strapping	First aid: Advise the athlete to rest. The treatment is the same as for tennis elbow. Overhead movements should be avoided for up to 12 weeks. The use of ice massage can be beneficial. Ultrasound can also help: this is a tool that produces sound waves and deep heat, and is used widely by physiotherapists in the treatment of injuries

Sprains

A sprain involves over stretching or slightly tearing a ligament. Sprains can occur in many sports but are particularly common in gymnastics. They are a frequent injury of the ankle or wrist.

WRIST SPRAINS			
Causes and risk factors	Signs and symptoms	Minimising risk of injury	Treatment
Sprains can be caused by: • a sudden twist • overstretching • stress on ligaments They are very common in: • gymnastics • boxing • pole vaulting • falling on an outstretched arm when the wrist is hyperflexed (this may occur as force is applied during techniques such as vaulting or floor exercises in gymnastics)	• Pain during the activity • Pain on performing passive extension of the wrist • Swelling in the wrist	• Use strapping or a support • Reduce intensity of training • Strengthen the muscles of the wrist and forearm	First aid: Use the R.I.C.E. method rest, ice, compression and elevation)

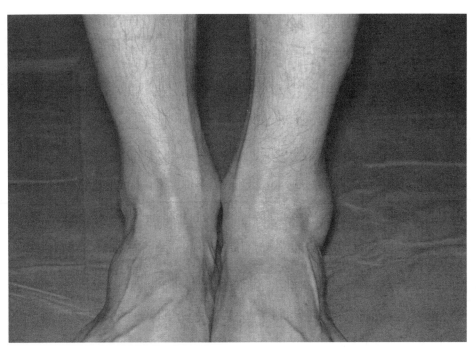

A badly sprained ankle

ANKLE SPRAIN OR TWISTED ANKLE

Causes and risk factors	Signs and symptoms	Minimising risk of injury	Treatment
Ankle sprain is caused by stress that is placed on either side of the ankle joint, which then forces the ankle from its 'normal' alignment. The ligaments that hold the joint in place are then torn or over stretched. For example, a runner may unintentionally land on the side of the foot, resulting in the ankle being forced from its normal position. This type of injury in common in the following sports: • running • basketball • football • skiing • running or playing sport on a rough surface • any sport where the athlete may 'go over' on his or her ankle	The main symptoms are: • pain at the ankle joint at the time of the injury • a feeling of popping or tearing of the ankle joint in the outer region Some other symptoms are: • swelling and tenderness in the area • slight loss of function with slight injuries to the ankle joint • more severe loss of function with more severe injury • bruising, which usually appears a few hours after the injury has occurred	• Perform thorough warm up prior to training • Wear protective shoes • Tape or strap the ankle	First aid: • Use the R.I.C.E. method (rest, ice, compression and elevation). After the initial treatment of the area, apply ice to the injury for 20 minutes, three or four times per day

Strains

A strain involves tendons that attach muscle to bone. A strain usually occurs when a tendon or muscle has been torn or stretched suddenly, or with some degree of force.

ADDUCTOR MUSCLE STRAIN (INNER THIGH)

Causes and risk factors	Signs and symptoms	Minimising risk of injury	Treatment
Adductor muscle strain is caused by quick changes in direction during running, taking the adductor muscle beyond the point of alignment or range of motion. Footballers are prone to this type of strain	● Sharp pain in the groin area, which may increase as the activity continues ● Weakness during flexion of the hip and adduction movements	● Perform thorough warm up prior to training	First aid: ● Carry out ice treatments immediately ● Stretching and gentle massage will reduce discomfort

TRICEPS STRAIN

Causes and risk factors	Signs and symptoms	Minimising risk of injury	Treatment
Triceps strain is most commonly an over use injury, where prolonged action has been experienced by the muscles and tendons of the strained area. The action could be constant extension when throwing a ball, for example. A single force to the area can also cause damage to the soft tissue of the area of the arm and elbow. Triceps strain is most common in the following sports: ● baseball ● football ● throwing sports ● weight lifting	● Pain experienced during motion of the elbow or during a forceful extension of the forearm at the elbow joint ● Muscle spasm ● Swelling around the injured area	● Perform thorough warm up prior to training	First aid: ● Use the R.I.C.E. method ● Advise the athlete to rest, so that the damaged soft tissue has time to repair itself ● Give ice treatments immediately, to reduce and prevent further swelling, as these treatments won't be effective 24–48 hours later ● Once swelling has stopped, heat treatments can be applied

 Think about it

Discuss some of the injuries you have learned about with others in your group. Have you any personal experience of them. If so, how were you treated? Was the treatment given correct for your injury?

Torn cartilage of the knee

Cartilage is the tissue that covers bones and acts as a shock absorber.

Causes and risk factors	Signs and symptoms	Minimising risk of injury	Treatment
Cartilage tears of the knee usually occur as a result of: • a direct blow to the knee • a collision • movements which involve excessive deep knee bending • twisting • previous knee injuries They are most common in the following sports: • football • weightlifting • running	• Swelling • Pain • Locking in of joints • Knee giving way	How to minimise the risk of cartilage tears of the knee: • Strengthen the muscles around the knee • Wear protective strapping when training or competing • Avoid training or running on concrete surfaces	First aid: • Use the R.I.C.E. method • Minute cartilage tears sometimes heel by themselves. In many cases, however, surgery is required

Dehydration

Dehydration can be described as a loss of water and salts from the body.

Causes and risk factors	Signs and symptoms	Minimising risk of injury	Treatment
Dehydration can be caused by: • excessive sweating whilst training or participating in a sporting activity • training during hot weather • inadequate fluid intake • the use of drugs	• Dry mouth/tongue • No urine (or very little) • Drowsiness/confusion • Deep sunken eyes • Dry skin • Tiredness or even collapse	Athletes should maintain a regular fluid intake when training or during physical activity, and small but frequent amounts of fluid in hot weather	First aid: Give the athlete small amounts of water to drink and refer him or her to a medical person. If the dehydration is severe, the athlete may need to go to hospital in order to receive intravenous fluids to replace lost fluids and essential salts

Hypothermia

Hypothermia can be defined as a dramatic fall in body temperature to below 35 degrees Celsius.

Causes and risk factors	Signs and symptoms	Minimising risk of injury	Treatment
Hypothermia can be caused when an athlete trains in extreme cold conditions for a prolonged period of time	Shivering Muscle rigidity Cramps Low blood pressure Low pulse and breathing rates Confusion Disorientation Cold, pale, dry skin	Be equipped for all kinds of weather Wear extra, thin layers of clothing Wear a waterproof and windproof outer layer of clothing Wear a hat and gloves Eat extra energy foods and warm drinks	First aid: Cover athlete with foil blanket Replace any wet clothing with warm dry clothing If the athlete is otherwise fit and healthy, bathe him or her in a warm bath to increase body temperature In the case of severe hypothermia, send for medical help straight away and keep the athlete warm and dry

Key point

Death usually occurs when the temperature falls below 25 degrees Celcius.

Soft tissue injuries

These are injuries that occur to the soft tissues of the body, and include things like cuts, grazes, blisters, sprains and strains. Soft tissue injuries can occur in any sport.

Cuts

Clean cuts with cold water to help stop the bleeding, then dry the cut and cover it with a sterile dressing

Grazes or abrasions

These usually occur during a slip or fall on a rough surface when playing sport. The superficial layer of skin is usually rubbed off. Treat grazes in the same way as cuts.

Blisters

A blister can be described as a 'bubble' which forms on the skin, and which is caused by friction or heat. If the blister is broken then it needs to be protected and covered by a dry, non-adhesive dressing to prevent infection. The dressing will also allow the blister to reduce and heal of its own accord, without further irritation from clothing or shoes.

Bruises

A bruise usually occurs as a result of direct contact or a hard blow. The capillaries under the skin become damaged and bleed into the tissue. As a result the skin becomes discoloured, swelling occurs and the area becomes painful to touch.

To treat a bruise, elevate the injured area and apply an ice pack for 10 to 15 minutes. Check the area after a few minutes for any increased swelling or discolouration. Also feel to check the temperature of the skin.

If there is increased swelling or discolouration, apply the ice for a further 10 minutes. If swelling still does not cease, you will need to get medical help.

Assessment activity 3: Common sporting injuries

P List five common sporting injuries and for each one:
1. identify the signs and symptoms
2. explain the immediate treatment.

M From your list compare the different methods of treating common sporting injuries.

D In small groups evaluate the effectiveness of treatment methods that are used for common sporting injuries, offering further recommendations and alternatives. You can record your findings in writing or by videoing your group discussion.

Assessing an injury or accident situation

When an injury or accident occurs it is extremely important to assess the situation quickly, carefully and safely. When it is safe to do so, the casualty or the injured athlete must be quickly examined to check for any life threatening conditions that may need urgent attention. You should be prepared to resuscitate if necessary.

If you are first on the scene, it is your responsibility to provide first aid. When medical help arrives you will need to give a report of the casualty and what treatment you have given. If the casualty is responsive, try to get as much information as you can to give to the paramedics or doctors. A checklist of relevant information should include the following:

- casualty's name and age
- details of any injuries
- time the injury occurred
- details of other individuals involved
- first aid treatment given.

You may not always be able to gather this information from the casualty. If there are people around, they may have seen what happened or know the casualty. Do not be afraid to ask.

Let's do it!

Devise an injury report form that could be given to a medical professional with information filled in about an injured athlete.

Key points

Remember the four Ps!

Preserve – Preserve your own life first by ensuring that you are not in any danger of being harmed. Never put yourself at risk. Also, preserve the life of the injured.

Protect – Protect the injured from further danger by ensuring that the area is safe.

Prioritise – Prioritise urgent matters and assess injuries to determine treatment priorities. You must treat any condition that is deemed to be life threatening first. For example, imagine a situation in which two football players both go to head the ball and collide. Both players fall to the ground. You need to quickly assess the situation. If one player has stopped breathing and the other has concussion, prioritise and treat the player who has stopped breathing.

Promote recovery – Help the injured to recover by applying the necessary first aid to relieve pain or discomfort, or to control bleeding and so on.

The five checks

Before making any type of diagnosis it is important to quickly go through the following five checks.

1 Check for unconsciousness:
Gently shake the casualty's shoulders and say, 'Hello, I'm (your name), can you hear me?' If there is no response the casualty may be unconscious

2 Open the airway:
- Place one hand on the casualty's forehead and two fingers of the other hand under the casualty's chin.
- Gently tilt the head backwards to open the airway.
- Open the mouth and remove any obstructions that might be affecting breathing.

3 Check for breathing:
- Place your ear by the casualty's mouth and nose and listen.
- Look at and feel the chest, to ascertain whether it is rising.

4 Check for circulation:
Feel for a pulse in the neck or at the wrist

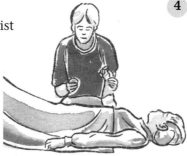

5 Check for any signs of bleeding:
Blood loss needs to be controlled. If it is not, the blood won't be efficiently transported to the vital organs of the body and the casualty could go into shock.

Key points

Perform the five checks and establish if the casualty is:
- conscious, breathing, with a pulse
- unconscious, not breathing, with a pulse
- unconscious, not breathing, without a pulse
- unconscious, breathing, with a pulse.

Then give the immediate necessary treatment without delay.

What to do if the casualty is ...

... conscious, breathing and has a pulse

↓

Make the casualty comfortable

↓

Place the casualty into the recovery position

↓

↓

↓

**... unconscious, not breathing
and has a pulse**

Call 999

Lay the casualty on his or her back and
tilt the head back to open the airway

Remove any obstructions and start
mouth to mouth ventilation

Once breathing has started unaided, place
the casualty in the recovery position

**... unconscious, not breathing
and does not have a pulse**

Call 999

Tilt the head back and ensure the airway is
open and free from obstructions

Start mouth to mouth ventilation

Apply 15 chest compressions
(cardio pulmonary resuscitation)

Give another two breaths

Apply another 15 chest compressions

Performing chest compressions

Repeat this process until the client starts
breathing and there is a pulse. If the client
does not respond, continue with this until
medical help arrives

... unconscious, breathing and has a pulse

↓

Call 999

↓

Place the casualty in the recovery position with the head tilted to ensure the airway is open

↓

Keep on monitoring breathing and pulse until medical help arrives

 Key points

To perform mouth to mouth ventilation:
1. Pinch the casualty's nose and seal your mouth around the casualty's mouth.
2. Breathe into the mouth and watch to see if the chest rises.
3. Perform this technique twice.
4. If there is still a pulse and the chest has risen, continue with ten breaths per minute until breathing is unaided.

 Key points

To perform chest compressions (cardio pulmonary resuscitation):
1. Find where the lower ribs meet the breastbone.
2. Place your middle finger on this spot and your index finger above it.
3. Place the heel of your other hand on the breast bone.
   Move it until it reaches your index finger.
4. Link fingers and apply a downward pressure leaning over the casualty with arms straight.

Let's do it!

Ask your tutor for a first aid box. List everything it contains, and describe what each piece of kit is for.

Assessment activity 4: Assessment checklist

Choose two different types of injuries. Prepare an injury report form like the one below, which could be given to a medical professional with information filled in about an injured athlete.

Injury Report Form

Date and Time of injury: 05/05/2004 2pm **Pulse:** 85 bpm
Venue: Barracks Lane Sports Ground **Breaths per min:** 23
First Aider: Milly Smith **Breathing:** quiet
Time of Observation: 2.01 pm

	General Information	Details of the injured party	Additional Comments
1	Name and age of injured	Nathan Murray – 14 yrs	
2	How did the injury occur/cause of the injury	Two football players went to head the ball at the same time. Collision of heads	Nathan fell to the fall clutching his head
3	The insured's symptoms, for example a) Numbness b) Blurred vision c) Severe pain d) Mild pain etc	He is conscious but is complaining complaining about severe blurred vision, dizziness and a throbbing headache	Nathan feels scared
4	Visual Signs, for example a) Swelling b) Bleeding c) Dislocation d) Discolouration e) Redness f) Bruising g) Breathing difficulties h) Unconsciousness i) Concussion j) Others	A lot of swelling at the front and side of the head	
5	Speech a) Respond well to questions b) Confused c) Other	Confused	
6	First Aid Treatment given	Ice pack for head Kept calm and warm	
7	Ambulance/Medical help sent for	Ambulance called	2.04 pm
8	Referred to hospital	Yes	Parents contacted – minor
9	Resume play	No	
10	Advice Given	Reassurance, kept talking/kept awake, felt sleepy	
11	Home treatment Plan	N/A	Referred to hospital

Injury report form

P With the help of your tutor, prepare an assessment checklist to find out the level of need for the two different types of injuries you have chosen.

M On your own prepare an assessment checklist that will help you find out the level of need for two more different types of injuries.

D Critically analyse the assessment checklist you created in **M** , identifying methods to evaluate its use and suitability to the target audience.

Alternative methods of treating injuries

Increasingly, sportsmen and women are turning to different forms of alternative medicine to help the healing process and to recover more quickly from an injury.

Method	Description	Picture
Acupuncture	A method of healing using needles, developed in China thousands of years ago. The needles are used to influence the balance of the body's natural health by stimulating points on the channels of energy (Qi) that flow through the body	
Homeopathy	This method uses medicines that are given in an extremely dilute form, and which work by influencing the energy level of the body. Homeopathy tends to see illness as an expression of disharmony within the whole person	
Chiropractic	This method specialises and focuses on muscular and skeletal problems through manipulation of the spine	
Medical herbalism	This method treats disorders with medicines that have been derived from plant materials	
Physiotherapy	A physiotherapist is crucial in the rehabilitation stages after injury. He or she will provide advice, assess and diagnose injuries, prescribe exercises, and perform massages and other manipulative techniques to aid the injured person back to full recovery	

Let's do it!

Carry out some further research on the methods of alternative treatments described on page 93. Devise a leaflet stating how these treatments may help an injured athlete in the recovery process following an injury.

Risk assessment

It is essential that at any sporting venue, facility or stadium, any hazards that could cause harm to participants, staff and visitors are identified. The risks must then be dealt with to prevent injuries occurring. It is the responsibility of the owner, manager and coach to work together to assess health and safety hazards and risks.

There are many potential health and safety hazards within all sporting environments, which, if not dealt with promptly, could cause serious injury to others or could even be life threatening.

What is risk assessment?

A risk assessment is an inspection carried out to identify hazards and to prevent accidents or injuries occurring within a facility or environment in which you are working or playing. There are six steps to a risk assessment:

1. identify the hazard
2. identify who will be harmed
3. give a risk rating
4. record existing measures being taken
5. suggest other measures that could be taken
6. record, review, monitor and evaluate.

Step 1 : Identify the hazard

Be observant and alert to anything that could possibly cause harm to others. If a hazard is reported, ask people what they saw, when and where. If an accident occurs due to a hazard, report it and put measures in place to ensure that it does not affect anybody else.

Step **2** : Identify who will be harmed

State who uses or works in the facility and who may come into contact with the hazard. Those persons who may be harmed will normally be staff, visitors and users of the facility.

Step **3** : Give a risk rating

In this section, the severity of the risk and the probability that the risk could occur need to be identified.

Severity of risk, rating 1–3:
1. high risk – where the outcome would be death or serious injury
2. moderate risk – where the outcome would be an injury requiring hospital treatment
3. low risk – where the outcome is a treatable injury, which would not incapacitate.

Probability of risk, rating 1–3:
1. good chance of it happening
2. could occur
3. not likely to happen.

Step **4** : Record existing measures taken

Identify any existing measures that are currently in place, if any. Note what is already in place to stop the hazard from harming others. If there is currently nothing in place, then state that on your risk assessment form.

Step **5** : Suggest measures that could be taken

In this section, state what can be done to prevent an injury occurring, or what further actions are required to control the risk.

Step **6** : Record, review, monitor and evaluate

Everything recorded on a risk assessment must be reviewed, to ensure that the suggested measures are being effectively employed and are still working. Risk assessments must be reviewed and evaluated on an ongoing basis.

Let's do it!

Possible health and safety hazard	Environment	How to minimise risk of injury	Purpose
Faulty equipment	Leisure and sports centres; gymnasiums	Report faulty equipment to a duty manager or health and safety officer as soon as it is identified. Record the fault in a log book. Withdraw the equipment, or display a notice on it stating that it is 'out of order'	To minimise the risk of injury to users To protect participants To maintain a safe environment To protect those leading the activity
Misuse of chemicals/ Chemical spillages	Swimming pools (pool plant chemicals); cleaning agents in sports and leisure centres	Train staff who use chemicals in COSSH procedures. Ensure staff know how and where to use specific chemicals properly. Regular staff training and observations are required. Report chemical spillages or misuse of chemicals immediately to a superior	To protect the users and staff from chemical burns and/or inhalation of dangerous chemicals To maintain a safe environment
Wet floors	Around swimming pools; in changing rooms; in the case of spillages	Display appropriate signs, warning that the floor is wet. Mop or dry area	To ensure that all staff, users or visitors are aware of the dangers To prevent slips or falls To maintain a safe environment

The table above shows some potential health and safety hazards within leisure, recreation and sporting environments. Extend the table, using the same headings, for the following hazards:

- fire
- electricity
- fumes
- equipment falling from shelves
- ventilation
- protective headgear and clothing.

Risk assessment procedure

Risk assessment procedure will always be the same, whether it is conducted by a sports coach or a duty officer. The completed risk assessment must be shown to the relevant person or people (for example, a manager or health and safety officer) who will then work with a team of people to reduce the likelihood of the risk occurring. The sporting activity should not commence until the risk is eliminated.

Certain rules or procedures may be implemented by an organisation to try to eliminate risks occurring. These must be monitored and reviewed regularly, to ensure they are effective.

 Key points

The benefits of maintaining a safe working environment are:
- repeat business
- good reputation
- happy customers
- less risk of accidents
- no fines!

A safe working environment is a safe learning environment

Let's do it!

1. Using the risk assessment layout in the table below, conduct a risk assessment for the following sporting situations (ensure that you identify all possible risks):
   - A crowded swimming pool with one pool attendant.
   - A football match on astroturf with inadequate lighting.
   - A 60 year old joining the gym, with no health screening undertaken.
   - A boxing participant without the correct PPE (personal protective equipment).

Step 1 Identify the hazard	Step 2 Who will be harmed?	Step 3 Risk rating (severity/ probability)	Step 4 Existing measures	Step 5 Suggested measures	Step 6 Record, review, monitor and evaluate

2. Arrange to visit a sporting facility, swimming pool, leisure centre, gymnasium or sports stadium. Working in pairs, conduct a thorough risk assessment. Record your findings as well as your suggested measures, and present this to the rest of the group.

Assessment activity 5: Risk assessments

Choose a sport or activity from the following list:
- football
- hockey
- netball
- karate
- ice skating
- weight lifting.

P Independently, prepare and carry out a risk assessment. Then explain the relevant laws, rules and regulations regarding your selected sport.

No extension to merit or distinction is possible for this assessment activity.

Key points

Here are some useful terms and explanations of methods involved in injuries:

Acute injuries – A single force is directed upon a structure that produces an injury.
Chronic injuries – Repeated force or loading, over a period of time, resulting in an injury.
Compression – A force directed along the length of a structure, a bone or soft tissue.
Cryotherapy – A therapy which uses cold application methods to reduce swelling and pain.
Ice massage – Massage technique that uses iced water in a foam cup. The ice protrudes from the cup and massage is performed over the area in circular movements. Usually carried out three or four times per day for approximately 15 minutes, for the initial 24–72 hours after the injury has taken place.
Laceration – A wound that opens the skin and goes through to the subcutaneous layer of the skin, muscles, associated nerves and blood vessels.
Spasm – Temporary muscle contractions.
Sprain – Injury to soft tissues e.g. ligaments.
Strain – The amount of deformation that a structure goes through compared to its original shape and size.
Synovitis – Inflammation of the synovial membrane that surrounds a synovial joint.
Tendonitis – Inflammation of a muscle tendon.

CHECK WHAT YOU KNOW!

Look back through this unit to see if you can you answer the following questions:
1. Define the following terms: health, safety, risk, hazard, risk assessment.
2. What are the key intentions of the Health and Safety at Work Act 1974?
3. Identify five risk factors which can cause sporting injuries.
4. If a sports facility maintains good practice, what do you think the benefits are to that organisation?
5. What are the key intentions of the COSSH regulations?
6. What are the risk factors associated with a busy swimming pool?
7. Describe the steps of a risk assessment, and state why it is important to carry out a risk assessment before any sporting activity.
8. Describe two common sporting injuries and the immediate basic treatment for them.
9. Name two methods of alternative medicine.
10. Why is it important to have a qualified first aider at sports events and training sessions?

Preparation for sport

Introduction

In this unit you will gain a better understanding of how the body is affected by various factors in training and performance. You will look at lifestyle and its relevance to training and performance, and analyse changing training practices. You will find out how knowledge of nutrition and psychology can improve performance if integrated into the training programme.

How you will be assessed

Throughout the unit you will have lots of tasks and activities to perform, to help you learn and remember information as well as prepare for assessment. These include case studies with questions. This unit is a compulsory unit to the BTEC First Diploma in Sport. It is assessed internally, so the centre delivering the qualification will assess your learning outcomes.

After completing this unit you should be able to achieve the following outcomes:
1. Explore the **fitness level and lifestyle** of an individual in a selected sport.
2. Plan a simple **fitness training programme** for an individual sports performer.
3. Examine the **nutritional requirements** of sportspeople.
4. Investigate the **psychological factors** that affect sports training and performance.

Fitness level and lifestyle

Components of physical fitness

Physical fitness can be described as having the ability to carry out day-to-day activities or tasks without the onset of unnecessary fatigue. This encompasses sportspeople and non sportspeople. There are different components that make up fitness. These components contribute towards the different needs of different sports.

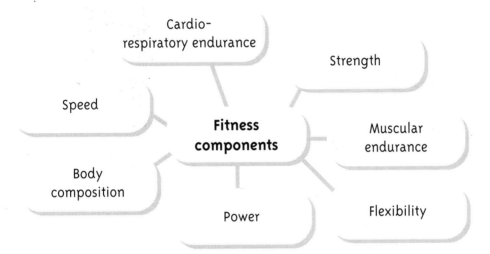

 Key points

There are four major components of fitness: these are strength, flexibility, speed and cardio-respiratory endurance. The amount of each component that each person possesses will vary. Some people are born with more flexibility than others and will develop this component through maturation. This will obviously help in following certain sporting careers, for example, gymnastics.

Strength

Strength can be described as the maximum force a muscle, or group of muscles, can produce in a single movement or contraction.

Key points

There are three categories of strength:
1. **maximum strength** – needed to produce a single movement against a resistance, for example, power lifting
2. **elastic strength** – needed to produce movements that are very close to each other in time, such as floor routines in gymnastics, or the triple jump
3. **strength endurance** – needed to produce repetitive movements of a muscle, or muscle group, and to withstand fatigue while doing so.

 Think about it

Can you think of examples of three sports which use the three different types strength described above?

Speed

Speed is required in many sports and can be described as the ability to move the body or body parts quickly over a set distance. It is important to note that speed is not only concerned with running, but also the speed at which other body parts can move. For example, you need to move your arms quickly when you catch and pass a ball during a game of rugby, to avoid it being lost in a tackle.

Let's do it!

In a group, write down a list of the sports that you regularly take part in. Then list the different requirements for speed for each sport. Which parts of the body have to react quickly?

Cardio-respiratory endurance

Cardio-respiratory endurance is the ability to continue exercising aerobically or for a prolonged period of time. To do this, the body needs to transport and use the oxygen that is breathed in during exercise. Cardio-respiratory endurance relies on the efficiency of the cardiovascular system to deliver oxygen. All long distance sports depend on this component of fitness to supply and maintain the energy that is required.

A marathon runner requires good cardio-respiratory endurance

Muscular endurance

Muscular endurance is a muscle or muscle group's ability to sustain repetitive contractions over a period of time. There is a rich blood supply to the muscles that helps to prolong the onset of fatigue or the build up of lactic acid.

Flexibility

Flexibility is the range of movement that a joint or series of joints can perform. There are many factors that can determine the range of movement around a joint, including:

- the elasticity of the ligaments and tendons at the joint
- the strength of the opposing muscle group (antagonistic muscle group)
- the shape of the articulating surface of the bones that make up the joint.

The degree of movement is also associated with the type of joint at which the movement is taking place. Joints are designed for stability, movement, or both. The hinge joint at the knee, for example, is designed primarily for stability; therefore the movement that can be produced is only in flexion and extension.

A gymnast with good flexibility

Body composition

The study of body composition distinguishes between the body's fat mass and its lean mass, and their distribution around the body. Body composition is an essential consideration, not only for sports but for health and well-being.

A body that contains more fat mass than lean or skeletal muscle mass can suffer from severe health problems, such as obesity, cardiovascular disease and other associated complications. For sportspeople, a high fat mass can result in the reduction of muscle mass. This will lead to a reduction of performance due to the drop in efficiency of skeletal muscle because more energy is required to move a greater mass. In other words, more energy is being used to move the mass than to perform.

Key points

Body shape, or somatotype, can be categorised into three main groups:

1. Endomorphs – rounded or pear-shaped body (this category may also be classed as overweight).
2. Mesomorphs – lean body shape, predominantly muscular and athletic in appearance (mesomorph body shapes often appear as a spinning top shape).
3. Ectomorphs – tall, slender and more angular body shape (long distance runners and high jumpers commonly have this body shape).

Mesomorph   Ectomorph   Endomorph

The three basic somatotypes

Power

Power is the ability to produce a large amount of force in a short period of time. It is the result of strength and speed. The amount of power required by different sports varies. A rugby player, for example, requires more strength and speed than a 1500 metre runner, although both sportspeople will need to include strength and power training in their training programmes. Most sports need strength and power for optimum performance, but in many actions it is power that is most important.

Assessment activity 1: Physical fitness and lifestyle factors

Choose two contrasting sports.

P On your own, use what you have learned to identify physical fitness and lifestyle factors for each of your two contrasting sports, and comment on the effects of these factors on sports performance.

M Define the components of physical fitness and explain how lifestyle factors can affect sports performance.

D Evaluate the effects of lifestyle factors on sports performance and provide recommendations for changes.

Fitness levels and fitness tests

Fitness is a term that has different meanings for different people, depending on the goals they set themselves to become 'fit'. Fitness levels vary, and 'getting fit' could mean anything from attending exercise classes twice a week, to training for running a marathon.

 Think about it

What is your idea of 'fitness'? In a group, discuss the goals you set yourselves, and your training regimes for a typical week.

The current fitness level of an individual needs to be established before any improvements can be made.

The best way to measure an individual's fitness level is to carry out field tests of physical fitness. Fitness tests are designed to measure changes in the body through the stresses that exercise places upon it. The two changes that need to be defined are:

- response to exercise – the short term changes that occur when the body exercises. (In other words, the immediate change in the body's systems to maintain a balance of the internal environment when required to exercise after a period of rest)
- adaptation to exercise – the long term changes that occur in and to the body when it has been exercised over a period of time.

Changes last only as long as the exercise or training continues. It can take up to six weeks to change your fitness level, and only two weeks to lose those changes.

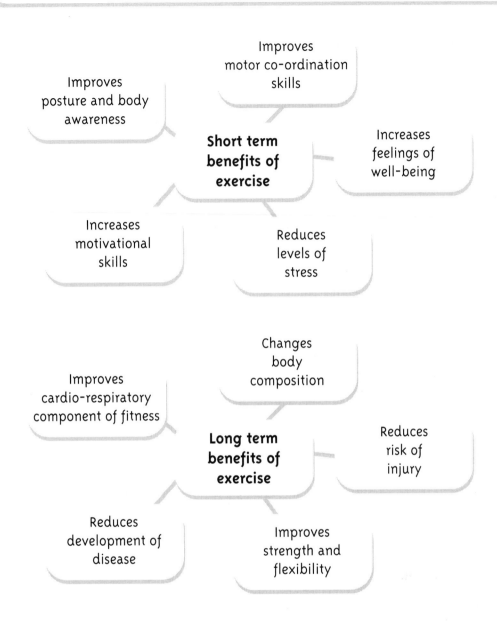

Improves motor co-ordination skills

Improves posture and body awareness

Short term benefits of exercise

Increases feelings of well-being

Increases motivational skills

Reduces levels of stress

Changes body composition

Improves cardio-respiratory component of fitness

Long term benefits of exercise

Reduces risk of injury

Reduces development of disease

Improves strength and flexibility

Let's do it!

Consider the list of sports given below. Rank the components of fitness that each sport requires, in order of their importance. Give reasons for your choices:

- weight lifting
- parallel bars in gymnastics
- shot putt
- 1500 metre running.

Fitness tests

Fitness tests help to assess the various components of fitness. Some of these tests are complex to administer, others are easily carried out.

 Key points

The benefits of carrying out fitness tests are as follows:
- the strengths and weaknesses of the sportsperson can be identified
- the information provides a benchmark against which future performance can be compared
- the sportsperson's motivation may increase as a result of the previous two points
- the information can be used to help make changes to, or design, training programmes.

Two tests for strength

The hand grip dynamometer and 1RM tests

The table below shows two tests for strength.
1. The dynamometer test is specific to one muscle group.
2. 1RM (one repetition maximum) tests various muscle groups. For this test, only one repetition can be completed for the weight that is being lifted.

Test	Muscle group being measured	Description of protocol	Advantages	Disadvantages
Hand grip dynamometer	Muscles in the forearm	Three attempts of the test from each hand (left and right), keeping the hand by the side of the body	A simple test; an objective measure	Not a total measure of strength because it is a measure of the forearms only
1RM (1 rep max)	Various, depending on exercise being performed	One possible maximum force to lift free weights or other gym based equipment	Accessible equipment	Greater possibility of injury due to the maximum weights that are required

The hand grip dynamometer

Grip strength scores

Classification	Non-dominant (KG)	Dominant (KG)
Women		
Excellent	>37	>41
Good	34–36	38–40
Average	22–33	25–37
Poor	18–21	22–24
Very poor	<18	<22
Men		
Excellent	>68	>70
Good	56–67	62–69
Average	43–55	48–61
Poor	39–42	41–47
Very poor	<39	<41

Fitness testing for speed

The 30 metre sprint

Test	Description of protocol	Advantages	Disadvantages
30 metre sprint	To run as fast as possible along an obstacle free distance of 30 metres on a non slip surface, from the call of the timer, '3,2,1, GO!'	A simple test; easy to administer	• Timing can be affected by error • Condition of the running surface can affect speed

Sprint test scores

Time (in seconds) Male	Time (in seconds) Female	Rating
<4.0	<4.5	Excellent
4.2–4.0	4.6–4.5	Good
4.4–4.3	4.8–4.7	Average
4.6–4.5	5.0–4.9	Fair
>4.6	>5.0	Very poor

Two tests for cardio-respiratory endurance

The VO2 Max NCF multi-stage shuttle run test

This is used to predict the maximum amount of oxygen that a person can take in and use during exercise. This test requires participants to complete 20 m shuttle runs in time to a pre-recorded cassette. As the test goes on, the speed at which they are required to run gets faster each minute. The test stops when the participant cannot keep up with the speed. At this point you can measure their estimated VO2 max or record the number of levels and shuttles completed – both will give an indication of aerobic fitness.

Test	Description of protocol	Advantages	Disadvantages
VO2 Max NCF multi-stage shuttle run test	Individuals must line up on the 20 m mark, on hearing the triple beep that starts the test, the subjects must start to run to the other line 20 m away. The subjects must reach the 20 m target before or on the single beep that signifies each suttle run. Subjects must continue to run arriving at each line on the beeps. Each subject can be given 3 chances before they either stop running or they are pulled out. This is a maximal test therefore subjects must run until they feel that they can not run any further.	● Comparisons can be made to published data ● Large numbers can be tested at once ● Limited equipment required	● Relies on subject's motivation and honesty to perform the test until exhaustion ● Not an absolute measure, only a prediction ● A running test, so may favour subjects that participate in activities that involve running

The three minute step-up test

This looks at the recovery rate of the heart rate, which can also determine cardio-respiratory fitness.

Test	Description of protocol	Advantages	Disadvantages
Three minute step up test	Step on and off a 45 cm high box or bench at a rate of 30 steps per minute. The speed can be set with a metronome. The test should last 3 minutes. Heart rate is taken before the test starts, to establish resting heart rate, at the end of the test, and on three occasions during the test: 1–1.5 mins 2–2.15 mins 3–3.15 mins	Requires minimal equipment; easy to administer	● Taking the heart rate at the set times; may rely on the experience of the experimenter to find the pulse rate at each stage ● Relies on other experimenters to monitor the accuracy of the steps

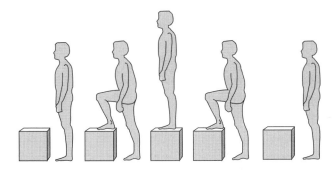

The three minute step-up test

The three minute step-up test scores

Classification	Male	Female
Superior	<118	<121
Excellent	119–133	122–136
Good	134–143	137–154
Average	144–166	155–175
Poor	167–193	176–205
Very poor	>194	>206

Two tests for muscular endurance

The press-up test

Test	Muscle group being measured	Description of protocol	Advantages	Disadvantages
The press-up test	Pectorals, triceps and deltoids	To perform as many press-ups in a minute as the subject can manage. The body must be lowered to approximately 5 cm away from the ground	• Easy to administer • Limited equipment required • Not time consuming	Level of accuracy of the press-ups and body position that is required relies on the motivation and honesty of the subject

Press-up test scores

Classification	Male	Female
Excellent	>45	>40
Good	41–45	35–40
Average	31–40	25–34
Fair	21–30	15–24
Poor	10–20	5–14
Very poor	<10	<5

The curl-up test

Test	Muscle group being measured	Description of protocol	Advantages	Disadvantages
The curl-up test	Abdominals	To perform as many curl-ups in a minute as the subject can manage. The upper body must be raised off the ground to an angle of 30–40 degrees, with the knees bent at 90 degrees, and feet on the floor. Place your arms across your chest or by the side of your body	Easy to administer Limited equipment required Not time consuming	Accuracy of the curl-ups and body positions relies on the honesty and motivation of the subject

A curl-up

Curl-up test scores

Classification	Male	Female
Excellent	>50	>40
Good	45–50	36–40
Average	35–44	26–35
Fair	25–34	16–25
Poor	15–24	10–15
Very poor	<15	<10

Fitness testing for flexibility

The sit-and-reach test

Test	Muscle group being measured	Description of protocol	Advantages	Disadvantages
Sit-and-reach test	Hamstrings and lower back	Subject sits with both legs flat against the floor and feet against the sit-and-reach box. Subject then stretches arms forward, to push the cursor on the box as far as possible, in a smooth action. This stretch must be held for two seconds	Easy to administer	Limited area of muscle being tested; muscle temperature can affect the scores

Sit-and-reach test scores

Classification	Male	Female
Excellent	>35	>39
Good	31–34	33–38
Fair	27–30	29–32
Poor	<27	<29

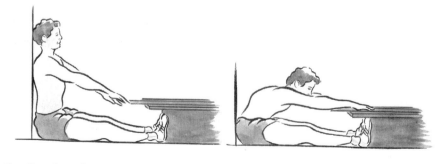

The sit-and-reach test

Fitness testing for body composition

The BMI (Body Mass Index) test

Test	Considerations being measured	Description of protocol	Advantages	Disadvantages
BMI (Body Mass Index)	Weight against height	Take measurements for subjects height and weight: $$BMI = \frac{weight\ in\ kg}{height\ in\ m \times height\ in\ m} \times height\ in\ m$$ The higher the score, the greater levels of body fat	Simple and easy test	It does not always apply to sports people; not an accurate test to distinguish between fat and lean mass

Ratings for the Body Mass Index

Classification	Rating
Healthy	20–25
Overweight	25–30
Obese	>30

The skinfold test

Test	Muscle group being measured	Description of protocol	Advantages	Disadvantages
Skinfold measures	Biceps Triceps Sub scapular Supra iliac			Results can change depending on the reliability of each tester

Fitness testing for power

The vertical jump test

Test	Muscle group being measured	Description of protocol	Advantage	Disadvantages
Vertical jump test	Legs	Place belt around the waist of the subject. Ensure the string attached to the foot mat (which stays on the ground) is taut. The subject bends the knees and jumps upwards in a smooth action. Score appears (in centimetres) on the electronic clock on the belt. Can be repeated three times with the best score taken.	Simple and easy to use	None

Vertical jump test scores

Classification	Male Distance (in cm)	Female Distance (in cm)
Excellent	>60	>47
Good	51–59	36–46
Average	41–50	29–35
Poor	27–40	25–34
Very poor	<26	<24

Let's do it!

With the help of your tutor, describe a fitness test for each of the following components of fitness. Ensure it is suitable for the fitness component and also for the area of the body you wish to test:

- flexibility
- power
- muscular endurance.

Assessment activity 2: Fitness tests

Choose a sports performer from your group.

P With the support of your tutor, carry out suitable fitness tests for the sports performer, and record the tests accurately. Assess the level of fitness of the sports performer according to the accepted norms and standard protocol.

M On your own, carry out suitable fitness tests for the sports performer. Record the test results accurately and comment on them.

D Critically analyse the results you get from carrying out a fitness test on the sports performer of your choice, drawing valid conclusions and making any suitable recommendations.

The effects of lifestyle on fitness

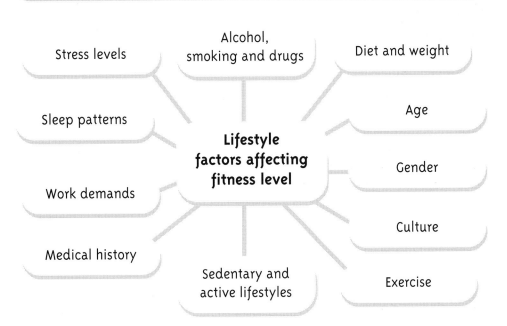

Stress levels

Alcohol, smoking and drugs

Diet and weight

Sleep patterns

Age

Lifestyle factors affecting fitness level

Gender

Work demands

Culture

Medical history

Sedentary and active lifestyles

Exercise

Stress levels

Stress is an emotional response to situations that we experience. Stress has been related to health problems such as heart disease, high blood pressure and lowered efficiency of the immune system. The body needs time to relax from day-to-day stresses to allow it to recover before the next demanding situation. Exercise has been found to be a beneficial method of reducing stress and decreasing health related illnesses.

The effects of alcohol

Alcohol has both short term and long term effects. The short term effects include:

- dizziness
- loss of motor control
- reduced ability to make decisions
- reduced perception of movement.

These symptoms will increase as more alcohol is consumed, eventually leading to unsafe, even life threatening, behaviour.

The long term effects of regular drinking beyond the recommended amounts can increase blood pressure and the efficiency of the heart. Symptoms that may be experienced include:

- breathlessness
- swelling of the legs
- muscular fatigue
- an increase in body weight
- joint problems
- liver damage
- heart failure (in extreme cases).

The effects of smoking

Aerobic fitness can be reduced by between 5 and 10% due to smoking. Smoking introduces carbon monoxide into the body. This is an odourless gas that takes some of the space of oxygen in the blood. A smoker, therefore, has less oxygen available during exercise. Smoking can also increase the risk of cancer, heart disease and respiratory disease.

The effects of drugs

Fitness levels can be increased by removing harmful substances from a lifestyle. Harmful substances include smoking, drinking alcohol and taking drugs for recreational use. Banned substances are used to increase capabilities for training and rapid recovery between exercise sessions. However, they can be harmful to health. If drugs are abused or incorrectly taken, they can reduce fitness levels.

Sleep patterns

These may vary due to the pattern of training or other external demands on life, such as family and work. Younger people commonly need at least eight hours sleep. As you get older, the amount of sleep that that you need usually decreases. However, as training intensity increases, the need for sleep will increase accordingly. If sleep is not balanced with work then the effects of training will not be seen.

Work demands

In modern society, work hours have increased and the time available to relax or partake in non work activities has reduced. This increases stress levels and the onset of health-related diseases.

Medical history

Our fitness levels are partly inherited from our parents, as are some of the the health related problems that may be experienced through the years. Training can increase levels of fitness but only to the capacity that has been passed down from generation to generation.

Sedentary and active lifestyles

The more active an individual, the greater will be the level of fitness he or she possesses. Sedentary lifestyles are related to many diseases, such as obesity, heart disease, high blood pressure and joint and bone problems. An active life style can help reduce these problems and increase the quality of life.

Diet and weight

A healthy diet will ensure a balance between the nutrient value that you consume and the energy that you use for muscular activity. Two results are possible if there is an imbalance between these two factors:
- less food and more exercise will result in weight loss
- more food and less exercise will result in weight gain.

Age and lifestyle from birth

As puberty approaches, young people discover the social factors of the world and move the importance of studying, eating and in some cases, exercise, further down the list of their priorities. Experimenting with drugs, alcohol, smoking and sex are just some of the activities that replace exercise.

Age range (in years)	Reason for participating in physical activity	Suggestion for activity
15–25	Preventing the onset of disease during later life	Regular exercise at a sports club or centre at least five times a week for no less than 30 minutes of moderate exercise
26–35	Weight management (as age increases the rate at which the body uses body fuel decreases, so activity is essential to manage body weight)	Regular exercise at a sports club or centre at least five times a week for no less than 30 minutes of moderate exercise
36–45	Reducing the risk of medical conditions such as coronary heart disease	Regular low impact aerobic exercise, to avoid possible strain and stresses on the heart and joints
46–55	Improving heart and lungs and keeping fit generally	As above, approximately 30 minutes a day of swimming, cycling, walking and even jogging
56+	Improving the quality of life	As above, including gentle mobility exercises that assist in joint efficiency

Doing exercise later in life helps improve your quality of life

Your family will also influence the type of lifestyle that you follow. If the older members of the family do not regard exercise as an important part of everyday life, there is a greater possibility of its younger members not having a high regard towards exercise, either.

Culture

Fitness levels are different for individuals from a variety of cultures for many reasons. For example, exercise may be seen as a lower priority than pursuing a career or developing a family, or exercise and an increase in fitness levels may be perceived as a predominantly male activity.

Gender

The fitness level of males and females differs due to the structures of their bodies. These differences are most noticeable after puberty has occurred. The two genders are also psychologically different. They cope differently with the stresses of physical demands made by work and exercise. There is a high drop out rate in physical activity in females aged between 16 and 21 years old. This could be due to social pressures, for example to succeed in personal relationships and careers, or financial pressure.

Participation in sports activities

Participation in competition and sports activities can overtake the importance of maintaining fitness levels. Too many competitions hinder fitness levels and stress the body without providing adequate recovery. Exercise can be become an addiction, where increasing participation can reduce the effects of training, resulting in reduced fitness levels.

Fitness training programmes

Principles of training

The major principle of training is to stimulate the adaptations that the body and mind go through during participation in sport, with the aim of improving performance. These adaptations must be controlled through the specific principles of training. Individuals react differently to training programmes, due to the differences in physiological, psychological and inherited factors. The design of the training programme should allow the body and mind of the individual to cope with the demand of the sport during participation.

Overload

If an athlete's body experiences the same intensity or stress each time he or she trains, his or her performance will not improve. The body learns to cope with stress over time. As a result, it is necessary to keep increasing the level of challenge, in order for changes to occur and improvements to be made. Overloading the body encourages these further developments.

Think about it

Get together with other members of your group.

- Can you think of times when you have pushed yourself in training?
- Can you think of times when you have carried on with the same routine too long?

Discuss your experiences.

Reversibility

A training programme must be exciting. If it isn't, the sports performer will not be motivated to follow it. If a sports performer stops an activity, then all the hard work that has gone into improving the body's ability to cope with the stresses of the sport will be lost. For example, how long does it take to lose 10 weeks work of aerobic training?

Specificity

A training programme should be specific to the sport that it is attempting to improve. It should be closely related to the activities that the sports performer will experience on the field. If not, the programme will be irrelevant, and the required changes to the body may not occur.

Choose a sport that you regularly participate in. Write down the exercises that your coach encourages you to do as part of your training programme. Can you think of other exercises that might be specific to the sport?

Progression

If there is too sharp an increase of the demands made on the performer the overload principle could result in injury. The higher levels of challenge should be organised in progressive steps, to allow the body to cope with the increased intensity of the demand placed upon it.

Variation

Any training programme should involve variation of the activities that the individual is required to perform. All the activities should take into account the specificity of the components of fitness and skills required by the sport.

Recovery

All long term training programmes should have recovery as an integrated principle. As the training programme increases the intensity of the demands, recovery becomes more important. Recovery allows the body to recuperate and rejuvenate from the stresses placed on the muscles and joints.

Key points

The volume and the intensity of the exercise must be considered during planning. If not, adaptations will not take place. The following four factors can be used to help in the design of a training programme, and are commonly known as the FITT principles:

- Frequency of activity
- Intensity of activity
- Time or duration of activity
- Type of exercise that will be used.

Fitness training methods

Flexibility training

Training for improvements in flexibility include:

1. Static flexibility training, involving slow, sustained stretching of a joint – stretches can be classed as:
   - **active** – where a muscle is lengthened in a position without assistance but requires the strength of other muscles to hold the position
   - **passive** – where a muscle group is assisted through the stretch by an external force, such as a partner or physical object.

2. Dynamic flexibility training, involving stretching during active contraction of the muscle tissue. This includes **ballistic** stretches, which are performed using a fast, bouncing action so that the momentum of body weight can assist in taking the joint beyond its range of movement. This method of stretching carries a high risk of injury to the muscle group concerned and is not recommended. It is still used in specific sports, however, such as dance and karate, to gain a greater range of motion to the joint area.

 Key points

Stretching to warm up and cool down

There is a difference between stretches used as part of the warm up and cool down of a training session and a flexibility training session. The stretches used in a warm up are to prepare the muscle groups that will be used for performance. The stretches used in cool down are primarily for relaxation and the reduction of muscle soreness after performance. Neither of these types of stretches is for the improvement of flexibility.

- **Maintenance stretches** are held between 6–20 seconds, usually during a warm up as part of a training or competitive session.
- **Developmental stretches** are usually held between 15–30 seconds during the cool down section of performance or training.

Strength, muscular endurance and power

Training for improvements in **strength**

- **Circuit training** – can be designed to improve general and/or specific strength. Circuits are deal for people new to strength training because they use body weight rather than external loads and are therefore safer. Work periods are short but at a high intensity and the rest periods are longer. To improve strength, intensity needs to be greater than 80% of the maximum effort.

- **Weight training** – this is carried out using weights equipment or machines.
- **Specific strength training** – this includes exercises that are specific to the sport, for example slinging a medicine ball in shot putt.
- **Plyometric training** – this improves either the strength or the speed at which muscle contracts (shortens). After undertaking plyometric training, performers in sports like rugby and football will observe improvements in sprinting, throwing and jumping movements.

Training for improvements in **muscular endurance**

- **Circuit training** – for this component, the exercises need to be carried out over a set period of time, during which as many repetitions as possible are carried out.
- **Resistance machines** – these can place further intensity on an exercise but should only be used when the exercise can be performed over a period of 30 seconds or more.
- **Reps** – between 12 and 15 reps will improve muscular endurance.
- **Sets and resistance** – between three and five sets at approximately 60–75% of the maximum effort will improve muscular endurance.

Speed and speed endurance training

Training for improvements in **speed**

Repetitive short bursts of maximum effort for set periods of time.

- **Hollow sprints** – these consist of two sprints divided by a recovery period of walking or jogging. For example, you might sprint for 30 metres, jog for 30 metres and then sprint again for a further 30 metres. You would then finish with a recovery period for a distance of 100 metres, before repeating the sprints again. This is ideal for games players.
- **Acceleration sprints** – these gradually increase in pace from a rolling start, to jogging, to striding out and then to maximum effort. Rest intervals, either by walking or jogging, should be included to ensure that full recovery has occurred. The runs can be completed in repetitions of about 3–6 and grouped in sets, for example three sets over a given distance on a sports pitch or court.
- **Interval training** – this is the most common form of training to improve speed endurance. There needs to be a balance between the intensity of the exercise and its duration. There also needs to be an adequate recovery period integrated into the training. You need to take into account the work length and pace/rest ratio. If the length of work is longer than in competition, the pace of the exercise needs to be slower. Decreasing the rest periods and decreasing the work intensity will develop the endurance component. Increasing the rest periods and increasing the work intensity will develop speed.

Aerobic endurance training

Training for improvements in **cardio-respiratory endurance**:

- **Distance training** – slow but over long distances.
- **Interval training** – set periods of work at high intensities with incorporated recovery periods (the work time can vary from 30 seconds to 5 minutes and the recovery phase can be complete rest, walking or jogging).
- **Fartlek training** – continuous intensity maintained for a period of time and then varied, for example, running continuously but at varying speeds. There is no complete rest period and the activity is continuous.
- **Continuous training** – exercising for a period beyond 30 minutes at a steady pace, during which time the intensity of exercise keeps the heart rate between 130–160 beat per minute.
- **Heart rate training zones** – calculating heart rate percentages allows the body to work in different heart rate training zones, which helps affect long term changes. To improve cardio-respiratory endurance an individual must attempt to train at close to 75% of their maximum heart rate. This can be done by swimming, running or cycling at an intensity that increases the heart rate to this zone.

Many swimmers use interval training to develop their aerobic endurance

Specific training programmes

All training programmes must include the principles of training discussed in this unit (overload, specificity, progression, individual differences, variation and reversibility). Every training programme should include sufficient warm ups, including exercises that work on the larger muscle groups with lighter weights, and then moving on to heavier weights. It is helpful to spread the exercises so that the different muscle groups are being worked.

Strength training programme

Chest press:
10 reps at 75% of max effort (10 × 75%)
8 × 80%
5 × 85%
3 × 95%
1 × 100%

This can be repeated 4–5 times for leg press, rowing, shoulder press and bicep curls.

 Key points

There are two types of strength programmes that can be followed: 3 sets of 6 repetitions and pyramid training. The number of repetitions in each set during pyramid training is decreased as the weights used are increased.

Speed programme

3 sets of 6 × 60 m at 90–100% effort
5 minute rest period
3 × 100 m acceleration runs (25 m jog, 25 m striding, 25 m at 75% and 25 m at 100% effort)
3 × 100 m hollow sprints (30 m sprint at 100% effort, 30 m jog, 40 m at 100% effort).

Continuous programme

Maintain a steady pace (walking pace) for about 40 minutes. The pace should be at a level where the time can be completed. The distance should be monitored so improvements can be recorded. The same distance can then be completed in less time or the distance can be increased.

Circuit training for muscular endurance

1. Bicep curls
2. sit-ups
3. shuttle runs
4. press-ups
5. squats
6. back extensions
7. step-ups
8. lateral raises
9. dead lifts

1 × set 60 seconds with 20 seconds rest between each station
1 × set 45 seconds with 10 seconds rest between each station
1 × set 30 seconds with 60 seconds running between each station.

Describe a training programme you have taken part in. Can you identify the principles of training integrated into it?

Designing a programme

When designing training programmes, the year is divided up into three phases of training:

1. **Pre-season phase** – preparation for the season's competition is being considered but a general, all round fitness regime may be followed (especially during the initial part of this phase). There will probably be a strong focus on the aerobic components to begin with, followed by a focus on strength, speed and power as this phase moves into the competition phase.

2. **Competition phase** – concentration on the maintenance of the components of fitness that have been developed through the previous phase of the training programme. If there is a long break before competition then further training programmes can be included, but it is important to avoid overtraining.

3. **Recovery phase** – Relaxation after the year's competitions. This phase is essential for optimal recovery and repair of the body, in order to improve performance for the following year. It will include active rest, although participation in other sports is encouraged. This is to ensure that fitness levels are maintained and that time during the preparation phase is not wasted in building up fitness levels from scratch.

This method is known as periodisation of training and its main concern is to ensure that phases one and three help optimise performance for competition. The time spent on each phase varies for different sports because the competition phase differs. Some sports have a very limited recovery phase and a longer competition phase. This may lead to an increase in injuries for the individual and the sport as a whole.

Assessment activity 3: Planning training programmes

Design a two week training programme for one of the following sportspeople:
- an experienced rugby player who wants to increase her strength and maintain the other components that she needs as a hooker
- a long jumper who needs to increase the speed of her run up before the take off
- a woman who needs to improve her cardio-respiratory fitness in order to run the London marathon, and who has never run more than six miles
- a goal keeper returning back to football, who needs to increase his flexibility and power.

P   Plan the training programme with the support of your tutor.

M   Plan the training programme independently.

D   Using the training programme you planned in **P** or **M** critically evaluate it, providing medium- and long-term recommendations for improvement.

Nutritional requirements

The subject of nutrition looks at the components of the food that we eat and how these components affect our everyday activities. A diet can be described as the pattern by which we eat the food, for example, a wheat-free diet or vegetarian diet. The way that a diet is organised can affect how fast and how well an individual will develop.

Our reasons for eating can be:
- **physical** – our bodies need food to function and develop. Food is necessary for muscle contraction, cell function, brain function, muscle development and growth, repair and recovery of tissues and to satisfy hunger
- **psychological** – we eat because it makes us feel safe and because it is a pleasurable experience
- **social** – the environment in which eating takes place is also important, we often eat because others are eating.

Think about it

List all the occasions you have eaten over the last two days.
1. When did you eat for physical reasons, or in other words, because you were hungry?
2. When did you eat for psychological or social reasons?

Nutrients

Each food component is called a nutrient. Each of these nutrients is essential to the diet and has a main function or role in the body.

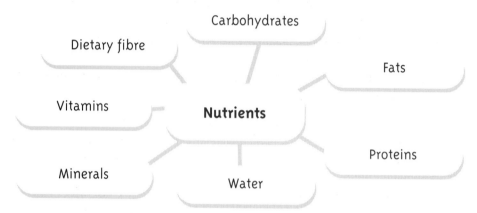

Carbohydrates, fats and proteins are called the energy nutrients because they are used as food fuels during metabolism.

Carbohydrates

The main role of carbohydrates is to provide the body with energy. Carbohydrates are stored in the muscles and liver as glycogen, and can be found in the blood as blood glucose. The body uses glycogen and blood glucose as its food fuels.

Carbohydrates (CHO) are broken down by the body to a simple form of glucose. This is then stored as glycogen in the muscles and the liver, along with about three times its own weight in water. There is approximately three times more glycogen stored in the muscles than in the liver. The body can only store a small amount of glycogen – glycogen stores are very limited compared to fat stores found in the body.

The body can only hold a certain amount of fuel, just as a car can only hold a certain amount of petrol. The total store of glycogen in the average body is 1600–2000 kcal. This is enough energy to last up to one day if nothing else is consumed. There are small amounts of glycogen present in the blood and brain and the concentrations of these are kept within a very narrow range, during rest and exercise. This allows the systems of the body to continue to function.

There are two types of carbohydrate:
- **simple sugars** (monosaccharides) – found in sweet foods such as jam, confectionary, fruit and sugar
- **complex sugars** (polysaccharides) – found in wheat based foods such as pasta and bread, and also potato and rice based products.

Fats

Fat can be divided into two categories:

- **stored fats** – found in the subcutaneous layer of the skin, as adipose tissue. The supply of this store of fat is much greater than the stores of glycogen. A small amount of fat is stored in the muscle tissue and is called intramuscular fat, but the majority can be found around the organs and beneath the skin
- **essential fats** – needed for the healthy function of the body. These fats are not stored and so need to be consumed.

The amount of fat that is stored around specific areas of the body is mainly determined by your genetic make-up and hormonal balance. Your fat deposits will generally be in line with one or both of your parents. Males usually take after their fathers – hormones tend to favour fat storage around the middle. Females usually take after their mothers – their hormones tend to favour fat storage around the hips and thighs. This explains the 'pear shape' associated with females and the 'apple' shape associated with males.

Excess fat is stored in different places in men and women

Fats are stored in the body as triglycerides. Triglycerides are found in the skeletal muscle and fat cells that make up adipose tissue. Fats are a form of fuel and are made up of glycerol and free fatty acids. They have many functions in the body:

- they help the absorption of the fat soluble vitamins A, D and E
- they regulate body temperature
- they encourage brain growth
- they are the main source of energy for cell function.

Fats provide almost twice as much energy for one gram compared to the same amount provided by either carbohydrates or proteins.

Amount of nutrient	Nutrient	Unit of energy supplied (in kcals)
1 gram	Carbohydrate	4 kcals
1 gram	Fat	9 kcals
1 gram	Protein	4 kcals

Fats can be divided into saturated and unsaturated fats:

- **Saturated fats** – these are found in many animal products and can be harmful to health if consumed in large amounts on a regular basis. Foods in this category include meats, dairy produce, cakes, pastries and confectionary.
- **Unsaturated fats** – these are less harmful and many foods in this category can help promote the consumption of the essential fats that are necessary for many of the bodily functions. Foods in this category include oily fish, such as mackerel, sardines and salmon. For those following a vegetarian diet, foods such as flax seed, pumpkin seeds, walnuts and dark green leafy vegetables contain smaller amounts of unsaturated fat.

Proteins

Protein is not stored by the body in the same way as fat and carbohydrate. Protein forms muscle and organ tissue. It is predominantly used as a building material rather than an energy store but proteins can be broken down to release energy if required. The muscles and organs, therefore, represent a large source of potential energy.

As with the previous nutrients, proteins can also be divided into two categories:
1. high value or animal proteins
2. low value or plant proteins.

All animal products, such as meat and dairy, contain the essential amino acids that form proteins. These amino acids are the building blocks of proteins, and are essential for their function in the body. The low value proteins are important but they do not include all of the amino acids in one food. If you do not eat meat and dairy products you need to eat a careful combination of low value proteins to ensure that all of the essential amino acids are obtained. Low value proteins include beans, lentils, peas, nuts, seeds and soya bean products.

Vitamins and minerals

These are essential for all bodily functions. Most of the fruit and vegetables that make up the western diet include most of these vitamins and minerals. The exceptions are certain vitamins, for example Vitamin B12 and Vitamin D, which are obtained from animal products.

Dietary fibre

This is essential for the regulation of the gut. Dietary fibre is not digested by the body but is used to maintain the function of the gut. Most of the foods that contain dietary fibre are also rich in carbohydrates.

Water

Water is one of the most important nutrients that the body requires. This is because many functions in the body rely on the presence of water. These include:

- cell function
- maintaining body temperature through sweating
- transportation of nutrients and the movement of blood
- removal of waste products via urination and breathing
- lubrication of the joints.

Water is found in many of the processed foods that the western diet is made up of, as well as in fresh fruit and vegetables. It is important to ensure that sufficient amounts are consumed to avoid the body deteriorating.

 Key points

The body can survive longer without food than without water.

Let's do it!

Look at the list you made of all occasions you have eaten over the last two days (on page 129). What foods did you eat? List them, and categorise them into the different food groups. Don't forget to make a note of drinks, too. Compare your list with others in your group.

Healthy diet

Recommended nutrient intake

Not all nutrients are taken in the same amounts, as this could have a detrimental affect on health and physical fitness. For example, fat provides the most concentrated form of energy to the body but it is not necessarily the best form of energy. Most of the energy provided by fats in the western diet is supplied by saturated fats that are harmful to health. There are national recommendations that encourage individuals to consume a balanced diet encompassing all of the necessary nutrients in the correct amounts.

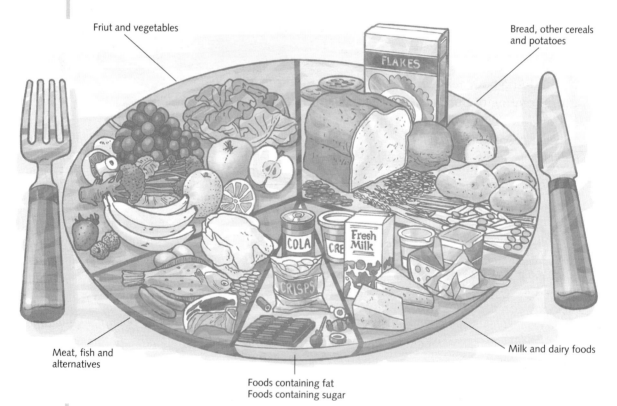

Friut and vegetables

Bread, other cereals and potatoes

Meat, fish and alternatives

Foods containing fat
Foods containing sugar

Milk and dairy foods

A balanced diet

Eating patterns pre- and post competitions, events or training

Your body uses most energy when the muscles are working during breathing, digestion, circulation and exercise. A balanced diet will be different for each individual. The amount of energy, and therefore food, you need will depend on your age, gender and body build, and also your activity level.

If you are preparing for a competition, diet must be a planned part of your training regime. Your programme should include what you should eat and when you should eat it, and this will be different for training and competition. If this part of your programme is planned for carefully, it should result in optimum performance during training and competition.

Nutrition strategies

Recommended dietary guidelines

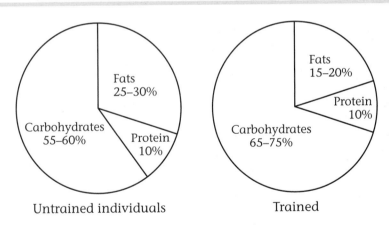

The percentage of different nutrients that should be consumed by trained and untrained individuals

Let's do it!

Look at your list of foods eaten over the last two days. How does your list compare with the national recommendations shown above? What foods do you need to eat more of? What foods do you need to eat less of?

Timing of food intake

Imagine that your body is like a car. A car must have a full tank of fuel in order to reach the end of its journey. If it doesn't, it may stop before the destination has been reached. Similarly, your body needs a full tank of fuel before starting a training session. You will then be able to maintain the intensity of the training and complete the task. If your tank is only half full, you are likely to reduce the training intensity or stop before the task is completed.

The primary fuel that the body requires is the energy gained from carbohydrates. As you know, carbohydrates are stored as glycogen, which is found in the muscles, blood and liver, and fats are stored in the adipose tissue found beneath the skin. The stores of glycogen are limited compared to fat stores.

It is important to refuel after exercise to ensure that the body maintains good levels of glycogen. The optimum time to refuel is directly after exercise has stopped, and for up to two hours afterwards. The refuelling process is faster during this time. It then starts to slow down, making the refuelling process less efficient. The body needs to recover from exercise and eating after exercising helps this recovery process, even if it is late at night.

Key points

- The efficiency of refuelling carbohydrate stores can be improved by training and increasing fitness levels.
- Carbohydrate is the only fuel that is used by the brain.

Eating for competition

Eating strategies should change in the lead up to a competition, in order for the sportsperson to reach optimum fitness. A high carbohydrate diet should be maintained to ensure that the glycogen stores remain full. Tapering, or reducing, training days before a competition can help to maintain glycogen stores for competition day. This strategy is especially important for athletes competing in events that may last for 60 minutes or more, and athletes competing in a number of heats over a short period.

Hopefully, by the morning of the athlete's competition, the previous day's eating will already have filled his or her glycogen stores. The pre-competition meal should be high in carbohydrate, low in fat, low in protein, low in fibre (i.e. not too bulky and filling), enjoyable and familiar.

Complex carbohydrates should be eaten as part of the pre-competition meal as these release energy slowly. Simple carbohydrates should be avoided as these release energy quickly but also stimulate the release of insulin, which can soon make the athlete feel tired.

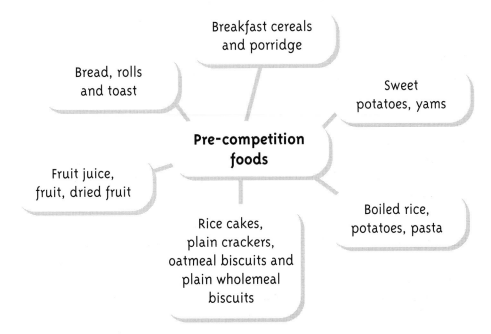

Breakfast cereals and porridge

Bread, rolls and toast

Sweet potatoes, yams

Pre-competition foods

Fruit juice, fruit, dried fruit

Boiled rice, potatoes, pasta

Rice cakes, plain crackers, oatmeal biscuits and plain wholemeal biscuits

There are many myths regarding eating before a competition. You may feel nervous on the day of the competition and not want to eat. If you avoid food altogether your liver glycogen stores will be low. These provide the body with fuel before the activity starts, so you will be starting the journey without a full tank of fuel. This could affect your performance, especially in the latter stages of an endurance event (or in one that lasts over one and a half hours).

 Key points

- The liver can only store enough glycogen to last 12 hours. Eating nothing after the previous day's evening meal can result in the liver glycogen stores being depleted.
- Studies have shown that eating certain types of carbohydrates just before competition helps to delay fatigue and improve endurance. If exercise starts within about five minutes of eating, an increase in insulin will be prevented and your blood-sugar levels will remain slightly raised for longer.
- Studies have also shown that if you exercise for more than an hour, taking extra carbohydrates during training or competition may help delay the onset of fatigue and maintain exercise intensity.

Let's do it!

Design a pre-competition meal for an individual who will be competing throughout the day in heats. The first heat will start at 11 o'clock. Consider the types of nutrients, the foods and the size of meal that will make up this pre-competition feast.

After the competition or event, it is important to refuel the body with the energy that has been used for the activity. Glycogen and water stores need to be refilled for the next training session or competition.

Immediately after exercise has finished, the performer should eat foods high in complex carbohydrates. The optimum time to eat is within two hours of the exercise stopping. Foods such as baked potatoes and pasta dishes are great meals to eat after exercise, as long as the fat content is not too high.

It is also vitally important to ensure that the fluid that has been lost during exercise is replaced. This can be done by drinking isotonic drinks. The body can then replace its carbohydrate and water content rapidly. If water only needs to be replaced after exercise, however, then a hypotonic sports drink would be more beneficial.

Keeping hydrated

Hydrating the body is a very important factor in helping to gain the best performance. Keeping your body well hydrated can help prevent muscle fatigue and problems to health after exercise has finished. Hydration should be maintained during training sessions and for competition. The body needs to be trained to cope with continuous hydration and exercise.

Key point

If you feel thirsty you are already dehydrated!

Sports drinks

Sometimes glycogen levels can be best replenished through consuming carbohydrate drinks. There are various carbohydrate drinks that serve different purposes.

Type of drink	Amount of glucose	Purpose of drink
Hypotonic drinks	Low levels of glucose	Replenish fluids – hydration
Isotonic drinks	Same amount of glucose to fluid	Replenish fluid and carbohydrates
Hypertonic drinks	High levels of glucose	Replenish carbohydrate levels

Let's do it!

Find one example of each of the above sports drinks.

Nutritional requirements for different sportspeople

Individuals following different types of sports will have different nutritional requirements.

Endurance sportspeople require a mixture of fuels to supply the body with energy. The fuels that are supplied predominantly come from fats and muscle glycogen (carbohydrates). Due to the limited supplies of glycogen stores in the body, as exercise continues energy must be supplied by fats as well. As exercise intensity increases there is a greater demand on energy being supplied by glycogen stores, this results in the glycogen store depleting faster as this intensity is maintained.

Exercise intensity	Main fuel source	Percentage of the fuel being used
Low intensity	Fat	Approximately 80%
Moderate intensity	Carbohydrate Fat	50% 50%
High intensity	Carbohydrate	80%

Power athletes participate in activities that last for short periods of time, lasting no longer than 4 minutes, with effort being close to maximum. It is very important to ensure that muscle glycogen stores are full before exercise or competition. Power events predominantly use glycogen to provide the body with energy, and this needs to be replenished after activity especially if the training session has been hard. It takes longer to replenish the stores if muscle damage has occurred. Therefore sufficient time is needed between events for the body to fully recover.

Nutritional supplements

The best nutritional advice is to make sure your diet is varied and balanced, and to ensure that you are consuming all the nutrients. However, some groups of people are at risk of nutritional deficiencies. Such groups include:

- **athletes** – if training is not balanced with food intake, or if injury is experienced and inadequate recovery has taken place
- **young adults** – because of the social influence of fad foods, the image of certain foods, or lack of money
- **females** – because of hormonal changes during adolescence, with the onset of menstruation
- **vegetarians** – due to a lack in vitamins B12 and D, iron and possibly zinc. (If the diet is not balanced there will be a risk of replacing proteins with high fat foods)
- **the elderly** – may have deficiencies of vitamins and minerals due to a lack of fruit and vegetables in the diet
- **the socially and economically deprived** – may not be educated about balanced diet, may lack a variety of methods to cook foods and may be unable to afford certain foods (especially organic foods). This group is also more likely to smoke and drink heavily
- **people with eating disorders** – reducing the intake of nutrients will inevitably increase the risk of disease and deficiencies
- **people who suffer from illness** – because the immune system is low, and replacing nutrients is difficult when the appetite is suppressed
- **people with allergies or intolerance to certain foods** – alternatives must be found with which the body can cope and which have the same nutritional value
- **people following calorie restricting diets** – such individuals will be consuming less calories than is recommended by national organisations such as The British Nutrition Foundation
- **pregnant women** – the unborn baby is feeding from the mother so the mother must replace these nutrients, to supply her own body and that of her baby.

There are different types of supplements that can be taken, and these are summarised in the table opposite:

Supplements	Description
Energy bars	A convenient way to obtain further carbohydrates during endurance exercise and immediately after exercise
Vitamin and mineral supplements	Usually taken to maintain the immune system rather than for energy during exercise – for example, vitamin C tablets
Creatine powders	Creatine is naturally produced by the body – it is used for high intensity exercise and is stored as phosphocreatine in the muscles. It enables the body to perform maximal exercise for longer. It also speeds up recovery between exercise bouts, which results in an increase in lean muscle mass
Protein powders	These can be mixed with water or milk and are usually used by power or strength athletes during very heavy training. Protein powders stimulate the immune system and can spare the use of muscle tissue during heavy exercise

Before taking a supplement, take the following factors into account:

- think of food first – is there any way you can supply the deficiency within your diet?
- choose a supplement that is closer to 100% of the recommended value for the day's intake (except for minerals, such as calcium and magnesium)
- avoid supplements that have excessive amounts of vitamins and minerals, as this can offset the benefits of other minerals in the body
- choose supplements in the precursor stage of the vitamin or mineral, for example. beta-carotene is the precursor to Vitamin A and this acts as an antioxidant
- make sure the supplement has not expired
- ignore claims of natural vitamins as they may have been produced with synthetic ingredients
- avoid any vitamin or mineral that does not state on the label that it has passed the 45 minute dissolution test. This may mean that it will not be absorbed by the body
- optimise the absorption of the supplement by taking it just before a meal or immediately after.

Assessment activity 4: Dietary guidelines

Choose an athlete from two of the following categories:
- endurance events (e.g. marathon, decathalon)
- speed events (e.g. running, swimming)
- power or team events (e.g. football, shot putt).

Prepare dietary guidelines for your two selected athletes, including suitable daily meal plans.

P On your own, prepare dietary guidelines for your two selected athletes, including suitable daily meal plans and present your guidelines to your class.

M Prepare dietary guidelines for your two selected athletes, including suitable daily meal plans – remember to explain your dietary guidelines and meal plans.

D Compare the dietary requirements of the two athletes you have chosen, and draw suitable conclusions.

Psychological factors

Motivation

The term motivation describes the level at which an individual is directed and influenced to complete a task. Motivation can be:
- **intrinsic** – affected by an individual's inner drive
- **extrinsic** – affected by the external environment that sport is carried out in
- **aroused** – affected by the energy with which a task is carried out; the stronger the arousal, the greater the effort put into the task.

Intrinsic and extrinsic motivation

Intrinsic motivation	Extrinsic motivation
Performer strives inwardly to develop optimum performance; self directed or determined	Performer strives to achieve optimum performance because of rewards that come from external sources. Rewards can be tangible and non-tangible: - tangible rewards include trophies, money, medals, badges and certificates - non-tangible rewards include positive comments (from teacher, coach, peers, spectators), media recognition, winning/glory and social status.

A sports performer's desire to win may be a strong motivator

Extrinsic motivation can be both beneficial and detrimental to performance. Rewards may become meaningless or worthless if they are over used. Conversely, if there are not enough rewards, the sports performer may no longer see the worth of performance.

There is a link between intrinsic and extrinsic motivation. A sports performer may think of extrinsic rewards as a way of *controlling* his or her behaviour, rather than *praising* or *rewarding* it. Good behaviour does not necessarily lead to successful performance.

If you are planning to increase intrinsic motivation through the use of extrinsic rewards:
- make sure that rewards are dependent on performance
- give praise both verbally and non-verbally
- provide a variety of rewards during training and competition-type situations
- provide opportunities for the sports performer to make decisions on performance
- encourage the negotiation of goals, to match up with a performer's skill level.

Let's do it!

List all the reasons why you started to participate in a particular sport. Then list the reasons why you have continued with the sport. Have your reasons changed?

Arousal and anxiety

Arousal is the combination of physiological factors and psychological factors. Taking part in a competition can give you a mixture of feelings that either excite you or cause you to become anxious. Placing stress on your body, whether physiologically or psychologically, changes your arousal levels. This in turn affects the way you process incoming information and the quality of your output, or final performance.

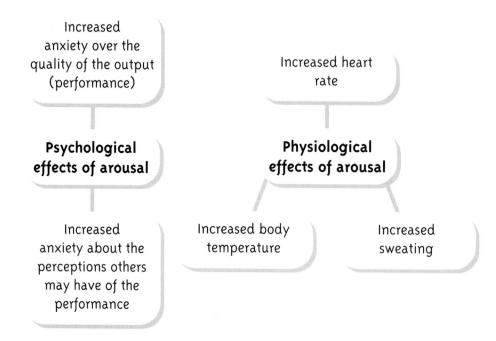

 Think about it

Get together with your group. Discuss your personal experiences of taking part in competitions.
1. How did you feel?
2. Did you suffer from any of the psychological or physiological effects described above?
3. How did this affect your performance?

Drive theory

This attempts to define a relationship between arousal and performance and states that as arousal increases, performance increases. This theory does not take into account arousal levels reaching a point that has a detrimental effect on performance.

The inverted 'U' theory

This theory does take into account the negative affects of high levels of arousal, It states that levels of arousal need to be high for simple tasks that do not require complex thought processes. More complicated tasks, however, need lower levels of arousal, so that concentration can be focused on the task in hand.

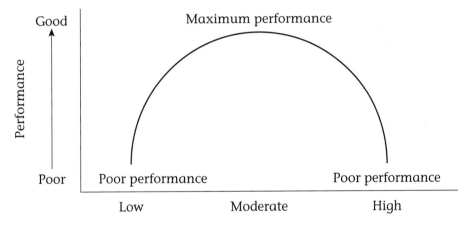

The inverted 'U' theory

The catastrophe theory

This moves one stage further than the inverted 'U' theory. It explains how performance is affected by arousal and looks at reducing levels of arousal in order to maintain the quality of performance. There are obvious symptoms that can be observed if this reduction does not take place.

Personality

Personality is a major influencing factor in sport. This does not mean to say that an individual must fall into just one category to become a top sportsperson. The traits that make up different personality types are relatively stable for each individual but they could change in a changing environment, even though personality traits are said to be innate.

Individuals can be divided into two groups according to the personality traits that they show:

1. **Introverts** (or type A) are more inward in their behaviour, and do not require high levels of arousal to achieve optimum performance. Introverts often favour sports that are classed as individual, and that require precision for success. Introverts often have low pain thresholds.
2. **Extroverts** (or type B) require high levels of stimulation to achieve the optimum performance. They thrive in highly competitive situations, where there is a great amount of noise and input from the audience. Extroverts often favour team sports rather than individual sports. Extroverts often have high pain thresholds.

Let's do it!

Look at the list of athletes below:

- Jonny Wilkinson – Rugby
- Denise Lewis – Athletics
- Andrew Flintoff – Cricket

Consider the sports that they are in and the media attention that they may experience.
1. What personality type do you think each has?
2. Explain your choice giving examples of their behaviour to justify your reasons.

Concentration

Any performer participating in sport is constantly being bombarded with different information. A performer's ability to cope with this depends on his or her experience, either in performance or through training under similar conditions.

When a performer processes information, he or she has to do two things:
1. make sense of it
2. decide the best action to take.

To carry out these two tasks, the incoming information first has to be filtered. Irrelevant information is discarded, leaving only relevant information to be dealt with. If this process is not carried out efficiently, it can hinder decision making. Each of us can only handle one thing at a time – this is termed limited channel capacity, or limited concentration capacity. An overload of information will hinder performance.

A sports performer will go through different phases to achieve efficiency in the execution of a skill. When you learn a new skill, concentration on all aspects of the skill may be given equal billing. With practice, each part of the skill will become second nature, and more concentration can be placed on the performance of the skill. Experienced players perform skills automatically. This means they are able to attend to other information, such as changes in the oppositions' performance, more efficiently than a beginner.

Bandura's self-efficacy theory

In 1977, Albert Bandura looked at success and failure of performance in relation to the self-confidence of the performer. Bandura found that the perception a sportsperson has of his or her ability is not constant, but can change in different situations.

Let's do it!

List the tasks or skills that you perceive to be strongest in your performance. Then list the tasks or skills that you think are weakest. Discuss these lists with your coach, teacher or team players.

Assessment activity 5: Psysiological factors

P Identify the basic psychological factors that affect training and performance.

M Identify and describe the basic psychological factors that affect training and performance.

D Critically analyse the psychological factors that affect training and performance in the short and long term.

In summary

Preparing for sport and training can be a big commitment, and life-changing. Changes to your sleeping, drinking, eating and training patterns need to be planned and implemented over a prolonged period of time – optimum performance does not happen by accident!

Understanding the factors that affect performance is essential to ensure proper planning and training, bringing you that one step closer to achieving your highest potential.

CHECK WHAT YOU KNOW!

Look back over this unit and see if you can answer the following questions.

1 Flexibility is one component of fitness. What are the others?
2 Identify a test for static strength.
3 What test can be used to identify muscular endurance?
4 During a 12 week fitness programme, what considerations must be taken in to account?
5 How long does it take for adaptations to the body systems to be made?
6 How long does it take for the body to lose the adaptations that have been made over a period of time?
7 Name the two main fuels that are used for energy in the body
8 Give three examples of foods containing the following nutrients: proteins, fats, and carbohydrates.
9 Name the type of motivation that involves gaining financial rewards for participating.
10 Using the inverted 'U' model, state what happens to an athletes' performance when:
   a) under aroused
   b) over aroused.

The body in sport

Introduction

Knowledge of the body and how it works is essential in the field of sport. Unit 4 will help you to understand more about human anatomy and how the body systems change due to the effects of exercise. Anatomy is the study of the structure of the body. Physiology is the study of how the body structures work.

To perform skills in sport your body has to move in a variety of ways. Knowledge of the body's positions and movements is of vital importance for any sports performer, coach, teacher or student involved in sport. Without this knowledge, it is difficult to improve performance.

When you train and perform in sport, many changes occur in the body. The performer and the coach have to ensure that the performer's body develops through training, rests between training and performance, and is given the opportunity to recover if injury occurs. In this way, the performer will able to achieve his or her optimum performance levels.

Let's do it!

For your safety you need to check your suitability to undertake the practical activities in this unit using the health status questionnaire in Appendix 1. Complete this questionnaire now before you read any further.

How you will be assessed

This unit is internally assessed by your tutor. After completing this unit you should be able to achieve the following learning outcomes:
1. Explain the structure and function of the **skeletal system** and its role in producing sports movement.
2. Identify the **major muscles** in the body and their role in producing movement in a variety of sporting actions.
3. Identify the structure and function of the **cardiovascular and respiratory systems.**
4. Investigate the **short term effects of exercise** on the cardiovascular and respiratory systems.

The skeletal system

Describing the body's parts and position

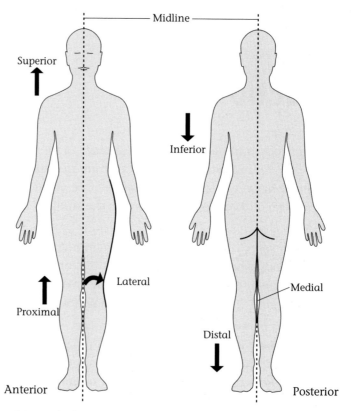

Anatomical positions in both anterior and posterior views

The parts and position of your body can be described in relation to its mid-line, using the following terms:

Anterior – body parts or position found at the front of the body.
Posterior – body parts or position found at the back of the body.
Superior – body parts or position found closer to the head.
Inferior – body parts or position found further away from the head, or closer to the feet.
Superficial – closer to the surface of the skin.
Deep – further away from the surface of the skin.
Medial – body parts or position found closer to the mid-line of the body.
Lateral – body parts or position found further away from the mid-line of the body.
Proximal – body parts or position found nearer to the point of attachment to the main structure of the body.
Distal – body parts or position found further away from the point of attachment to the main structure of the body.

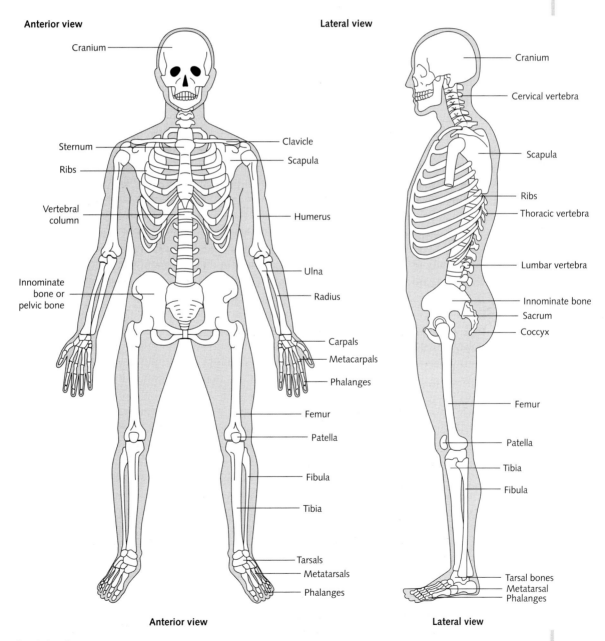

Let's do it!

Look at yourself in a mirror, or look at a partner. Place an imaginary line down the centre of the body. Identify one body part in each of the following positions: anterior, posterior, lateral and distal. Use general terms if necessary, for example, the jaw or the knee-cap.

The skeletal system

Anterior view

- Cranium
- Sternum
- Ribs
- Vertebral column
- Innominate bone or pelvic bone
- Clavicle
- Scapula
- Humerus
- Ulna
- Radius
- Carpals
- Metacarpals
- Phalanges
- Femur
- Patella
- Fibula
- Tibia
- Tarsals
- Metatarsals
- Phalanges

Lateral view

- Cranium
- Cervical vertebra
- Scapula
- Ribs
- Thoracic vertebra
- Lumbar vertebra
- Innominate bone
- Sacrum
- Coccyx
- Femur
- Patella
- Tibia
- Fibula
- Tarsal bones
- Metatarsal
- Phalanges

Anterior view

Lateral view

The skeletal system

Functions of the skeleton

Your skeleton has many different functions to enable you to live and survive. These include:

- shape
- support
- movement
- protection
- calcium storage
- blood cell production.

Shape

Your skeleton provides the framework to give your body its shape. Without it, you would look like a blob of jelly.

Support

Your skeleton also supports the visceral organs within your body. These important organs are held within the body structure by a network of tissues. As with all of the body's systems, these tissues do not work in isolation. They are attached to the matrix of the bones' structure and this enables them to support the body's organs.

Movement

Your body is able to move because of the co-operation between its muscles and bones. The muscles are attached to the bones of the skeleton, creating a lever and joints system that allows the body to move.

 Key point

It is important to remember that many of the other systems of the body are also required for the production of movement.

Protection

The organs that are supported by the tissues and the skeleton also need to be protected throughout life. The organisation of your skeleton's bones allow for this. Many of the internal organs are protected by adipose (fatty) tissue and also by the hard structure of bone. The flat-type bones that your body possesses function in this way. For example, the pelvic girdle provides protection for the female reproductive organs and the cranium provides protection for the brain.

Calcium storage

Bone is your body's largest storage tank for the mineral calcium. Calcium is important for bone formation and maintenance. Calcium is also used for muscular contraction.

 Key points

> Your bones are constantly changing in structure, and to do this they require specific amounts of certain nutrients. It is essential to follow a diet that is specific to your needs to ensure your bones develop and maintain the correct level of bone density and strength.
>
> It is also important to participate in regular physical activity. By doing this, your bones will develop a greater density. This means your bones will become stronger and able to bear more weight.

Blood cell production

Bone also produces blood cells. This occurs in the marrow of the bone that is found in the epiphysis region and the shaft (diaphysis) of all long bones.

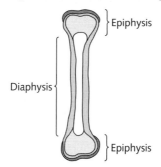

Cross section of a long bone

The two parts of the skeleton

The skeleton can be divided into two parts:
1. the axial skeleton, which forms the main axis or core of the skeletal system
2. the appendicular skeleton, which forms the appendages of the limbs.

The axial skeleton comprises:
- the vertebral or spinal column
- the cranium or the skull
- the thoracic or rib cage.

The appendicular skeleton comprises:
The shoulder girdle, which includes:
- the clavicle or the collar bone
- the scapula or the shoulder blade
- the arms (i.e. the appendages that hang off these structures).

The pelvic girdle, which includes:
- the pelvic bone
- the legs (i.e. the appendages that hang off this structure).

Let's do it!

Can you identify the bones that form the two parts of your own skeleton?

The vertebral column

Your vertebral column, which is also called your spine, is used for posture, movement, stability and protection. It is a strong and flexible structure and one of its primary roles is to protect the spinal cord. If the cord is damaged in any way it can cause considerable problems to the movements of the rest of the body, or can even lead to death.

Your spine is made up of 33 bones that fit together to form its shape. Some of these bones allow for movement at the joints where the bones fit together, and some allow for no movement at all. Between these joints are discs, which work as shock absorbers during impact.

The 33 bones that your vertebral column is made up of can be divided into five categories.

Category	Number of bones	Movement
Cervical	7	Yes
Thoracic	12	Very limited movement to create a stable structure for the organs found inside the cage
Lumbar	5	2 lumbar vertebrae are movable, 3 are fused, therefore no movement
Sacrum	5	Fused, therefore no movement
Coccyx	4	Fused, therefore no movement

The cranium

Your cranium, or skull, sits on the vertebral column and is attached by a pivot joint (see page 158). It comprises many flat and irregular bones that give your head and face their shape.

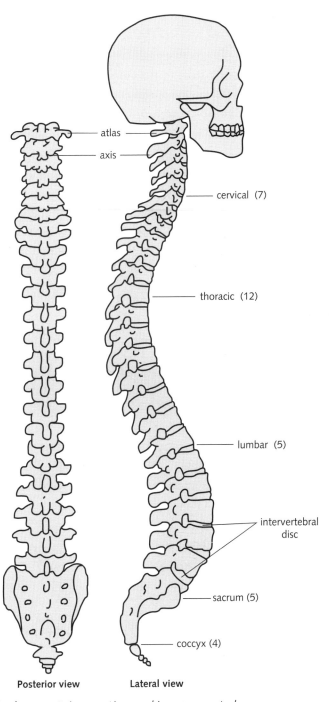

atlas

axis

cervical (7)

thoracic (12)

lumbar (5)

intervertebral disc

sacrum (5)

coccyx (4)

Posterior view   **Lateral view**

The vertebral column contains 5 sections making up 33 verterbrae

 Key point

The shape of the spine allows for the absorption of impact, for example during sport. It is mainly the lumbar region of the spine which absorbs the impact and this area is where many back problems can be located.

Bone formation and development

The bones of an unborn baby start to develop from soft connective tissue. This is when the shape of the skeleton starts to form. After the baby is born, the bone of the skeleton becomes harder, firmer and more resilient to physical stresses. This process of bone formation is known as ossification.

Humans are born with more bones than they die with. At birth, a baby possesses over 300 bones yet the adult body is made up of approximately 206 bones. This is because some of the bones that make up the skeleton, especially those that are used for protection, fuse together to form a solid structure. A good example of this is the skull, which at birth is made up of six parts, and seven parts for the face. As the baby matures, the bones join together, to provide protection for the brain.

Bone structure

There are two main types of bone tissue that make up your skeleton:

1. **Compact bone** – this is found at the shaft or diaphysis of long bones. It is the external layer of bone that copes with the physical stresses experienced through life.
2. **Cancellous bone** – this is also referred to as spongy bone and is found under the external layer of compact bone. This section of the bone is where bone marrow is found.

Types of bone

The bones that make either the axial or the appendicular skeleton can be placed into groups according to their shape and function.

Types of bone	Example found in the body	Example of function
Short bones	Carpals Metatarsals	Small movement
Long bones	Femur Humerus	Large movements Cell production
Irregular bones	Vertebrae	Protection Support
Flat or plate bones	Pelvic girdle Cranium	Attachment of muscle Protection
Sesemoid bones	Patella	Prevention of hyper-extension of the femur

Let's do it!

Complete the following table:

Description of the bone	Type of bone	Main function of the bone
Humerus		
	Sesamoid	
		Muscle attachment and protection
Phalanges		
		Protects and support internal organs

 Key point

Exercise increases the strength of bones. They adapt to the stress imposed by exercise by laying down more calcium.

Joints

Joints are found when two or more bones meet. Not all joints provide movement. Bones that work together to provide movement are joined by soft tissues called ligaments.

 Key point

Ligaments attach bone to bone.

Joints can be divided into three main groups:

Types of joint	Movement	Example of joint
Fixed joint	No movement	Cranium Sacrum
Slightly movable joints	Limited movement	Vertebral column (thoracic vertebrae)
Synovial joints	Free movement	Ball and socket Hinge Sliding Saddle Pivot

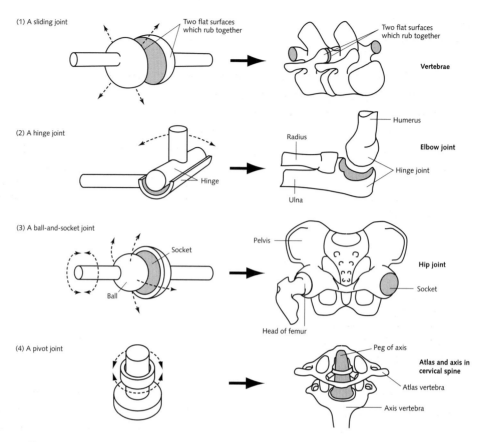

Different types of synovial joint and where they can be found in the body

Features of synonal joints

All synovial joints, whatever their type and degree of movement they afford, contain the following common features:

- **A joint cavity** – the space within the joint.
- **Articular cartilage** – this covers the end of the bones. It provides a smooth sliding surface for the bones assisting in reducing friction and improving the shock-absorbing qualities of the joint.
- **A synovial membrane** – this lines the whole of the interior of the joint with the exception of the bone ends, and secretes synovial fluid.
- **Synovial fluid** – the fluid that nourishes the cartilage and cells, and lubricates the joint to reduce friction as the joint operates.
- **A joint capsule** – forming the outer membrane surrrounding the joint. It holds the bones together and encloses the joint cavity. It is strengthened on the outside by ligaments that help to stabilise the joint.

Let's do it!

Produce a clearly labelled poster of a synovial joint and identify the function of each feature.

Let's do it!

Look at the list of skills in the following table. For each one:
- identify the joint(s) used to perform the skill
- state where you would find the joint in the body
- identify the bones that make up the joint(s)
- give an example of another joint(s) of the same type, and where it can be found in the body.

Skill	Joint	Location	Bones	Example of another joint
Squatting (lower body) from the ankle				
Throwing a javelin (upper body) from the wrist				
Trail leg of hurdling (lower body) whole leg				

Joints need the help of muscle to produce movement. The muscle pulls on the bone to allow for the movement to happen. The muscle is attached to the bone by another soft tissue known as a tendon. Tendons are linked strongly to bone by fibres that are extensions of collagen (protein) fibres. The fibres are attached to the periosteum layer of the bone.

Key point

Tendons attach muscle to bone.

Cartilage

There are three categories of cartilage found in the body. Each has a specific role to play in relation to the movement of the joints within the body. The three different categories are:
1. articular (or hyaline) cartilage
2. fibrocartilage
3. elastin cartilage.

Key point

Each type of cartilage has the same basic structure – a ground matrix of cells and protein fibres. The protein fibres are known as collagen and elastin and are found in varying quantities in each type of cartilage.

Articular cartilage, also known as **hyaline cartilage**, is bluish-white in appearance. It is found at the end of the surfaces of the long bones as a lining where movement occurs between bones. This type of cartilage is also found within the structures of the respiratory tract, where movement is essential for breathing.

Fibrocartilage is tough and resistant to compression. This type of cartilage makes up the vertebral discs found between the joints of the vertebrae. Fibrocartilage is also used to join together the different sections of the pelvic bone.

Elastin cartilage is strong but supple. This type of cartilage can be found in the epiglottis and the outer ear.

Types of movements at specific joints

Your body can move in a variety of ways and these movements link your skeleton and muscular system together. The table below shows the terms that are used to describe the movements that different parts of the body perform.

Movement term	Description of movement
Abduction	The limb moves away from the mid-line of the body
Adduction	The limb moves closer to the mid-line of the body
Circumduction	A limb moving in a circular motion around the joint, giving a cone shaped movement
Rotation	The limb moves towards the mid-line and changes the position of the body, e.g. medial rotation results in the anterior surface of the body moving medially
Dorsiflexion	The toes point upwards, movement towards the head
Plantarflexion	The toes point downwards, movement away from the head
Extension	The joint angle of two or more bones increases, or the limb straightens
Flexion	The joint angle of two or more bones decreases, which results in a bending position
Supination	Movement of the fore-arm, in which the palms of the hand face upward
Pronation	Movement of the fore-arm, in which the palms of the hand face downward

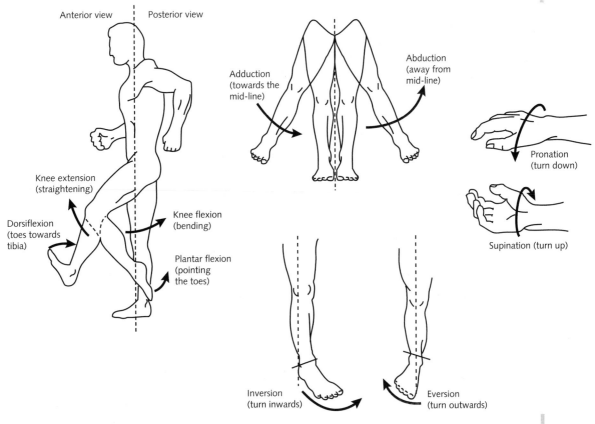

Terms relating to muscle action

 Think about it

Choose two of the terms in the table on page 160. Think of one joint movement for each of them.

Let's do it!

Complete the following table.

Structure or movement	Functions	Examples in sport
Long bone	Mineral storage	Provides calcium needed for muscular contraction
Fixed joint		
Hip and socket joint		
Adduction		

Major muscles

Your body has over 600 muscles to enable it to move.

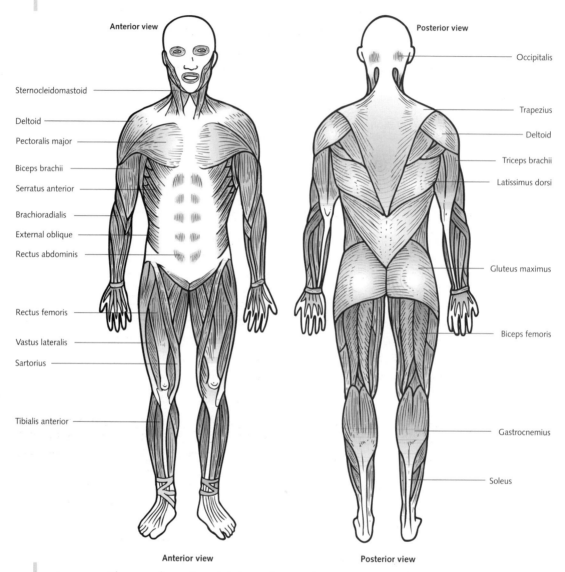

Anterior view

Sternocleidomastoid

Deltoid

Pectoralis major

Biceps brachii

Serratus anterior

Brachioradialis

External oblique

Rectus abdominis

Rectus femoris

Vastus lateralis

Sartorius

Tibialis anterior

Posterior view

Occipitalis

Trapezius

Deltoid

Triceps brachii

Latissimus dorsi

Gluteus maximus

Biceps femoris

Gastrocnemius

Soleus

Anterior view   Posterior view

The muscular system showing major muscle groups

Classification of muscles

Three different types of muscle tissue make up the muscular system:
- cardiac muscle, which is only found in the heart
- smooth muscle, also known as involuntary muscle
- skeletal muscle, also known as voluntary muscle.

The structure and function of each of these muscle tissues are very different, and they are controlled by different methods.

Cardiac muscle

This type of muscle is found only in the heart. It has a built in 'pacemaker', known as the sino-atrial node, that controls the rate of the heartbeat. The rate of the heart beating is an involuntary action but can be influenced by factors such as stress, medication, illness and exercise. These influencing factors change the reaction of the nervous system and the hormones that are released, which results in a change in heart rate.

Involuntary or smooth muscle

Examples of this type of muscle can be found in the visceral organs, propelling food through the digestive system, and the blood vessels that aid the blood flow away from the heart to all parts of the body. These muscles are controlled by the autonomic nervous system.

Skeletal muscle

This type of muscle is attached to the skeleton of the human body and its major functions are to provide movement and stability. It is also called striated muscle, because of its stripy appearance under a microscope. These muscles are controlled by the central nervous system. These are the muscles that you will concentrate on through this section.

Muscle type	Muscle structure	Primary function of muscle	Control mechanism of muscle	Location of muscle
Cardiac muscle	A combination of striated and smooth muscle tissue	Allows the pumping action of the heart, during rest and exercise	The heart's automatic nervous system, assisted by the central nervous system (C.N.S.)	In the heart
Involuntary muscle	Smooth	Maintains the different functions of many vital organs of the body	C.N.S. without conscious thought Autonomic nervous system (A.N.S.)	Blood vessels and visceral organs
Skeletal muscle	Striated or striped	To provide movement of the body	C.N.S. with conscious thought	Attached to the bones

The structure of skeletal muscle

As a result of a great deal of research, we now know that skeletal muscles are made up of many thousands of fibres rather than just one. Each skeletal muscle in the body consists of many individual fibres. These in turn are made up of even smaller fibres called myofibrils. It is within these smallest fibres that the contraction of muscle takes place. Actin and myosin are the proteins in myofibrils that are responsible for muscular contraction.

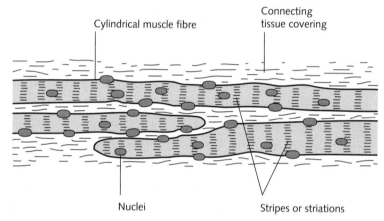

The microscopic structure of skeletal muscle

 Key point

Skeletal muscle performs any visible movement that your body makes. Movements that are not visible are the result of other muscular tissues performing a job that you do not have to think about. You can sometimes feel these movements, in your abdomen or chest, for example.

Muscle movement

Skeletal muscle has a vast supply of nerve and blood vessels. It is one of many links between the systems of the body, which work together to help movement to occur. Skeletal muscle is also termed voluntary muscle because movement is created via conscious thought processes.

There are many factors that help produce muscle movement. Nutrition is one that is often over looked. Muscles pull to produce movement. In other words, the cells of the muscle tissue contract and then relax to their original size. The cells of the body use chemical energy to work. This energy is created from the foods that we eat. Carbohydrate foods are the main fuel provider for muscle contraction. Minerals such as calcium are also essential.

Antagonistic pairs

Muscles work in pairs to provide movement for physical activity:

- Prime movers – these muscles determine the movement of an action via contraction. For example during the bicep curl, the prime mover during the flexion phase is the bicep.

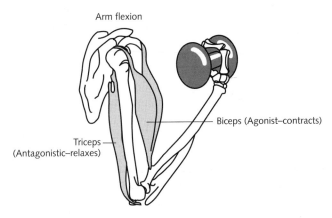

Arm flexion

Biceps (Agonist–contracts)

Triceps (Antagonistic–relaxes)

The upward phase of a bicep curl

- Antagonistic – this muscle works together with the prime mover but creates an opposition action. Using the example of the bicep curl again, during the flexion phase the triceps enable the arm to bend at the elbow joint for the bar to move toward the shoulder girdle.

Muscle contraction

Muscles contract to produce movement. There are three main types of muscle contraction: two where obvious movement occurs and one where there is no obvious movement visible.

- **Isometric contraction** is where the muscle stays the same length during contraction, or when the activity is being carried out. A good example of isometric contraction is during the crucifix position on the rings in gymnastics. Tension occurs in the muscle but the distance between the ends stay the same.
- **Isotonic concentric contraction** is where the muscle shortens when performing an action. There is obvious movement when the ends of the muscle move closer together. A good example of isotonic concentric contraction is the leg kicking or striking a ball.
- **Isotonic eccentric contraction** occurs when the muscles lengthen under tension. The ends of the muscle move further away during an action. A good example of isotonic eccentric contraction is when the bicep lengthens during the downward phase of a bicep curl.

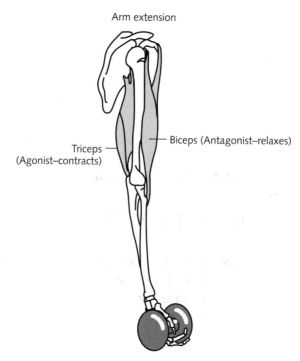

Arm extension

Biceps (Antagonist–relaxes)

Triceps
(Agonist–contracts)

The biceps lengthen during the downward phase of a bicep curl

Think about it

The different types of muscle contraction are constantly being performed during sport. The table below shows the different types of muscular contraction that you can see during a game of rugby.

Phase of play	Muscle group	Prime mover	Contraction
The lock after the scrum has engaged	Quadriceps Hamstrings Gastrocnemius	Quadriceps	Isometric contraction
The arms after the ball has been thrown in from a line out	Triceps Biceps	Triceps	Isotonic concentric contraction Isotonic eccentric contraction
The draw back of the leg as it prepares to kick the ball	Hamstrings Quadriceps	Hamstrings	Isotonic concentric contraction Isotonic eccentric contraction

Get together with other members of your group. Think of more examples of these different types of muscle contraction.

Muscle tone

Muscle tissue never really relaxes and is in constant partial contraction – this is what gives the body its muscle shape, or tone. A sedentary lifestyle can decrease the tone of the body's muscle tissue. Training, on the other hand, can increase the tone of the muscle tissue to become firmer even during resting conditions, to the point at which the shape of a muscle can be seen. If you stop training, maybe due to injury, some of the muscle tone will be lost. You will need to start training again to regain muscle tone.

The importance of posture

The curves of the spine provide a range of movement and potential movement to occur. The majority of the back problems that people experience are due to an imbalance of muscle strength around the torso area. Posture is vitally important, whether you are moving or not.

Good posture has the following characteristics:
- the body is upright and erect
- the head is in the mid-line and perpendicular to the shoulders and the vertebrae
- the shoulder and pelvic girdle are aligned
- the arms hang freely from the shoulders
- the feet point forward when they are planted firmly on the floor
- the vertebrae shows a concave curve at the cervical and lumbar regions
- the vertebrae shows a convex curve at the thoracic region.

 Key points

Everyone has a preferred side of working. For this reason, the two sides of the body are very rarely symmetrical.

Levers

You are able to move because of the relationship of the systems found in your body. Each system is dependent on the other systems. The skeletal system requires the muscles to be attached and the joints to function to allow for various movements to be successful. Efficient movements are possible due to a further system of levers. Movement is produced through a fixed point that allows a turning action to occur. Think of it in this way:
- bones are the **levers**
- joints are the **fixed point** or **fulcrum** that allows the turning motion
- muscle contractions provide the **force** that allows movements to take place.

There are three types of levers that are found in the body. These are categorised as first, second and third class. Each has three common elements:
1. the fulcrum (the point at which the lever turns or is supported) (F)
2. the effort or force that is applied for the movement to be carried out (E)
3. the load or resistance that is placed on the structure (L).

Each class of lever is arranged differently, according to where the fulcrum is found.
1. First class lever: the fulcrum lies between the effort and the load or resistance.
2. Second class lever: the load lies between the fulcrum and the effort.
3. Third class lever: the effort is between the fulcrum and the load.

It is the third class lever that determines the majority of the movements in your body – it produces movement the quickest.

The two main functions of the lever system are to increase the resistance against an opposing force, and to increase the speed of body movements.

Let's do it!

Identify the levers that are being used to carry out the following actions:
- standing on your toes
- the head, when heading a soccer ball
- flexion at elbow in an arm curl.

Let's do it!

Produce a poster presentation on three well known sportspeople of your choice, for example Tim Henman, David Beckham or Paula Radcliffe. The presentation should focus on one specific movement action in the performance of each of their sports, e.g. the actions of the muscles involved and the muscle fibres used in striking the ball in taking a penalty or serving or hitting a volley.

Working independently, or in small groups of three or four, use a video recorder and film a range of different sportspeople in action. Suitable sports to choose from would include gymnastics, soccer, tennis, track and field events or golf. If access to sportspeople is difficult visit your local leisure centre or health club and film people using resistance training equipment. Ideally footage for a minimum of three contrasting sports should be obtained. Please note that before filming it is always important to gain the consent of those being filmed first for ethical reasons.

Following filming, review the data you have captured and analyse the sportspeople in action. To do this, devise a simple movement analysis checklist concentrating on the bones, joints, muscles and movement patterns responsible for bringing the body into action in the sporting activities you have chosen.

P Using your movement checklist, identify the relevant muscles, joints and movement patterns.

M Using your movement checklist, compare the functions of relevant muscles and joints and their effects on movement patterns.

D Using your movement checklist, critically analyse the functions of relevant muscles and joints and their long term effects on movement patterns.

Let's do it!

Take five minutes to consider all the movements your muscles have contributed to in the last hour. List the different activities you have identified. How many are there? Discuss your findings with other members of your class.

Energy needs for muscular contraction

Your body requires energy for all its movements and for any muscular activity that takes place. Every living cell in your body requires energy to function. Your body does not produce its own energy. It obtains energy from the food that you eat. Foods that are high in carbohydrates, such as rice and pasta, help your body to maintain energy supplies. Foods that contain fat, such as oily fish and nuts, also help to keep up your energy levels. This energy is what your body uses for muscular contraction.

Key point

Proteins are normally used for fuel under starvation conditions.

Energy cannot be created or destroyed. It is converted from one form to another. The body converts the food it consumes into chemical energy through a series of chemical reactions. The chemical energy is used to perform body movements. These actions convert the chemical energy into mechanical energy, or muscular contractions. Any energy that is not used is then stored as potential energy.

Your body's immediate source of energy is A.T.P. (adenosine triphosphate). Energy is released by the breakdown of A.T.P. The A.T.P then needs to be re-synthesised so that the process can start again. Stores of A.T.P. are found in the muscle and liver as the stored form of carbohydrate, glycogen, and in the blood as blood glucose.

 Key point

A.T.P. consists of one adenosine molecule and three phosphate groups. These groups have a high energy bond between them. This bond can be released through a chemical reaction. The reaction enables the re-synthesis of another A.T.P. molecule.

ATP being re-synthesised

The three energy systems

The body uses three energy systems to produce A.T.P. Each of these systems works by re-synthesising the molecule of adenosine triphosphate (A.T.P.). The three systems are:

1. the A.T.P.-P.C. system
2. the anaerobic or lactic acid system
3. the aerobic system.

The A.T.P.-P.C. system

The body stores a chemical compound in the muscles called phosphocreatine (P.C.). This compound breaks down to release a phosphate molecule. This free molecule joins with adenosine diphosphate (A.D.P.) to re-form the compound of A. T. P. There is a very limited amount of P.C. found in the muscle so this energy system can only be used for short bursts of activity.

The advantages of this system are that:

- A.T.P.-P.C. is found directly in the muscle tissue
- it is an anaerobic system and so does not require oxygen
- no waste products (such as lactic acid) accumulate because none of the energy gained from food is used.

The disadvantage of this system is that there is a limited store of the energy supply that does not allow for continued high intensity work beyond 10 seconds.

The sports that predominantly use this type of energy system are sprint and power sports, for example the 100 metre sprint, the high jump and the long jump. It is also used regularly for certain elements during team sports, such as kicking, jumping, twisting, turning etc.

This athlete is using a short burst of energy

Think about it

Can you think of any other sports or events where the activity is completed within the 10 seconds that this system provides energy for?

The anaerobic or lactic acid system

The anaerobic system requires the breakdown of carbohydrate-type foods to form A.T.P. from the energy bonds found in the muscle. Carbohydrates are broken down to form glucose and are stored as glycogen in the body. The breakdown of the glucose or glycogen, to gain the energy required to form the A.T.P. molecules, is called glycolysis.

The anaerobic system does not require oxygen to provide the body with energy. The lack of oxygen results in a build up of lactic acid. Lactic acid is formed as a waste product of glycolysis and causes fatigue if not removed.

If exercise continues beyond 10 seconds at the same intensity there will be a build up lactic acid and carbon dioxide. These waste products need to be removed, either by reducing the intensity of exercise or stopping the activity. If neither action is taken, the muscles become tired and breathing rate increases. This will eventually result in the activity stopping.

The advantages of this system are that:
- the chemical reactions are very short
- it is an anaerobic system and therefore does not require oxygen.

The disadvantages of this system are that:
- there is a limited store of the energy supply that does not allow for continued high intensity work beyond 180 seconds
- there is an accumulation of lactic acid that can stop the exercise from continuing.

The sports that predominantly use this type of energy system are high intensity events that last for approximately 180 seconds. Such sports include, for example, races between 200 and 400 metres, 100 metre swimming events, hurdles and interspersed activities in sports such as rugby and basketball.

World class swimmers in 100 m swimming events use anaerobic energy

The aerobic system

The aerobic system is a long term energy system. It requires oxygen to ensure that sufficient energy is available for the re-synthesis of A.T.P. molecules. This involves the use of the simple units that make up carbohydrates and fats, known as glycogen (or glycerol) and free fatty acids respectively. It also uses energy supplied from proteins.

The aerobic system provides energy for continued low to moderate intensity exercise. There is a much greater amount of energy available during this system, compared to the other two systems, to help in the re-synthesis of A.T.P. The aerobic system goes through various chemical reactions that produce carbon dioxide and water as by-products. The aerobic system makes available vast amounts of energy during exercise.

The advantages of this system are that:
- it has a great capacity to store energy
- energy provision is available from the three main fuels – carbohydrates, fats and proteins

- energy for low to moderate activities that can be sustained
- because oxygen is present, there is no build up lactic acid
- waste products (water and carbon dioxide) are removed via the breathing process.

The disadvantages of this system are that:

- the chemical reactions are greater and therefore, slower to change levels
- it is an aerobic system and therefore requires the presence of oxygen.

The sports that predominantly use this type of energy system are low to moderate intensity events that last longer than five minutes. An example is the 1500 metres running event.

Let's do it!

Identify when each of the energy systems are being used during a game of hockey for a player on the right wing.

Think about it

Analyse a sport of your choice and identify when each of the energy systems is being used in the activity.

How the body uses the energy systems

All three systems operate to enable your body to carry out the normal functions necessary for living, and for completing day-to-day tasks. If you exercise, the demands on your body increase. The energy that is required to complete the exercise or the task will determine which of the energy systems dominates the provision of energy. The factors that determine which energy system leads an activity are:

- the type of activity or sport
- the speed of the task
- the intensity of the task
- the standard or level of the sport
- individual factors, such as personal fitness level and the type of training that an you carry out
- duration of task.

Under resting conditions your body obtains the majority of the energy it requires from the aerobic pathway. This enables the cell functions that keep you alive to be carried out. During rest, there is enough time for the aerobic system to break down fats which then provide the energy required at a steady rate and for a prolonged period of time.

During exercise, your muscles require more oxygen. If the intensity of the exercise continues to increase, the demand for oxygen continues to increase. Eventually, the point will be reached at which the demand exceeds your body's ability to provide sufficient levels of oxygen to complete the task. The body then calls on the anaerobic system to provide the necessary energy for exercise. This point is termed the 'anaerobic threshold'.

As the anaerobic pathway continues to provide the energy for exercise, there is an increase in the production of lactic acid within the muscle tissue. Lactic acid build up can change performance. If the intensity of performance is reduced then the lactic acid can be dispersed; if the intensity of performance continues at the same level then lactic acid can prevent further contraction of the muscle.

Let's do it!

Using the knowledge you have gained about the skeletal and muscular systems, visit your local health club or leisure centre to observe and analyse the range of fitness equipment available. Draw a chart of your research to include information on:
- the range of fitness equipment available
- the muscle groups targeted by this equipment
- the muscle actions brought about by the execution of the range of exercises utilising this equipment.

Assessment activity 2: Skeletal and muscular systems

P Re-read the sections on the skeletal and muscular systems. Produce a poster that simply describes the structure and function of either one of these systems. To assist you in this task you may find it useful to search the Internet and relevant textbooks for suitable resources.

No extension to merit or distinction is possible for this assessment activity.

The cardiovascular system

This system is the body's delivery and transport system, where blood moves from the heart and delivers oxygen and nutrients to every part of the body. On the return trip the blood picks up waste products so that they can be removed from the body.

The cardiovascular system is made up of three components:
1. the heart
2. the blood vessels
3. the blood.

The heart is a muscular pump, the size of a clenched fist, which can increase in either size or thickness as a result of training. It is made up of special cardiac muscle, which contracts regularly without tiring. Cardiac muscle becomes bigger and stronger if regular exercise is carried out. This means the heart becomes more efficient in pumping blood around the body.

Structure of the heart

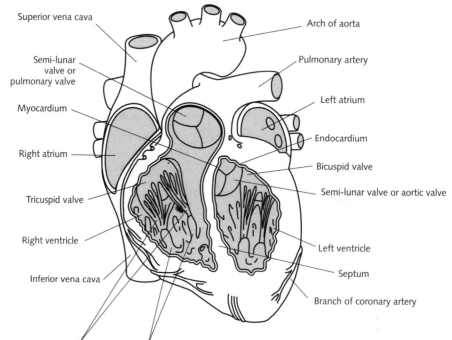

Superior vena cava

Semi-lunar valve or pulmonary valve

Myocardium

Right atrium

Tricuspid valve

Right ventricle

Inferior vena cava

Arch of aorta

Pulmonary artery

Left atrium

Endocardium

Bicuspid valve

Semi-lunar valve or aortic valve

Left ventricle

Septum

Branch of coronary artery

The *chordae tendineae* and *papillary muscles* tie the edges of the valves to the ventricular wall and stop the blood from flowing backwards.

A section through the heart

 Key points

- The atria are the top chambers of the heart. They are commonly known as the collecting chambers.
- The ventricles are the bottom chambers. They are commonly known as the pumping chambers.
- The right side of the heart collects and pumps de-oxygenated blood (blood with less oxygen).
- The left hand side of the heart collects and pumps oxygenated blood (blood carrying more oxygen).

Function of the heart

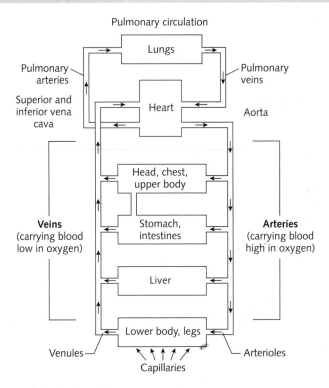

Double circulation of blood through heart

The cardiac cycle

There are two phases of the cardiac cycle, diastole and systole.
1. Diastole is the first phase of the cardiac cycle. Blood enters the atria and fills the two chambers – de-oxygenated blood into the right atrium and oxygenated blood into the left atrium – before moving into the ventricles. Diastole is the relaxation phase of the heart.
2. Systole is the second phase of the cycle. Blood is squeezed into the ventricular chambers from the atria. The right atrium squeezes the de-oxygenated blood to the right ventricle ready to be moved to the lungs and the left atrium squeezes the oxygenated blood to the left ventricle ready to be distributed to the rest of the body.

 Key points

> **Cardiac output** can be defined as the amount of blood pumped out of the left ventricle per minute.
> **Stroke volume** is the volume of blood pumped out the left ventricle per beat.

Measuring your resting heart rate can determine your fitness level, although many other factors must be taken into account. These factors include gender, health status and life style. If you compare the resting heart rates of females and males with similar training regimes and life styles, you usually find that the females have faster resting heart rates. This may be a result of females having a smaller heart size. As a result, the heart needs to beat faster to supply the body with sufficient amounts of blood.

Let's do it!

For this activity you will need an open space in which you can run or walk, or a sports hall or fitness facility with a treadmill.

Before you start:

- Calculate your maximum heart rate using the formula: **220 − age in years**.
- Take your pulse and calculate your heart rate at rest in beats per minute.

Then:

- Walk for 2–3 minutes. Remain standing and immediately take your pulse using a 10 second count and times by six to give beats per minute. Record your reading.
- Increase your pace to a jog for 2–3 minutes or as long as you can sustain your chosen pace. Remain standing and immediately take your pulse using a 10 second count and times by six. Record your reading.
- Increase your pace to a run for 2–3 minutes or as long as you can sustain your chosen pace. Remain standing and immediately take your pulse using a 10 second count and times by six to give beats per minute. Record your reading.
- Now perform 30 burpees (squat thrusts) or as many as you can. Remain standing and immediately take your pulse using a 10 second count and times by six to give beats per minute. Record your reading.
- Take 5–10 minutes to do a thorough warm down and then consider the body changes that you have experienced during all the above activities. Record your thoughts for later discussion with your tutor.

Key points

- The heart has its own nervous control. If the central nervous system is damaged, the heart can still function.
- The left ventricle is the largest chamber of the heart. One of the changes brought about by endurance training is that the cavity of this chamber increases in size.

The structure and function of blood vessels

The blood vessels are the routes that the blood travels to carry nutrients and gases to all of the many body parts.

There are three types of blood vessel in the body:

1. **Arteries**– these are thick and elastic in texture. They carry blood away from the heart. The muscle action of these vessels pushes the blood through the arteries to the relevant stops.
2. **Veins** – these are two layers thick, carry blood back to the heart and contain pocket valves to ensure that blood returns back to the heart.
3. **Capillaries** – these are narrow and thin, and connect the veins and the arteries. Delivery of nutrients and the removal of waste products occurs via the diffusion of chemicals and gases in the capillaries.

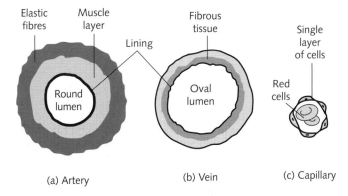

Major blood vessels

 Key points

The blood passes through the arteries using the Windkessel 'pressure chamber' function. The blood is pushed forward as contraction occurs within the vessel.

Damaged pocket valves can result in varicose veins.

Types of blood cells

The total volume of blood in the body differs between individuals. It depends on your gender, body size and fitness level. Men on average have between five and six litres of blood, compared to the average four to five litres that women have.

The blood is made up of 55% plasma and 45% formed elements. The 45% formed elements consist of red blood cells (erythrocytes), white blood cells (leukocytes) and platelets (thrombocytes).

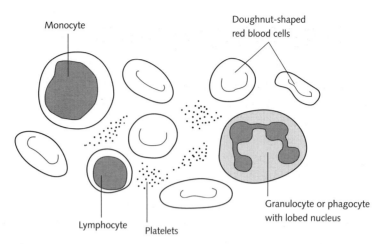

Different types of blood cell

Plasma

Plasma is a watery liquid, pale yellow in colour, which contains substances such as salts, calcium, nutrients (including glucose), hormones, carbon dioxide and other waste from body cells.

Red blood cells

These cells are made in the red marrow of the long bones, sternum, ribs and vertebrae. They give blood its colour, and contain haemoglobin, which carries oxygen from the lungs to all our body cells. These cells have a very short life span of 120 days.

Platelets

These cells are made in the bone marrow and they stick together very easily. They produce clots when vessels are damaged.

White blood cells

These are made in the bone marrow, lymph nodes and spleen. There are fewer of these cells compared to the red blood cells. White blood cells are three times the size of red blood cells. The function of white blood cells is to fight infection and disease. Some of these cells eat the germs that cause infection. Others produce antibodies to destroy germs.

Blood pressure

Blood pressure is the force exerted by the walls of the arteries as the blood moves through them. The average blood pressure is 120/80 mmHg. This figure will vary due to your gender, age and fitness level as well as hereditary factors and health. Changes in blood pressure occur during exercise because there is a greater pressure on the vessels to force the blood through, especially as the increase of blood flow takes place.

The respiratory system

The respiratory system helps the body take in oxygen and remove carbon dioxide and heat. The average adult breathes in and out between 12 and 16 breaths per minute.

Let's do it!

Sit on a chair with a back rest and relax. Do not cross your legs or arms. Count how many breaths you breathe in and out in one minute. Count in and out as one breath. Compare your results with the rest of the group. Breathing rate is different for different groups of individuals. Some these differences are due to gender, age, health and fitness.

The structure of the respiratory system

The respiratory system is the breathing machine of the body. It includes the mouth, nose, larynx (voice box), trachea (wind pipe), lungs, diaphragm, intercostal muscles, and the thoracic cage (rib cage).

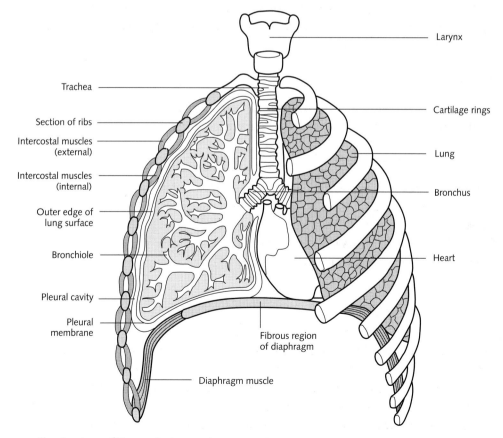

The structure of the respiratory system

When we breathe in, oxygen comes in through the nose and mouth. It travels down the trachea until it arrives at the bronchi. The bronchi can be described as thick trunks split into two parts. They direct the air into the right lung and the left lung. These trunks are divided further into smaller branches, known as bronchioles. The bronchioles have little air sacs (alveoli) at the tips. These air sacs allow oxygen and other nutrients to change places.

Oxygen and nutrients are used by the body. Blood takes them to the different body parts. Carbon dioxide and other waste products have to be removed from the body. Blood picks them up and returns them back to the heart. It then passes to the lungs to remove them when we breathe out (expiration).

Key points

The method by which oxygen and carbon dioxide change places is called **gaseous exchange**. These gases can only change places through the process of diffusion. This is where a high concentration of gas moves to a low concentration of gas. The exchange of these gases occurs in the capillary network.

The high concentration of oxygen found in the alveoli during inspiration (breathing in) moves to the smaller vessels of the pulmonary vein. This is so that the blood can take the oxygen to the heart for distribution. The high concentration of carbon dioxide in the smaller vessels of the pulmonary artery moves to the alveoli, so that it can be removed during expiration (breathing out).

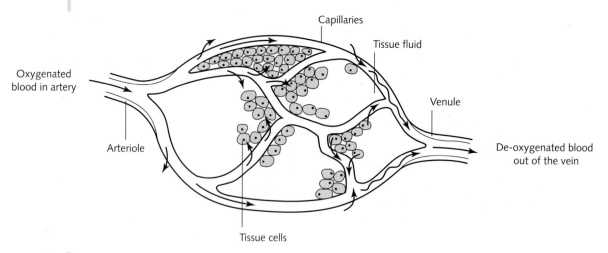

The capillary network

The mechanism of breathing

The respiratory system allows the passage of oxygen through the body and the removal of waste products. The diaphragm and the intercostal muscles help with the process of breathing. The diaphragm is found below the lungs. It contracts and flattens when you breathe in (inspiration). During breathing the intercostal muscles lift and expand the thoracic cage to allow for the lungs to fill up with oxygen. When you breathe out (expiration), the diaphragm and the intercostals muscles relax and the lungs deflate.

These intercostal muscles are classed as involuntary muscles because they relax and contract without conscious thought. You can over-ride this involuntary control, however, through conscious thought, for example by forcibly pushing out a breath further than a normal breath.

 Key points

Stretch receptors found in the lungs detect changes in the lung environment. They will initiate expiration to avoid the lungs from over inflating.

Term	Description	Amounts at rest
Breathing frequency	The amount of breaths per minute	12–16 breaths for an average adult
Tidal volume	The volume of air breathed in or out per breath	0.5 litres per breath
Minute ventilation	The volume of air breathed per minute	6 litres per minute
Vital capacity	Maximum amount of air that can be forcibly inhaled and exhaled in one breath	500 ml
Total lung capacity	All the air in the lungs after a maximum inhalation	6000 ml
Residual lung volume	The amount of air left in the lungs after a forced breath out	1200 ml

Assessment activity 3: Cardiovascular and respiratory systems

P Re-read the section on the cardiovascular and respiratory system. Produce a leaflet that simply describes the structure and function of either one of these systems. To assist you in this task you may find it useful to search the Internet and relevant textbooks for suitable resources.

No extension to merit or distinction is possible for this assessment activity.

Assessment activity 4: Effects of sport on oxygen and carbon dioxide levels

P With the support of your tutor, identify and use basic tests that demonstrate the main mechanics of breathing and the changes in oxygen and carbon dioxide levels in two contrasting sporting activities. Record your outcomes and results.

M Carry out the above activity independently. Explain the tests, and compare the outcomes and results.

D Carry out the above activity. Analyse the relationship between the different sports activities and their effects on the oxygen and carbon dioxide levels in the body. Critically evaluate the practical investigations you have undertaken and clearly describe the conclusions you have drawn. Include evidence of planning and executing your tests, your results and your interpretation of these. You may find it useful to present this information in the form of tables, charts and graphs.

The short term effects of exercise

The short term response of the heart to exercise

Your heart rate increases as you start to exercise and will continue to increase as exercise intensity continues to rise. Stroke volume also increases when exercise starts, due to the increase of oxygen demand by the working muscles. The volume of blood delivered to the working muscles increases with every beat of the heart and this delivery rate increases as heart rate continues to increase.

However, stroke volume does not continue to increase in the same manner as cardiac output and heart rate. Therefore, as exercise intensity increases, the increase in oxygen demand is supplied by the increasing beats of the heart (the heart rate).

In the short term, both heart rate and stroke volume increase, resulting in an increase in cardiac output. As exercise continues increasing in intensity, cardiac output continues to increase due to the continued increase in the heart rate rather than the volume of blood being pumped out per beat.

Factor of the cardiovascular system	At rest	During exercise
Heart rate	60–80 beats per minute	Max. 220 – age in years
Stroke volume	70 ml per beat	140 ml per beat
Cardiac output	5 litres per minute	20–25 litres per minute

Cardiovascular changes from rest to exercise

The short term responses of the respiratory system to exercise

Respiratory frequency, or breathing rate, is the amount of breaths breathed in and out per minute. The amount of breaths can depend on a number of factors, including age, fitness levels, lifestyles and gender. When you exercise your breathing rate becomes rapid and shallow. Respiratory frequency can double or triple during high intensity work. This is because of the increase in demand for oxygen, which is needed by the working muscles, and an increase in carbon dioxide accumulation. Breathing rate needs to increase to help provide the body with the oxygen and to remove the waste carbon dioxide and lactic acid.

The effects of exercise on muscle

There are two types of changes that muscles go through when they are exercised:
1. responses – these are the immediate changes that happen when you start to exercise
2. adaptations – these are the long term changes that occur due to regular participation in exercise.

Muscle responses to exercise

These include:
- an increase of blood flow to the working muscles due to the increased demand of oxygen from the working muscles
- an increase in the fuel demand for the movement to take place

- the creation of by-products or waste that need to be removed by the body. These are created by the energy that is produced for movement and include lactic acid and carbon dioxide
- an increase in body temperature, which is a result of energy from the fuels being broken down.

Muscle adaptations to exercise

If you exercise regularly, long term changes occur in the muscle tissue. Muscles become bigger and stronger depending on the type of exercise that you undertake. It can take up to six weeks for changes to be seen. However, it often only takes two weeks for these changes to be lost if exercise does not continue. Participation in strength-type exercise increases the size and strength of the muscle tissue. The size in muscle tissue can be termed 'hypertrophy'.

Think about it

For this activity you need to find somewhere to cycle for a 10 minute period. Warm up and then undertake this activity.

- While cycling, try to note the acute responses your body appears to make to this bout of exercise.
- Consider the chronic adaptions you would expect to occur if you were to cycle two or three times per week for a six week period.

Case study: Jeanette

Jeannette plays rugby regularly. When she injured her ankle during a game she was forced to stop training for seven days. After this period of time she began to perform gentle rehabilitation exercises.

After a period of four weeks, Jeanette realised that she could now lift as many weights with her lower body as she could before the injury. She was referred to physiotherapy. She was placed on a circuit training programme for 16 weeks to help build her body strength back to pre-injury levels. As a result of the training programme, Jeanette's performance improved:

- She increased the weight of the barbell curl for the biceps from 10 to 15 kg per 15 reps.
- Her performance of the leg extension exercise improved by 10%.

Jeanette continued with the muscular endurance training for six weeks after the initial programme. She found that her strength and her ability to continue with repetitive exercise for the major muscles groups increased.

Now answer the following questions:

1. What would happen to the other systems – C.V. and respiratory – if Jeanette does not vary her training?
2. State any different exercises that Jeanette could do to improve all her systems.

Assessment activity 5: Responses of the body to exercise

Identify, explain and compare the immediate and long term responses of the body to two contrasting sports activities from the following list:

- marathon running
- cricket
- power lifting
- hockey
- basketball
- golf
- rowing
- football.

P You may find it useful to present your findings as a table. Identify the immediate responses of the body to contrasting forms of exercise.

M Explain and compare the responses of the body to contrasting forms of exercise.

D Critically analyse the responses of the body to contrasting forms of exercise drawing valid conclusions.

In summary

Understanding how the body is structured and functions is vitally important if you want to maintain and improve your performance.

Knowing how the body moves and works in sympathy with other systems is essential knowledge for creating exercise programmes that will be beneficial, allow for improvement and will not put undo strain on the sports performer.

CHECK WHAT YOU KNOW!

Look back through this unit and see if you can answer the following questions:

1 Name the five functions of the skeleton.
2 Name the five types of bone.
3 Give one example of the function of each of the types of bone.
4 Name the three types of muscle found in the body.
5 Name the groups of common joints found in the body.
6 Hinge joints are limited in their movement. Name the types of movement that a hinge joint can make.
7 What are the common factors of a synovial joint?
8 If training continues over a period of time, what adaptations will cardiac muscle go through?
9 What structures help the breathing system become more efficient?
10 Name the three energy systems that the body uses to provide energy for muscular movement.

Sports leadership skills

Introduction

Many successful sports leaders combine performance and leadership skills, enabling themselves and others to achieve personal and team goals. There are certain traits that a sports leader must possess and develop. These are classed as common factors, or generic abilities and skills. The sports leader will show these qualities through the planning, delivery and evaluation of each sports session.

How you will be assessed

This unit looks at ways you can prepare for leading a group in a practical sports session. It suggests ways to improve your delivery and looks at how you can evaluate your own performance as a leader once the session has finished. It is an internally assessed unit, so the centre at which you are studying will devise the assessments that you will carry out.

After completing the unit you should be able to achieve the following learning outcomes:

1. Examine and use the **skills and qualities** required to lead a successful activity session.
2. Assist in **planning** an activity session.
3. **Deliver and review** an activity session.

Skills and qualities

All sports require leaders. Good sports leaders inspire and encourage the team at vital moments in a game and provide a good role model. As an effective sports leader, it is part of your role to develop the performance of each individual in the group. It is also important to encourage cohesion, so that your group of individuals works well as a team.

People who develop and encourage sports at grass roots level, helping coaches and teams, are also sports leaders in their own right. The role of these sports leaders is to develop and encourage young people and adults to participate, and continue to participate, in all types of sports.

Think about it

In groups, discuss the sports leaders you have come into contact with.
1. Who have you most admired?
2. Why?

Together, list the qualities that you think make a strong leader.

Personal qualities

Ability to make effective decisions

Strong leadership style (enthusiastic/ motivating/ communicative)

Personal qualities required by a sports leader

Good standards of appearance

Ability to relate to others

Key points

A good standard of appearance will gain you the respect of your group. You should also wear appropriate clothing to ensure that you are safe. Wearing baggy clothes or large jewellery, for example, can be a hazard in some sports.

The appearance of a sports leader needs to be confident, smart and safe

Personality

Sports leaders are usually confident in their approach to the sport and about what is required for success. They are also confident about organising others and giving advice and guidance.

Introvert and extrovert personality types

Personalities fall into two categories, extrovert and introvert (for a description of these two personality types, see Unit 3 *Preparation for sport*, p. 146). There is a strong link between an individual's personality type and the type of sport he or she is attracted to. Extrovert personalities are often found in team based sports, where situations are unpredictable and can change quickly. Introvert personalities tend to be found in sports that require low levels of stimulation but require high levels of accuracy in delivery. (This does not mean, however, that introverts only participate in individual sports and extroverts only stay in team game sports.)

Your personality type can be a key factor to success as a sports leader. Your leadership style will be determined by the type of personality you possess – you are likely to lead in a way that suits your personality type. Also, the personality types of the individuals you are leading will influence your leadership style.

 Think about it

Discuss introvert and extrovert personality types with your group.
1. Why do you think different personality types are attracted to different sports?
2. What category do you think you fall into?
3. What kind of sports do you participate in?
4. Are there any exceptions in your group to the tendency described above?
5. Can you think of any exceptions outside your group?

The co-operation and support of colleagues

To be a good team leader, you need to be positive. Leaders need to motivate their teams and a positive approach is the best way to achieve this. Team members feel more comfortable with a leader who is easy to get along with and pleasant to be around. A sense of humour can help to keep players interested and focused during practice sessions and matches. It also helps to ease the tension that can arise from intense sports sessions.

As a team leader, part of your role will be to impart knowledge and advice to team members. In order to do this, you need to have a positive relationship with your team mates. You also need to be positive about the area of delivery you are commenting upon but remember that this does not mean only offering positive comments. Your team members will not be able to improve their performance if you concentrate only on their strengths and neglect to highlight weaknesses. Such comments can be put in a positive way, however, by giving constructive advice and offering solutions.

Let's do it!

Choose a sport with a partner. Then role play the following scenario: a discussion between the team leader and a team member in which the leader highlights strengths and weaknesses in the performance of the member in a positive way.

You can directly influence a sports performer by discussing the activity with them

Part of your role as a sports leader is to help other performers to achieve their goals. You can directly influence a team member's performance by discussing it with them. You can also influence it by being a role model or inspiration in their sport. Pelé (in football) and Steve Redgrave (in rowing) were the world's best in their sports. Each continues to be an ambassador for his sport, showing great commitment and the positive attitude that is required for all sports.

Leaders are often chosen by the management structure of the club or by the players and are usually the captain of the team. However, senior players within the team can also be leaders. For example, Martin Johnson was the captain of the England World Cup winning team (2003), but Lawrence Dallaglio, Neil Back and Mike Catt offered advice and leadership as well.

Think about it

Think of captains or leaders in three different team sports.
1. How do they lead?
2. Are there other players in these teams who also lead?

Leadership styles

The way you approach specific tasks will determine how effective you are as a leader. Such tasks include planning your activity, delivering it and providing opportunities for feedback. Your success as a sports leader will be measured in terms of your team members achieving a set goal.

Leaders in sport all have different styles. These styles vary because of the personality of the leaders and also because of the demands and requirements of the sport.

Case study: team leaders

Martin Johnson (rugby), Roy Keane (football) and Nasser Hussain (cricket) are all leaders of their teams. Each of these leaders has a sound technical and tactical knowledge of their sport, and although there are some similarities in their leadership styles, there are also significant differences.

Each of these leaders:
- leads by example in his performance
- is aggressive in his performance
- is very verbal.

However:
- Martin Johnson is positive but firm in the guidance that he gives his team players
- Roy Keane forcibly directs the players around him
- Nasser Hussain, who is involved in a very different type of sport, is more verbal and his decision-making role is more strongly in evidence.

Nasser Hussain

Now answer the following questions:
1. Choose a leader in your sport who inspires you – he or she could be a team player or a captain.
2. List the reasons why you think that he or she is a good leader.

There are many different ways that sports leaders can be effective and successful. Different types of leader suit different situations. The table below lists some of the factors that you need to consider when you lead a team:

Task	Team	Individual
What needs to be done?	How do the group interact as a team? How does your team benefit from your leadership style?	How are the needs of each individual being met?

Three leadership styles have been identified: autocratic, democratic and *laissez-faire*.

Leadership style	Description	Benefits	Disadvantages
Autocratic	Does not involve others in the decision making process. Task oriented rather than team oriented	Decision making can be carried out quickly. Effective in team sports with large numbers. Can be very inflexible	Task becomes leader centred rather than performer centred. May not bring out full potential of individual team members
Democratic	Involves others in the decision making process. Is interested in the team members as individuals, developing close personal relationships	Less formal approach to leading a team. Team members more likely to develop	Decision making is time consuming, and may not be quick enough under pressure. Problems may occur in teams of large numbers
Laissez-faire	Acts as a consultant rather than a decision maker – the initiative is left to others	Flexible approach. Encourages others to take the initiative	Lack of structure to the task. Lack of direction or co-ordination. Risk of poor decision making

Let's do it!

Look back at the information given about the various leadership styles and the different personality types. Give examples of three sporting situations in which each of these leadership styles would be effective.

Case study: Leilah

Leilah is 8 years old and has been swimming for the last 18 months for the local swimming club. At present she is attending her club twice a week, at the weekends. Leilah enjoys all sports and participates in gymnastics and football at school. Leilah strives to be the best in any activity she gets involved in, and enjoys the praise that comes with her successes.

During training for swimming, Leilah's coach:
- does not dress in the formal club uniform
- praises the children in every attempt that they make in the tasks that are set
- does not highlight the mistakes that the children may make
- allows the children to dictate what they will do for the session.

Leilah enjoys the sessions and always comes back very happy. However, there has been no evidence of improvements in Leilah's performance in the time trials that she enters.

Now answer the following questions:
1. Describe the leadership style of Leilah's swimming coach, giving examples from the case study as evidence to support your decisions
2. Do you think Leilah should change her coach? (Discuss your answer with a partner.)

 Key points

Some of the key factors to success as a team leader are:
- the ability to communicate
- a positive attitude
- enthusiasm
- concern for others
- humour.

Enthusiasm and the ability to motivate others

Being enthusiastic and motivated is contagious! These qualities rub off on sports performers, other leaders, members of the coaching team and spectators. The coach or sports leader often creates the 'spark' that keeps the performance of other team members moving and creative.

Skills in sports leadership

Good communication skills (with team mates/officials/coaches)

Effective organisation of facilities and equipment

Effective management of time

Sports leadership skills

Thorough knowledge of the sport and equipment

Effective management of groups

Thorough knowledge of health and safety requirements

Let's do it!

In small groups, discuss the relative importance of each of the skills in the spidergram. If there are differences of opinion within the group, try rating each of these factors on a scale of 1–10, 1 being the least important.

Communication

If you can communicate at various levels you will be able to bridge the gap between players, other coaches, the opposition and officials. You can communicate:

- using verbal language
- using non verbal language, such as facial expressions and bodily gestures
- by listening.

Communication skills are essential for any leader to have, develop and use. A sports leader must have a clear voice and a command over the language that dominates the performers in the sport being delivered. Many people are chosen to be a captain or a coach in their sport due to their experience as a player at a very high level. However, although they may have an excellent understanding of the sport, if they cannot communicate effectively they will not be able to pass this knowledge on.

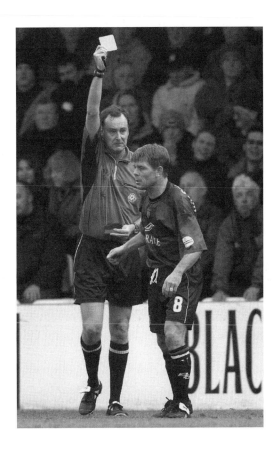

Non-verbal communication

 Key points

Effective communication skills are essential to:
- pass on information about what players must do for each skill
- use appropriate language to direct players to improve performance
- provide further information that helps the organisation of the sport to run smoothly off the training or playing ground.

Delivering information effectively is important, but to do this, you must also listen. Listening carefully to performers as they acquire skills may help you to improve the performance of the player. Listening to performers' experiences of playing may clarify areas of difficulty that you, as a leader, may not be able to see. Communication is a two way process for the improvement of performance!

Organisation

Organisational skills are essential to the sports leader. As a sports leader or member of a coaching team, it will be your responsibility to organise:

- each training session (including facilities and equipment)
- competitions
- paperwork, which may be essential if performers are to compete
- health and safety
- the evaluation of each meeting for the performer and their parents.

Key points

Time management skills are essential for a good sports leader. You need to allow time to plan your session. Also, your plan needs to include:

- the time the session starts
- the duration of the session
- the duration of each component activity or task.

During the session, you then need to stick to your plan as far as possible, to ensure you cover everything and achieve your aim.

Knowledge and skills

Knowledge of the sport you are coaching is a crucial factor to being a good sports leader. It is essential that you master the tactical and technical aspects of the sport being delivered. You must also have a good understanding of its laws and rules.

As well as sport specific knowledge, you should also know about basic fitness training and health and safety issues. You should have current first-aid knowledge and, if possible, an up-to-date qualification. You should also have a basic knowledge of the care and prevention of sports injuries.

As you gain more coaching experience, you will build up a personal 'knowledge bank'. Increasingly, you will draw on this when making decisions. Your playing experience is also important. It will give you, as a sports leader, a 'vision' for the game or sport that cannot be taught in a classroom environment. If you have played the sport yourself, you will also understand what it is like to be a player and what it is like to be coached – in other words, you will be able to put yourself into another performer's shoes.

It is obvious, then, that some of the knowledge you will need as a sports leader will be gained through experience. This experience can be specific to the sport, or may be gained through coaching and leading other groups. Some elements of coaching remain the same in any sport – for example, planning, preparation, organisation, evaluation and review of the session or programme.

Assessment activity 1: Using skills and personal qualities to lead activities

Choose two contrasting sport activity sessions that you have led.

P With the help of your tutor list the skills and personal qualities that you used to lead your group. Remember you need to show that you have also effectively used these skills while leading your sports activities.

M Independently use skills and personal qualities to lead two contrasting sport activities.

D While you are leading two contrasting sports activities modify and adjust your personal and leadership skills to suit the changing needs of participants.

Activities

Activities can be designed and used:
- for warm ups
- as skill drills
- for competitive situations
- to help performers learn skills specific to the sport
- to help performers learn the rules of the sport
- to practise working as a team.

There are many different types of activities for different groups participating in sport. The types of activities that you use will vary according to the sport in question, the size of your group and the age and ability of your group.

Individual and team activities

Some examples of individual activies include:
- circuit sessions
- passing against the wall
- shooting practice
- dribbling
- throwing.

Circuit training can be used for teams to train together and for individuals training in a group or on their own

The skills practised in these activities can be transferred to a competitive situation – for example, you could time or count successful attempts. Activities like the ones listed above can also help to promote team work, although they are practised individually. Passing and dribbling, for example, can be practised as an activity and then used in a competitive situation by defenders in a confined area.

The design of the activities can help each member of your group to understand the role of his or her specific position and the roles of others on the field. It is a good idea to gradually increase this sort of information as the activity progresses. In this way, the players will begin to understand their positions in more detail. They will also understand how they can contribute to the team's successful performance.

Rules and regulations related to activities

Activities are a useful way to introduce rules and regulations in a sport. However, you don't need to include all of the rules and regulations of the sport for each activity. The rules that regulate the sport can be included in a practice situation gradually. For example, when a player catches the ball in netball, he or she must stop travelling. The player can pivot on the landing foot but cannot move further in distance until the ball has been passed. For beginners to the game, it is appropriate to allow one or two steps. The number of steps can then be reduced, once the skill of stopping has been mastered. This kind of gradual approach can help the performer learn each skill and rule without feeling overloaded.

As already discussed, some activities are designed to encourage team work. If these activities do not produce the desired effect, then you could consider introducing rules which restrict the play but encourage the team work. For example, you could make a rule that all players must have a touch of the ball before shooting for goal in football. Another example might be that five passes from different players must be carried out in any one half of the pitch or court.

Activities related to recreation

Games with rules that have not been set by the Governing Body of a sport can be classed as improvised or unplanned games, or activities for recreation. For example, a full side football match in a league or a cup competition, played on a standard pitch with two sets of goal posts and a referee, is classed as a sport because:

- the teams play according to a standardised set of rules
- competition is an essential part of the game
- there is a result at the end of the game.

A four-a-side game of football, played on a non-standard pitch using posts for goals and with no official referee is classed as a recreational game because:

- the rules have been modified by the individuals participating on the day
- competition is not essential
- there is not necessarily a result.

The organisation of sport

A successful sports session depends upon good preparation. Being prepared will help you to cope with last minute hitches to the session, such as changes in weather, lack of equipment or changes in numbers. If your sports session is well organised, your group will be able to enjoy an activity where every eventuality has been considered. The session will be fun, fluent and educational.

Lesson plan

The lesson plan you design must be realistic and suitable for the group you are leading. At the planning stage of a session, you need to be thinking about:

- aims, objectives and target setting – the purpose of the session
- the different requirements of members of the group – making sure you have information about special medical, cultural or educational needs
- the facility, and any resources or equipment you may need
- how to sequence activities
- your target group
- preparation – e.g. carrying out checks of the venue and equipment
- clothing and equipment – ensuring the athletes' clothing is appropriate and that they are wearing the required protective clothing; providing adequate and appropriate equipment.

Let's do it!

In a group, think about a sports session you attend regularly. What would the sports leader have to consider when planning the session?

Aims, objectives and target setting

As a sports leader, you need to set goals for the short, medium and long term. This can seem a daunting task. Having an overall plan will help you to set goals over a period of time and in an achievable way. It will also help you to deal with the changes that you may come across during each session or programme.

Start by determining your long term 'aim', and then break this goal down into smaller goals, or 'objectives'. The goals of a sports leader must have input from the performers that he or she works with. The S.M.A.R.T. model will help you to set these goals. S.M.A.R.T. stands for: **S**pecific, **M**easurable, **A**greed, **R**ealistic and **T**imed.

Specific – This refers to the content of the goal. It must be specific to your chosen sport or event. For instance, a top 100 metre sprinter in athletics does not need a great deal of stamina. Even within a particular sport, different performers may have different aims. A football goalkeeper, like Tim Howard of Manchester United, will not need to practise shooting as much as the striker Ruud Van Nistelrooy.

> ### Let's do it!
>
> Consider the training of Paula Radcliffe (a marathon runner) and Ruud Van Nistelrooy (a football striker). In small groups:
> - discuss ways in which the training of the two sports performers might be the same and different.
> - discuss how these sports performers could measure how well they are doing.
>
> Bring your ideas back to the class for further discussion.

Measurable – Your goal needs to be measurable, that is, there must be some way to clearly see when it has been achieved. In athletics, measuring the achievement of goals can be very straightforward – you will run a certain time, or jump a particular distance, for example. The measurement is very objective. Changes in your fitness can also easily be measured by undertaking fitness tests.

For other goals, you will need to think of other ways to measure them. For example, you might look at reaching targets by a set date. Athletes will usually try to reach their peak performance at the same time as competing in major events, for example the Olympic Games. If they are able to 'peak' at the right time, they will hope to perform well. If they peak too early or too late, their chances of success will be reduced.

Agreed – Goals that you set must be agreed with your teacher or coach. This will involve sitting down and discussing what you might aim for, by when and how your success will be measured. Failure to agree these points will ultimately lead to confusion, conflict and failure.

Realistic – Any goal that you set must be realistic, i.e. you must be able to achieve it. This does not mean to say that the goal set is easy, but neither should it be too hard. It should be possible to achieve it, assuming that, for example, you stay free from injury, receive the required resources and so on. Be realistic in relation to the set timescale as well as the actual performance goal. Winning this year's London Marathon is unlikely to be realistic for you but completing the race in an agreed time may well be!

Timed – Your goals must be time constrained. This means that a deadline is set by which the goal should have been achieved. For instance, if you are learning to drive, the date of your exam is the deadline for learning and being able to perform all the various skills required. Deadlines should be flexible, they may need to be changed because of injury or illness. Deadlines can also be long term. Top athletes will often set a deadline a number of years away. For instance, a swimmer or runner may set goals for the Olympic Games four years in advance.

Target setting

The S.M.A.R.T model can be used for setting individual targets for performers. Each training session and competition should provide you with the information on the strengths and weaknesses of a performer in specific situations. This can be used to set targets for the performer.

Information about your group

It is important to collect information about your group, for example:
- how big it is
- the age range and gender mix
- the cultural background of its members
- the level of ability
- any relevant medical information.

The design of the session plan must be realistic for the sport and the group that are being coached. The type of delivery and leadership style you adopt will also be affected by the size of your group and the age-range you are coaching. You need to be aware that there are rules and regulations set by law that state the required ratio of leaders to children of certain ages.

You also need to be aware of the cultural backgrounds of the members of your group. Different cultures have different rules about the way individuals should behave and respond in various situations. The type of dress or clothing that is worn during sport may also be influenced by cultural background. For example, females in some cultures do not wear clothing that reveals certain parts of their bodies, including their arms and legs.

Each member of the group must complete a medical history form before participating in any activity. If the individual is under 18 years old, his or her parent or guardian must sign permission for him or her to participate. An example of a medical history form is given overleaf.

INCORPORATING PAR-Q

(A questionnaire for people aged 15 to 69)

Name: _____ Age: _____ Sex: _____

Address: _____ Postcode: _____

Occupation/Course: _____ Tel Wk: _____ Tel Hrn: _____

Person to be contacted
in case of accident: _____ Tel Wk: _____ Tel Hrn: _____

SECTION 1

Common sense is your best guide when you answer these questions. Please read the questions carefully and answer each one honestly. ✓ Tick – YES or NO.

YES	NO	
☐	☐	Has your doctor ever said that you have a heart condition and that you should only do physical activity recommended by a doctor?
☐	☐	Do you feel pain in your chest when you do physical activity?
☐	☐	In the past month, have you had chest pain when you were not doing physical activity?
☐	☐	Do you lose you balance because of dizziness or do you ever lose consciousness?
☐	☐	Do you have a bone or joint problem that could be made worse by a change in your physical activity?
☐	☐	Is your doctor currently prescribing drugs (for example, water pW's) for your blood pressure or heart condition?
☐	☐	Do you know of any other reason why you should not do physical activity?

If you answered Yes to one or more questions
Talk with your doctor by phone in person BEFORE you start becoming much more physically active or BEFORE you have a fitness appraisal. Tell your doctor about the PAR-Q and which questions you have answered YES.
- You may be able to do any activity you like as long as you start slowly and build up gradually. Or, you may need to restrict your activities to those which are safe for you. Talk with your doctor about the kinds of activities you wish to participate in and follow his/her advice.
- Find out which community programmes are safe to follow for you.

SECTION 2

Have you ever or do you have any of the following?
☐ Muscular pain   ☐ Diabetes   ☐ Epilepsy
☐ Arthritis   ☐ Asthma   ☐ Are you pregnant?

Any pain or major injuries particularly the following areas:
☐ Neck   ☐ Back   ☐ Knee   ☐ Ankles   ☐ Other

If you "✓" Please ask instructor for exercise class or programme guidance before starting
If your health changes so that you then answer YES to any of the above questions, tell your fitness or health professional. Ask whether you should change your physical plan.

What exercise type have you been doing recently?
Intensity: Hard – Medium – Light   How long?   How often?

Signature: _____ **Date:** _____

Example of the medical history form

Special needs

Special needs could refer to medical needs, for example allergies to sun creams, fluids or medication. It could also refer to any special educational needs (S.E.N.). Some performers learn differently and, as a result, you will need to adjust the way in which you deliver information. Performers can learn through instruction, through demonstration, or through a combination of the two. Some performers learn better if a demonstration is given first, followed by instruction. Others learn better with a number of small demonstrations, followed by feedback at the end of the performance.

Planning activities

The structure of your session and the sequence of tasks you deliver should be directed by:

- what you want to achieve in the session and how want to achieve it
- what the members of your group want or expect from the session.

Design your session to ensure that if quick progression is made by any individual, he or she can move on to further tasks. This helps small groups or individuals to progress at a faster rate than others in the group and keeps the performers physically and mentally active throughout the session. The progression of tasks should take into account the different needs of the group, for example those who are experiencing difficulties as well as those who are gifted or talented. It is possible that you may need specialised support for certain acitivities, or for certain individuals. Make sure you take account of this at the planning stage.

A session plan should also carry relevant information from the previous session and have space to evaluate the current session. An example is given overleaf.

Equipment and resources

You will need to check equipment and resources are safe before the session starts. During the session you will need to ensure they are used correctly, by referring to manufacturer's guidelines if necessary. If specialist equipment, such as a scrummaging machine, is used incorrectly, then the risk of injury is increased. If you want your session flow, make sure there is sufficient equipment available for the numbers in the group. If there is not enough equipment, you will need to consider how the task can be adapted, and make a contingency plan.

Activity	Introduction to rugby			
Venue: Sportsvilla Centre	*Health and Safety Checks:* ladders on the wall marked area for the activities to be away from the walls			
Date: 01.02.03	*Group size:* 15 (4 females/11 males)		*Age range:* 9–12 years	*S.E.N.* none

Duration *(Time in mins.)*	*Coaching element or skill*	*Coaching points to remember*	*Equipment*
10	Warm up Passing skills: in a grid	Hands out: ready to receive the ball Avoid contact with other group members	1 ball per group of 3
5	General stretches	Ensure that all stretches are carried out standing up	none
15	Passing the ball backwards Line work	Ensure that the individual reaches each one before a pass is delivered	1 ball for each line of 4
10	Tag rugby game	The ball must be passed back No hand offs	1 ball Tag and belts for each team
5	Cool down and summarise the session	Question and answer to ensure the group has learned the laws of the game	
Points from previous session	None, first session in this sport		
Evaluation of the session	Quicker progression to move the individuals forward and the ball back. Bring a whistle to control the group especially during the game. Work in smaller groups so less people are standing around waiting for their turn with the ball.		

An example of a session plan for the introduction to rugby

Using a scrummaging machine properly

Let's do it!

Choose a sport that you participate in. What equipment or clothing is required? Find the manufacturer's guidelines for correct use and maintenance of the equipment or clothing. Do you use the items in this way? Did any of the information surprise you?

The environment

If your sport takes place outdoors, weather conditions can hinder the delivery of a session. Rain and wind can increase the risk of injury, as can performing sport in the sun. You need to consider these factors and take appropriate steps. For example, during hot weather, encourage the performers to provide their own fluids, sun cream and hats; during cold weather, ensure that performers are wearing the correct footwear and outdoor clothing.

If your sport takes place indoors, book your facility in good time. Just before the event, check again that the facility will be available. A double-booked facility at the last minute can cause real problems. Check the facility before the session, to ensure that it is appropriate and safe to use.

Remember to protect yourself from the sun during outdoor activities

Using S.W.O.T. analysis

As a sports leader you need to assess your delivery of each session. A common way to do this is to conduct a S.W.O.T. analysis. This assessment method looks at:

- strengths
- weaknesses
- opportunities
- threats.

Strengths and weaknesses

Identifying strengths and weaknesses is a useful thing to do. In terms of your delivery of a session, you will probably identify your strengths in those aspects of the session which went smoothly. Your weaknesses will be identified in the areas that did not go too well, or did not work at all. Try to identify where things went wrong or right. For example:

- Were the tasks or activities chosen appropriate?
- Was the level at which the tasks were set appropriate?
- Was your verbal delivery set at the correct level? (In other words, did you communicate effectively for the age range and ability level of your group?)

You need to have a good understanding of your strengths so that you can play to these qualities and improve them still further. It is also important to recognise areas of weakness, so that you can work either to improve them or to avoid them.

Opportunities and threats

These are factors that may not be fully in your control. Opportunities can arise unexpectedly. For example, the increased confidence of one performer may have encouraged others to come and join the sports club. Threats can be equally unpredictable; for example, if a performer is accidentally injured during play, this can affect the confidence of the team.

Unit 9, (on the website; www.heinemann.co.uk/vocational) also looks at S.W.O.T analysis as a tool.

Checking the facility and equipment

A good sports leader will always allow sufficient time before the session begins to make the necessary checks of the area, facility and provision. Organising any complicated equipment prior to the start of the session can also save time during the session. The members of your group will want to participate, not watch their leader organising the props!

Health and safety

Health and safety is one of the most important responsibilities of any sports leader. Unit 2 of this book deals with health and safety in detail. You are recommended to read this unit to supplement the information given in the paragraphs below.

Carrying out risk assessments

Health and safety procedures are carried out to protect the leader and the performers from harm. The assessment of risks should be carried out on a regular basis. The results of each check should be recorded. The record should be signed and dated by the person responsible, and a note made of the time the assessment was made.

Safety checks

You will need to complete a health and safety check for each different venue you use and every activity that you deliver. You will need to identify hazards and take measures to reduce them before the activity is delivered. Any changes that you make should take into account the facility's recommendations and any relevant manufacturer's guidelines. Everything you note and decide upon must be recorded.

Check equipment at three stages:

1. before it is set up
2. once is has been assembled
3. just before it is used.

Check for:

- damage to the working parts of the equipment
- missing parts of the equipment that could cause damage
- lack of function.

Any damage that you note must be reported immediately. Repair should only be carried out according to the manufacturer's guidelines, or by a qualified technician. If this is not possible, the equipment must be removed from use.

 Think about it

List the safety considerations you have to take into account during your coaching sessions.

Let's do it!

Draw a plan of the area in which your sport takes place. Include ten unsafe obstacles and problems that would need to be considered if you were about to lead a group of children in a physical activity. Swap drawings with a partner. Try to identify the problems on your partner's drawing.

First aid

As a sports leader, you will need to be able to recognise various common injuries, and have sufficient first aid knowledge to help an injured person. It is your responsibility to ensure that someone holding a current first aid certificate is available during a session, in case of possible injury to a performer or the coach. A fully stocked first aid box should also be available.

You also need to find out where first aid resources are kept. The facility should have guidelines on what to do in the case of any injury occurring. Make sure you know what these are and what lines of communication you should follow when an injury occurs.

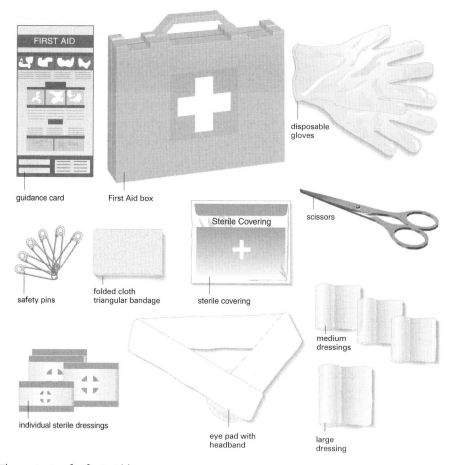

The contents of a first aid box

Think about it

Look at the first aid box above. Do you know what all the different things should be used for?

Emergency procedures

As a sports leader, you must also know the procedure for evacuation of the facility and ensure that any relevant individuals know too. For example, in case of a fire drill, it is important that you know the location of the fire exits. You should also check them regularly, to ensure that there are no obstacles to prevent access.

Legal responsibilities

There are various legal requirements which you, as a sports leader, are required to know about. You also have a responsibility to take steps to enforce the legislation. The legislation is found in various Acts passed by Parliament, to ensure the safety of groups of individuals undertaking physical activity.

The Children Act 1989

This Act concerns any provision of leisure, recreation and play services for children. It affects planning, delivery and management of these services. The Children Act enforces duties that must be carried out by the service providers. These duties include:

- providing care services and supervised activities for children
- publishing adequate information about these services
- reviewing and monitoring these services and consulting with the appropriate bodies (i.e. those bodies that deal with the protection of children)
- ensuring that registration is completed for all day care and supervised activities for children under the age of 8 years.

Before a service can be registered, the suitability of the organisation, all its employees and its premises need to be assessed. Organisations can seek help from the Child Protection Unit of the Institute of Sport and Recreation Management (I.S.R.M.). This organisation provides practical recommendations for service providers for children.

Data Protection Act 1998

Any business or organisation that holds personal information or details on staff or individuals using its facilities may be required to register with the Data Protection Registrar. The Data Protection Registrar places the business or the organisation on a public register of data users. It also issues the organisation with a code or practice, which must be adhered to. The code of practice states that:

- information must be kept in a secure location
- information must be accurate and relevant to the needs of the organisation
- if information is requested by an individual about his or her details, this must be complied with.

Activity Centre Act (Young Person's Safety Act) 1995

This Act requires that all facilities providing adventure activities for children under the age of 18 years have a licence. The Act applies to facilities run by local authorities and commercial businesses. It sets strict guidelines about:

- the qualifications staff should hold
- operating procedures and emergency procedures
- appropriate ratio of staff to children participating in any activity.

The licence aims to give assurance that good and safe practice is followed by the organisation holding it. This has had two beneficial results:

- facilities of this type have gained a good reputation
- there are now greater opportunities for young people to experience adventure activities.

The Activity Centre Act ensures safety for young people taking part in adventure activities

Target group

Sports leaders work with varous groups of people, including children, the elderly, individuals with special needs and people with different cultural backgrounds. When you are planning and delivering a physical activity you will need to take the needs of the different individuals in your group into account.

Children

There are many common factors in the development of children and many sports activities have been specially adapted to take these into account. It is important that you are aware of the limitations of the children that you are leading, so that you can aviod unsafe practice during the session. Children's physiological make up is different from adults, especially with regard to their body temperature regulation. For example, children need to be encouraged to drink fluids on a regular basis to avoid dehydration.

Although there are many similarites, there are also big differences between children as they develop. These differences are both psychological and physical. A sports environment will often highlight the special emotional and physical needs of individual children. When you lead children in sporting activities it is important that you are aware of each child's individual needs.

Teenagers

During adolescence, both males and females see changes in their bodies that are also visible to others.

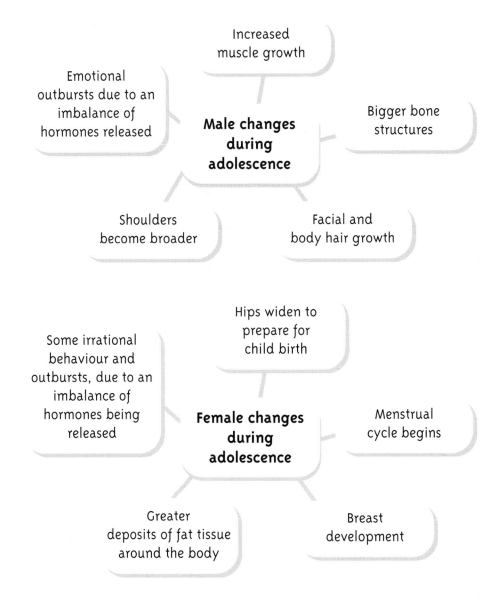

Not everyone develops at the same rate or in the same way. The way in which an adolescent deals with the changes in his or her body is influenced by:

- **external factors** – for example, peer group, family or coaches
- **internal factors** – for example, the hormones that are released during puberty, which can lead to emotional outbursts ot withdrawal from an activity.

Children who were well co-ordinated before the onset of puberty may become less so after, due to changes in their body structures. As a leader, you will need to be aware of this. Make sure you have prepared contingency plans, to ensure that all participants experience some success. This will also lessen the focus on these changes by others in the group.

You need to consider these factors when leading a group of teenagers in a sports session. Ensure that you:

- are aware of the physical differences between members of the group – don't avoid the subject but encourage tolerance of differences
- support children who show clumsy tendencies.

50+ groups

A 50 year old can often do as much as a 30 year old, depending on his or her personal level of fitness. It is important that you remember this, and treat this age group with respect. However, there are certain conditions that individuals in this age group become increasingly prone to:

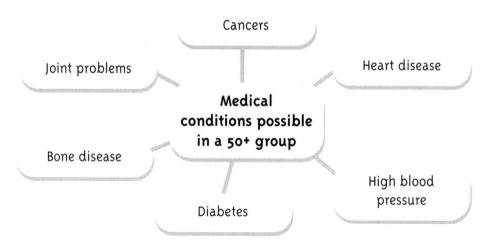

Medical conditions possible in a 50+ group: Cancers, Joint problems, Heart disease, Bone disease, Diabetes, High blood pressure

Although not all individuals in this category will be suffering from these problems, you still need consider them. Some, though not all, of your clients may need approval from their G.P.s to attend sports classes. This information can be gained from the history forms that all individuals must complete before participating in sport and exercise. Some clients may also be referred to an approved sports facility that caters for referral patients from the hospital. Facilities will have procedures in place for these types of initiative, so such information will be made available to you, as the sports leader.

Mixed or single sex groups

The choice of an individual to attend a session that only has a single sex participating must be respected and catered for. 'Women only' sessions may require a female leader, as well as female only participants. Do you think that there should also be male-only sessions? Why?

When you work with mixed groups, you need to be aware of different considerations for males and females, especially during and after puberty. It is also important not to stereotype individuals on the grounds of their gender. Certain sports are dominated by one gender, for example football is dominated by males. This does not mean, however, that only males play football, or that all males are more aggressive and competitive than females.

Assessment activity 2: Lesson plans

P With the help of your tutor, produce a lesson plan for a sports session. Make sure you:
- identify the target group
- plan the progression, timing and sequencing of activities
- take account of health, safety and legal requirements
- note down expected outcomes.

M Complete the activity in **P** on your own.

D If you are aiming for a distinction you will need to critically analyse your lesson plan, justifying the choices made and providing realistic alternatives and modification.

Contingencies

Your sports session might be going to plan but then something significant changes at the last minute. Such changes might include:
- too many or too few members turning up to your session
- a double booked facility
- an adverse change in the weather if you are working outside
- not having enough equipment
- equipment and facilities not being up to standard
- the need for specialist support or help.

Case study: Owen

Owen has completed his level 1 and level 2 coaching courses for rugby and plays for his team on Saturdays. He thinks that there is insufficient provision for rugby in the inner city areas for school children. He has decided to start a touch rugby session at his local school.

There are no grass fields at the school. Provision includes:

- a concrete yard about the size of a basketball court
- a hall that is also used for dinner time, morning school meetings and all P.E lessons – there is also some sports equipment left out, which could be a possible hazard.

Owen asked for help from the local rugby development officer, who has provided him with rugby balls, belts and tags.

Owen has so far attracted 20 Year 5 pupils, 6 girls and 14 boys, from a variety of cultural and social backgrounds. Many of the children attended the first session without sports kit. Owen thinks that participation is important, so he allowed them to take part in the hope that they would enjoy the session and be motivated to purchase kit.

The first session

Owen provided a warm up designed so that everyone could participate – even children without appropriate kit could progress to more strenuous activities.

Owen started with playground games, like tag and 'hot rice' (a version of tag using a soft ball). He then progressed to rugby activities in grids, using the concrete yard in the playground. He finished off with a rugby game. No rugby tackles were performed because the game that Owen introduced was tag or touch rugby. He also placed conditions on the game to ensure maximum involvement, for example he organised small sided games in which every player in the team had to touch the ball before a try could be scored.

Now answer the following questions:

1. Do you think Owen was right to let all the children get involved?
2. State three reasons why you have chosen your answer for question one.
3. If it had rained heavily during the first session, where could Owen have held the session?
4. How could Owen have made sure that the areas the session used were safe for the children, but would also allow them to enjoy the game of rugby at the end of the session?

You need to ensure that:
- you have thought carefully about what could go wrong
- you have done everything you can to prevent things going wrong – for example, checking that the facility is available, or ringing up the participants the night before to check they are all still coming.
- you have alternative action plan – in other words, a plan to help you cope with things that might go wrong.

Action plan

Your action plan needs to be neatly and logically laid out and easy to read. Using a word processor will help with this. It should give information about alternative facilities and venues, where to get specialist help if required, or notes on changes to equipment and clothing. Your action plan will also need to take account of all the factors highlighted in this unit so far, to ensure a safe and enjoyable session.

Assessment activity 3: Produce an action plan

P Produce an action plan for at least two contingency situations, listing alternative activities, resources and support, with the support of your tutor.

M On your own, produce an action plan for at least two contingency situations, listing alternative activities, resources and support.

D Using the action plan you created in **M**, critically evaluate and review the action plan, providing realistic modifications and alternative activities, resources and support.

Delivery and review

Successful delivery of your sports session depends largely upon the quality of your organisation and preparation. Once everything is in place, it is up to you as sports leader to deliver the session with confidence. Your aims and objectives should be clearly defined, you should have prepared the tasks thoroughly and have a secure knowledge of them. As a result of this, you should find that group control is easier. It is good practice to have a whistle close at hand – you may not need to use it once control of the group has been gained, but it is a good precautionary measure.

Planning and preparation are key factors of a successful session. Before the session starts, ensure that you have the appropriate resources and equipment available, and any other facilities that you may need. Also ensure that you have the permission of parents and carers if this is appropriate.

Delivery of the activity session

Different types of activity session

There are as many different types of activity session as there are sports leaders. The type of session you run will influence your aims and objectives. For example, you might be leading an introduction or taster course to a specific sport. Such programmes can be run either as a short course, from one to four weeks, or as a longer programme introducing the basics of a sport over six to ten weeks. For this type of session you will be dealing with people who are new to your sport. Your aims will be to motivate them to continue and to teach them the basics of your sport.

On the other hand, your group might be more experienced, and your aim might be to prepare them for competition. In this case, you will need to include activities with a competitive element, encouraging performers to use their skills in problem solving, as well as skills in the sport. Participants will also need to physically exert themselves. As you know, for improvements to occur, the body needs to be overloaded. The sessions leading up to a competition should be planned to progressively push the performer to a limit beyond the ordinary. At the same time, as sports leader, you need to ensure the safety of each individual in your group.

The structure of your session

Whether your session is for beginners or experienced performers, it will have three phases:
1. a start – usually a warm up,
2. a middle – usually a skill practice and competition
3. an end – usually a cool down.

These three phases should be well balanced and will not always take the same amount of time each. You will need to use your time management skills to control the session. Allocate times for all your activities in your plan, and then make sure that you stick to this. In this way, you will achieve the aim of your session and ensure that the session finishes as advertised.

The activities you have chosen should be designed for the number of participants, their ability, the venue and the equipment being used. However, when delivering the actual session, you will need to be flexible. You may need to adjust your plans on the day in response to the number of participants in the group, their behaviour on the day of the session, or changes to the venue or equipment.

Think about it

Get together with other members of your group. Can you think of an occasion when:
- you had to change your plans when you were leading a session
- you attended a session where the leader had to change his or her plans.

1. Discuss your experiences.
2. Why were the plans changed?
3. How were they changed?
4. Did the changed plan work? If not, why not?

Controlling your session

When you deliver a session it is not enough just to know about the sports and the activities. You also need to know how to control the group. In particular, you need to know how to start and stop activities. If you can successfully control your group, you will be able to supply useful feedback after each activity and further information to enable the group to progress to more advanced tasks. During the activity, there will be lots of personal and social interaction occurring. It is your responsibility as the leader to ensure that this is a positive experience for all participants in the session.

Your session must flow or you will lose the interest of your group. If a leader stops an activity too frequently because the group is unable to master the skill, or if the activity is carried out over a long period of time, the group may become bored and tired. Both situations can result in disruptive behaviour, after which, the leader may lose control.

Controlling your session ensures that it is lively, interesting and safe

Set the rules at the start of the session and make sure everyone understands them. When you explain the rules, highlight the possible consequences. There are various ways you could give warnings during a session. For example, you might consider using yellow and red cards during a session, as a quick, visual way for the players to recognise that they are not abiding by the rules.

Be careful when you organise your participants into groups. Ability groups or friendship groups can lead to single sex or single ability groups and may take some of the 'fun' out of the session. Take a flexible approach to the organisation of groups and keep making changes to groups if necessary. Be careful not to isolate individuals, or to penalise a participant for being too successful, or not successful enough.

 Key point

The most important thing to achieve during the delivery of any session is maximum participation of the individuals in the group.

It is not a good idea to allow children to choose their own team each session. This can result in the same individuals been left to the last each week, resulting in low self-esteem. Choose teams using your knowledge of the skills of each player gained through each session, or organise teams according to physical attributes, such as height. It is important to remember that sports sessions are about taking part – organise groups in a swift but fair manner.

Teaching methods

During the delivery of a session, your communication skills will be needed to control the group and pass on necessary information. Use language appropriate to the specific group you are leading. Remember that different individuals learn in different ways. As well as verbal instructions, give demonstrations, and use signs and equipment to help your group understand the task.

An important part of your role is to improve your group's understanding of skills and technique.

 Key point

A skill is a learned action that is delivered effectively in the right situation at the right time. The way in which you execute the skill can be defined as your technique.

The teaching methods you choose will depend on the individuals in your group, for example, their level of experience and the way they prefer to learn. Keep your objective in mind and ensure that your activity is organised to achieve it.

Let's do it!

Instruct your partner in a particular sports skill. Use different methods to do this, for example, using demonstration or verbal instruction. Record how well the performance went using the different methods of instruction.

At the end of the session

When the session is finished, draw the group's attention to future opportunities for involvement. If your session has been well-run and fun, participants will not only return for another session but may also spread the word, and bring others!

Your work as a sports leader does not stop at the end of the session. It is your responsibility to keep up-to-date with the changes in the sport or physical activity that you lead, and its health and safety requirements. There are various special educational programmes or courses that you can attend, designed to help sports leaders and coaches to develop. Examples include those organised by Sports Coach U.K. (National Coaching Foundation) and the Football Association, as well as more general courses on Child Protection and First Aid.

Reviewing the session

After each session and programme you should carry out an evaluation. This will help you to maintain a clear and accurate account of the progress that has been made. The evaluation process can also be used to compare the results from each session to the objectives that were set at the start. The information that is gained through this process needs to be interpreted, and made relevant to future plans.

A S.W.O.T. analysis (described on page 209) can be carried out again to gain this information. This will highlight the factors that have caused problems and help you to improve the delivery of future sessions. Act on any weaknesses that you find by making changes to you original plans if necessary. If you avoid changing them now, you may find that this leads to further disappointments for both you and the performers.

The influence that you have as a sports leader is massive. Your responsibility as a sports leader goes beyond the demonstration of skills in sport. You must also set, and show, high moral and ethical standards. By improving the performance of young people, your aims should include:

- identifying and meeting the needs of all individuals in your supervision
- improving performance through a progressive and safe programme for sport
- ensuring that the activities set include a guided practice, that a method is provided for measuring performance and that opportunities for competition are available
- creating an environment in which participation is continuous and challenging, and where improvements can be observed.

As you are delivering a session, you are constantly taking on board information about the session, the group and the activities. This information includes things that went well, for example, successful tasks and methods of delivery, and things that didn't go so well and that you will need to improve or change in future sessions.

There are different ways in which you can gather information about your session, for example:

- making a video of the session, which you can then play back and discuss with friends or with your tutor
- asking peers, colleagues or your tutor to watch the session – they may be able to highlight those elements that worked and those that didn't, and make suggestions for change; compiling a questionnaire about the session and asking peers or your supervisor to complete it.
- self-reflection – asking yourself questions, for example:
  - ➢ Did my session plan take into account the venue, equipment, group size and ability?
  - ➢ What changes did I make to the session plan during the delivery?
  - ➢ How flexible was I?
  - ➢ Did I communicate effectively?
  - ➢ Did the participants understand the instructions given to them?
  - ➢ Did the participants understand what they were meant to learn?

You need to use this information to formulate a review after the delivery has taken place. Your review should measure the delivery of your session against your original goals. Don't forget that these goals include the participants' objectives, as well as your own personal aims. The evaluation process is very important. You need to to find out whether changes need to be made to improve the design of the activities or their delivery. It is important that you see these changes as positive, and of great benefit to you, as the leader, and to the group.

Making modifications

The spidergram below shows some of the modifications you might make as a result of your evaluation.

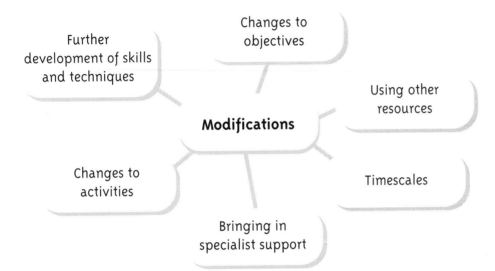

If you deliver the same session to another group, you may need to make changes because of the different ages, genders, ability levels or cultural backgrounds of the participants. However, if you lead the same group in a further session, you may need to change some of the activities to ensure that members of the group do not lose interest or so that they can progress to the next level.

Assessment activity 4: Delivery and review of the activity

P Deliver and review an activity session by:
- commenting on your own role in the session
- identifying any new skills that the participants learned
- note any changes you had to make to the activities during delivery.

M Deliver and review an activity session remembering to explain and justify any changes, modifications and amendments made to the acitivities.

D If you are aiming for a distinction you will need to critically analyse the activity session, drawing valid conclusions and providing effective solutions for your own and the participants' personal development and further skills acquisition.

Case study: football and basketball sessions

Twilight sessions for football and basketball have been running on Tuesday and Thursday evenings for the last year at the adventure playground. These sessions have been traditionally organised for 10–12 year old boys. The organisers have just started providing Monday and Wednesday tea time sessions to a mixed group of boys and girls aged 6–10 years.

The organisers contacted the sports development section of the local council, who guided them to the specific Governing Bodies of the sports. They gained information about the relevant health and safety and child protection laws. They applied for adapted equipment available for this age range, such as different-sized basketballs and adjustable basketball posts and nets.

The sessions are well attended. Some of the children also attend the Tuesday and Thursday sessions. The ability levels within the group are varied and this causes some problems in the participation of those who are less able.

There are three leaders of the new sessions, two of whom also lead the Tuesday and Thursday sessions. All three leaders met after the first week of the new sessions to evaluate the success of the activities.

Now answer the following questions:
1. Suggest how activites could be organised to allow for the different abilities in the group.
2. Suggest ways to ensure beginners and more experienced individuals can still participate fully
3. What are the benefits of the three leaders meeting and discussing the delivery of the sessions?

In summary

It is important to establish a leadership style that is not only appropriate to the individual or group, but also one that you are comfortable with. Leaders should not try to be someone else – you need to develop your own style.

Setting aims and objectives are also important as they guide practice and keep it focussed.

There should always be a balance of knowledge, understanding, enjoyment and safety through any training session or sporting activity that you lead.

CHECK WHAT YOU KNOW!

Look back through this unit to see if you can answer the following questions:

1 List five skills and qualities that a leader in sport should have.
2 Place these skills and qualities in order of importance, number one being the most important.
3 Explain how a quietly spoken sports leader can be successful.
4 List the considerations that a sports leader will need to make about the venue of the sports session.
5 Why is it important for a sports leader to dress appropriately for the sport that they will be leading?
6 Whose responsibility is it to check for damage of equipment that will be used for an activity?
7 What items should a sports leader always carry when leading a sports session?

The sports performer

Introduction

There are a vast number of different factors that can affect your ability to play sport well. Many things, both on and off the pitch, can have either a positive or negative effect on how well you play on a particular day. The aims of this unit are to:
- investigate these factors
- investigate where and how you can train for sport
- to look at planning, goal setting and external support in respect of your involvement in sport.

How you will be assessed

To pass this unit successfully, it will help if you play sport competitively outside of your school or college. This unit has a close link with Unit 11 – Practical sport. You may wish to use the two sports that you choose for Unit 11 as a basis for completing Unit 6.

After completing this unit you should be able to achieve the following learning outcomes:
1. Investigate the **factors that affect sports performance.**
2. Investigate **opportunities to train and compete** in two selected sports.
3. Produce and implement an **action plan to improve performance** in a selected sport.
4. Provide **evidence of possible progress.**

In order to achieve a good grade for this unit, you will need to:
- produce information on the factors that affect sports performance
- produce information on where you could train and compete locally, nationally and internationally
- produce a plan with goals and targets using the S.M.A.R.T. principle to improve your own playing performance
- implement your plan and note any improvements or changes over a period of one month, using a diary or similar record
- with your tutor, check your progress and highlight areas which need immediate improvements, and other areas that need to improve in the future.

Factors that affect sports performance

Factors that affect sports performance

Let's do it!

In small groups, choose a sports person of your choice. Draw up a chart and list all the factors that you think would affect this person's ability to play at the highest level.

When you have finished, discuss the factors as a class. What did other groups decide?

How many of the factors in the following diagram did you think off?

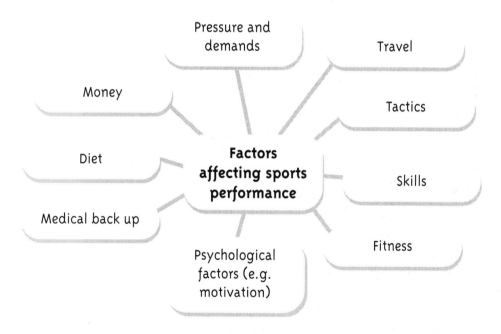

Skills

Skills in sport are all the various movements, strokes, shots and so on that you might need to use in a game.

It is important to remember that **skills** are learned. You are not born able to perform a somersault. You have to be taught how to do it by a teacher or coach. You do need to be born with the necessary physical and mental qualities that are needed to perform the skill. These are called **abilities**, and might include courage, height, good hand to eye co-ordination, or speed. Some of these can be improved but if they are not there in the first place, you will not reach the top!

Think about it

1. Look at this picture of Paula Radcliffe.

In pairs, discuss the skills that Paula Radcliffe needed to learn. What qualities did she need to be born with to become as good as she is? Share your thoughts with the rest of the class.

2. Now do the same for Lennox Lewis, the world heavyweight boxing champion. How are the skills and abilities that Lennox Lewis needs different from the ones Paula Radcliffe needs? Discuss this with your partner.

The following table shows one way in which the skills and abilities of the two performers might be compared. Do you agree with its conclusions?

	Skills	Abilities
Paula Radcliffe	Running at speed Race tactics	Stamina and determination Particular body size/shape Strong heart
Lennox Lewis	Throwing a variety of different punches Footwork Defensive movements	Courage Physical size Balance Fast hand speed

Let's do it!

Continue the table above, adding other skills and abilities that you may have thought of.

General and specific skills

Some skills are general and will be common to many sports. Such skills include running, jumping, throwing and catching. Others will be needed by only a few sports, or even only one sport. Such skills include a tennis serve, a badminton smash or a cover drive in cricket.

Let's do it!

Copy the table below, and complete it for basketball and netball. Which skills are common to both sports? Which skills are specific to each sport?

Sport	Basketball	Netball
Common skills	Catching	
Specific skills	The lay up shot	Defending a shot

Individual and team skills

Sports skills can be either individual, for example dribbling or passing, or team skills, for example a basketball fast break or scrummaging in rugby. Both types of skill need to be learned.

Let's do it!

Complete the table below with a partner. Think of as many individual and team skills as you can for each sport, and list them. Produce a chart to display on your classroom wall.

Sport	Individual skills	Team skills
Football		
Netball		
Athletics		
Badminton		

Other ways of classifying sports skills

Skill classification	Example
Self paced – The start of a skill is determined by the performer	Shooting a pistol at a target
Externally paced – The start of a skill is determined by an external source	The start of a 100 m race
Fine – Small muscle groups are used to produce delicate movements	Throwing a dart
Gross – Major muscle groups are used	Putting the shot
Open – The environment affects the skill	Passing the ball in a football match
Closed – The environment has no effect	Performing a routine in gymnastics
Discrete – The skill has a clear beginning and end	A serve in tennis
Continuous – There is no clear beginning or end	Cycling

Let's do it!

Now consider one of your chosen sports. Choose an example from it for each category above. Can you explain why you have made your choice?

Tactics

The Oxford Dictionary describes tactics as the *'Actions or strategies planned to achieve a specific end'*. Tactics in sport are the ways you play in order to overcome another team or individual. Tactics used in a match are dependent on many factors, including:

- your strengths and weaknesses
- your opponent's strengths and weaknesses
- the weather or match situation, for example it might be raining, or you might need to win the game
- the players you have available
- the game situation, for example is it the first set, the start of the second half, or a qualifying match in a World Cup group?

Think about it

Tactics apply to both individuals and teams. For example, some top tennis players are said to prefer to play from the baseline, while others like to 'get to the net' as soon as possible. Some football teams like to 'hit teams on the break', while others like to play 'through the middle'.

1. What do you think these phrases mean?
2. Why might teams or individuals want to play like this?

Let's do it!

In small groups, discuss what tactics you have come across in a sport of your choice.
- Explain the tactic used – why is it used and when?
- Describe its benefits.
- Describe its potential weaknesses.

Think of a way of displaying the results of your discussion. The table below provides an example.

Tactic	Description
Man for man defence in basketball	Each player on court defends one player on the other team at all times, whether they have the ball or not
Advantages	Places pressure on the skills of your opponent. Often forces the opposition to turn the ball over to your team. Allows you to match up your best player with the best/worst player on the other side. Can be used on the whole court (a full court press) or just in your half of the court (a half court press)
Disadvantages	Very tiring – fitness of your team is a factor. Need to concentrate very hard. Requires high levels of determination. Requires good skill levels in your players. Much harder to play well than a zone defence

Tactics will also include what particular shots you might use, or not use, against a particular team or individual and how you will play as a team when attacking or defending. For example, in a cricket match, the fielding side may try to bowl a ball outside a particular stump to tempt a batsman into a shot and set a field, in the hope the batsman falls for the trap! Obviously, the batsman will be trying hard to make sure that he or she does not play this shot unless it is absolutely necessary!

Has the trap worked in this photo?

Fitness

Fitness means many things to many people. In sport, fitness can involve many different factors. The level of fitness held by a team or an individual will have a dramatic effect on performance.

There are many factors to fitness. These are often referred to as the 'S' factors:
- speed
- strength
- stamina
- suppleness
- psychology.

Speed

Speed is the 'quickness of movement' that a person can produce.

Key point

It can be argued that speed is an inherited quality because it requires particular types of muscles, but training can improve your speed to a degree.

Think about it

Choose one of the sports you are studying. When and how would speed be needed in a game situation?

Speed might also include agility. Agility is defined as 'the ability to move quickly and easily' (Oxford Concise English Dictionary). This factor is best seen in gymnasts, when the gymnast moves their body position very quickly and in a variety of different ways.

Let's do it!

Ask your tutor about the Illinois Agility Test. This is one means of measuring a person's agility. Try it for yourself and see how you measure up!

Strength

Strength is the maximum force a muscle can exert. Lifting weights is a simple example of strength. Some sports require more strength than others.

Think about it

Can you think of some examples of sports which particularly require strength?

We all have strength in varying amounts!

Some sports require the performer to be able to produce power. This is a combination of strength and time. Imagine you are pushing a car along the ground. If another person can push the same car faster, then they are producing more power. Shot putters and weight lifters need to be able to produce huge amounts of power to be successful in their events.

Stamina

Stamina, or endurance, involves many different factors. Stamina is what allows us to keep an activity going for a long period of time – a marathon, for example, requires very high levels of stamina. There are other types of stamina, too. Local muscular endurance is the ability of a particular muscle or group of muscles to maintain a movement or position. Performing sit ups is an example of local muscular endurance. In addition, there are aerobic endurance and anaerobic endurance. 'Aerobic' means 'involving oxygen'. Going for a jog is an example of aerobic endurance. You might jog for five miles at a steady pace, which allows you to get enough oxygen to the working muscles to keep going without slowing down very much. If you jog too fast you will quickly become exhausted.

Anaerobic means 'without oxygen'. A good example of an event requiring anaerobic endurance is the 400 metre race in athletics. At the speeds at which athletes run, they are unable to supply sufficient oxygen to produce energy to the working muscles. Eventually, they will not be able to run any more. At this point in a race, you will see the athlete 'die'. Their legs give out because of a lack of oxygen, which is needed to clear a substance called lactic acid from the working muscles. Lactic acid is produced when you exert yourself physically and is what causes aches and pains after hard exercise.

Suppleness

Suppleness, flexibility or mobility refers to the amount of movement possible at a joint. The body has many different types of joints and these are necessary to allow a variety of movement. For example, the 'ball and socket' joint in your hip allows rotation through 360°. Again, it might be argued that this is an inherited quality but training can most definitely improve the flexibility of joints.

A very flexible and supple gymnast!

Flexibility not only allows gymnasts to adopt extreme positions, it also helps to prevent injuries in other sports. Limbs and joints that have limited movement are more likely to suffer pulls and other problems due to having limited movement. Performers in many different sports now spend much of their time improving their flexibility.

Psychological factors

There are many psychological factors that can affect performance in sport. These include:

- an individual or team's motivation
- the ability of a team or individual to concentrate
- the level of arousal in the team or individual
- the personality of an individual.

Motivation

This refers to factors that cause an individual to act in a certain way. For example, the motivation for you to seek out a drink is probably thirst. Similarly, you play sport for some reason that motivates you.

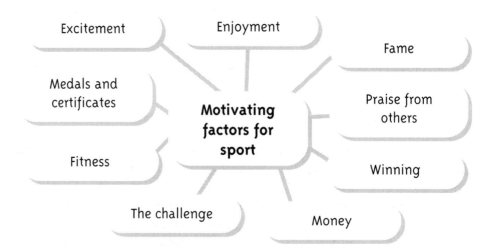

Key point

Motivating factors can be 'internal' or 'external'.

Internal factors come from within yourself. These are factors such as enjoyment or the challenge. **External factors** come from outside the individual and include winning trophies, earning money, or fame and glory!

Let's do it!

Do you agree that motivating factors can be divided into 'external' and 'internal' factors? See if you can sort the various factors identified in the spider diagram above into these two categories.

Different factors motivate different people in different ways. Some players may have been motivated by the fact that they are playing in their one and only Cup Final. Other people may be motivated by winning medals. For other people, the factor that spurs them on may be a large win bonus offered by the club.

Arousal level

Another 'mind' factor that can affect performance is the level of arousal that a player reaches. Arousal can be defined as how 'excited' a person is. For all sports there is an 'optimum', or ideal, level of arousal. This optimum level allows players to perform at their best. This can be best illustrated by a theory called the 'Inverted U' theory (see page 145).

Look at the diagram below to find out what happens to performance as the intensity of arousal increases (in other words, as the player gets more and more excited). To begin with, performance improves until it reaches a peak. The peak is the 'optimum' arousal level. After this point, if the player's arousal level continues to rise, the performance drops off. The player has become 'over excited'. He or she may have become 'psyched out', perhaps by his or her opponent, the event itself, or a fear of losing. Coaches need to understand their players so that they can make sure this does not happen.

The 'optimum' level of arousal or excitement is not the same for all sports. In some sports, such as snooker or shooting, players need to be very calm and collected, and so the optimum level of arousal is low. In other sports, such a boxing, rugby, or other contact sports, the player knows he or she is going to get hurt, so the optimum level of arousal is higher. So, for example, in the diagram below, Athlete A might be a Snooker player, such as Mark Williams the World Champion (2000, 2003), while Athlete B might be the former England Rugby Captain, Martin Johnson.

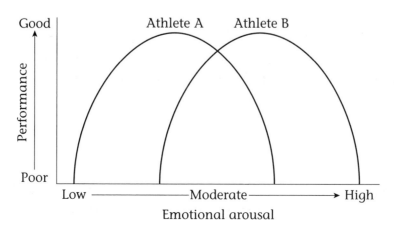

Optimum levels of arousal for athletes in two different sports

Concentration

Another psychological factor that will have a major effect on performance is the ability to concentrate. Concentration is defined by the Concise Oxford Dictionary as 'Focussing all one's attention or mental effort on a task'. In sport, there are many examples of where concentration is important to performance. In athletics, the sprinter must concentrate on the sound of the gun at the start. In football, a defender may need to concentrate on the movement of one particular player at a corner or free kick. Failure to concentrate fully on a situation could mean a goal being scored, taking a corner incorrectly in a Formula 1 race, or not seeing a punch coming in a boxing match.

Personality

Your personality type can also affect your performance in sporting situations. Personality can be described as the characteristics and qualities that form an individual's distinctive character.

Let's do it!

Look at your class mates. How would you describe each of them? A good mixer? A loner? Quiet? Noisy? All these qualities define an individual's personality.

Complete the chart below for all the people in your class. Do any patterns appear?

Name	Description of their personality	Sport(s) played
1		
2		
3		
4		
5		
6		

It may already be apparent from your chart that an individual's personality will have an influence on what sports he or she is suited or attracted to. For example, Formula 1 racing drivers are often very confident, occasionally arrogant, young men. A good pistol shooter might be the complete opposite – very quiet and happy to keep his or her own company.

Think about it

Look at the following old cliché: 'When the going gets tough, the tough get going'. What do you think this phrase means? In small groups, discuss this phrase in respect of some selected sports of your choice. Can you think of examples where a player's personality might affect their level of performance? Bring your group's ideas back to the class, to discuss further.

Diet

Diet can be regarded as everything that a person eats and drinks. It is an important contributory factor in sports performance. Diet has become increasingly more important over the past few years, as our knowledge of nutrition has increased. Now, most international sports performers have a nutritionist, whose role is to give advice about what to eat and drink.

The main food groups

The main food groups are:
- carbohydrates – e.g. bread, pasta, rice – which are high in energy
- protein – e.g. meat, dairy products, pulses – which repair and build muscles
- fats – e.g. oil, butter – which are high in energy and essential for regulating the body's temperature, and for other bodily functions.

The body also requires:
- vitamins and minerals – found in all fresh foods, these are substances essential for all bodily functions
- water – to prevent dehydration and maintain the body's fluid balance.

Some basic dietary guidelines are issued by the Food Standards Agency. These guidelines include the following:
- Eat a variety of foods – this way you will get a wide range of nutrients.
- Eat plenty of starchy foods, such as bread, rice, noodles, cereals, potatoes and pasta – starchy foods should make up a third of the food you eat, but try not to add too much fat (such as butter, oil, or creamy sauces).
- Eat lots of fruit and vegetables. Fresh, frozen, tinned, dried or juiced fruits all count. Aim to eat five portions or more a day. A portion is 80 g, which means, for example, one apple, two to three tablespoons of vegetables, or one glass of fruit juice (but remember that juice only counts as one portion however much you drink in a day). Potatoes count as starchy foods not fruit and vegetables. Try keeping a tally of your daily portions to help you increase the number you eat.

- Limit the amount of fatty foods you eat. Try eating small amounts, choosing low fat alternatives and/or cooking without adding fat. Also remember to cut the fat off meat, remove the skin from poultry, eat fish without the batter and choose half-fat cheese or semi-skimmed or skimmed milk.
- Only eat sugary foods in small quantities and preferably with a meal, to limit dental decay.
- Don't to add salt to your food – most people already eat too much.

Key point

You must never train or compete on a full stomach. Your body takes time to digest the foods you consume and turn it into energy. Current advice is to eat a meal high in carbohydrate between one and four hours before a match. This ensures the body has adequate supplies of energy for you to perform at your best. Look at the BBC website for some practical examples: www.heinemann.co.uk/hotlinks.

Fluid intake

It is important for everyone to drink plenty of fluids, but it is *very* important for sports performers to do so:
- Drink regularly before, during and after exercise to replace fluid loss.
- Choose a drink that includes approximately 70–1266 mg sodium (salt) and 14–17 g (6–7%) carbohydrate (glucose).
- Choose a drink that tastes nice!

Let's do it!

- Collect the containers for a selection of sports drinks, such as Lucozade. Look at the information given on the bottle or sachet. Do the drinks meet with the advice given about fluid intake for sport?
- Imagine a sports performer has asked for your advice on what to drink. Present your evidence in the form of an advice leaflet.
- List and describe the effects that dehydration could have on sports performance. Compare the effect of this factor on performance with two other factors of your choice. For instance, does it have a small or large effect? How much will performance deteriorate if the performer is dehydrated?

Financial considerations

Apart from the various personal factors that affect how well you play a sport, there are a number of other external factors that also need to be considered and one of the most important is money.

Sport costs money. Money is needed for equipment, for travel, for competing, even for basics like food and a home. In the initial stages of their development, most sports performers will be 'funded' by their parents. Later on, you might have a part time job that provides the money you need to play a sport. At the lower levels of sport, money may be available in the form of grants. The better you become and the higher the level at which you play, however, the more expensive sport becomes. At the very top, sports performers are training and competing full time – they live and breathe sport! Their income comes from sponsorship, prize money and being paid to appear at events.

Sponsorship

Sponsorship is a very important source of income. For example, the protective leathers of the World MotoGP Champion, Valentino Rossi are covered in his sponsors' logos. Each sponsor pays a large sum of money to be associated with Rossi's success.

All Premiership football teams have kit sponsors. Many players also have individual sponsorship deals to wear a particular make of boot, or to endorse a particular product. At a more local level, a local business or individual might sponsor a team or a particular sports performer. You may be able to think of local examples.

Appearance money

Top players and teams may also receive appearance money, for simply 'turning up'. If players who are not the very best were unable to earn a living from the game, they would not be able to play. This would mean that big tournaments would not be able to take place. There would not be enough players to allow the various rounds to take place and make the tournament what it is. This is particularly important to sports such as tennis and snooker, where tournaments require a large number of players to allow the tournament to take place.

Key point

At last year's Wimbledon Tennis Tournament, players who lost in the first round were awarded £8630. Women first round losers earned £6900. The men's champion took home a colossal £575,000! (These figures have been taken from the BBC sport website, you can view this on www.heinemann.co.uk/hotlinks)

A number of players make a living just by playing in a variety of tournaments. Appearance money is very important to sport and its future. Other examples include the contracts that are given to players to play for their country. The England Test Match Cricket squad are all on England contracts, which pay them a lucrative sum of money for playing for England. Obviously, the better the player, the better the reward from the contract!

In athletics, many big stars are paid a fee to run in a particular event. Big names draw crowds and sponsors to an event. Many people will go to see the London Marathon simply because Paula Radcliffe is competing. A golf tournament will receive bigger crowds and more publicity if a pro-golfer like Tiger Woods is playing.

Prize money

Prize money is paid to the winner, and often the runner up, in a tournament or event. In horse racing in the UK £94.1 million was paid in prize money in 2003!

If there was no prize money in horseracing:
- there would be no incentive to be the owner of a race horse
- there would then be no need for stables and trainers, or grooms and jockeys
- your high street bookmaker would struggle to stay in business.

Many different types of job are linked to the horse racing industry. Prize money keeps the sport alive. The same can be said of golf, Formula 1 and many other sports. These cash prizes allow individuals and teams to continue to play in the sport.

Grants

At a lower, more local level, there are a number of sources of funding that help to maintain sport in the UK.

SportsMatch Funding

The National Lottery

Funding from national Governing Bodies, for example The Football in the Community scheme

Sources of funding

Local authority grants

Local sponsorship

Let's do it!

Ask your tutor to arrange for your local Sports Development Officer to visit you. Ask him or her about sources of funding available in the area to local teams or individuals.

- Describe three different sources of funding and show the effect they could have on the performance of a team or individual. For instance, it may give an individual the chance to travel abroad for warm weather training, or a Formula 1 team to go winter testing.
- Describe the advantages of the opportunities you have identified for each of your three sources.
- Compare your three sources in terms of availability, what the money can be spent on, and any conditions that are attached.

Travel

The global market for viewing sporting events, brought about by the emergence of satellite television, has created a huge demand for sporting events around the world. You can see almost any sport at almost any time on television. For a top team or player to compete, they need to be able to travel around the world. This long distance travel creates a number of problems, the main one being a condition known as 'jet lag'.

Jet lag happens because the Earth is crossed by a number of time lines. When it is 12 noon in the UK, it is 9 p.m. in the evening in Sydney, Australia. Jet lag confuses the body. It may be the middle of the day, but the body wants to sleep because it thinks it is time to go to bed! A team or player needs time to allow their body to adapt and get used to the new time zone they are in. It is generally accepted that for every one hour of change in time between the country left and the country arrived in, you need one day to recover. Of course, if the next match or game is in another time zone, the whole process starts again!

Time difference isn't the only problem. Travelling around the country or the world means that players will experience different dialects or languages, different foods, different customs and even different climates and weather. All these factors can affect the level of performance that a player is able to display. Individuals and teams may take great steps to minimise the effects of these various changes.

Case study: Rugby World Cup 2003

The management of the England World Cup rugby team were well prepared for the potential problems that might have resulted from players travelling half way around the world to Australia for the competition.

Jet lag from the long flight

Self doubt in players' minds

Different climate

Lots of travelling to and from matches (England's matches were played in Perth, Brisbane and Sydney)

Factors which might have affected England's performance in the 2003 World Cup

Different culture

Injuries from playing and training

Adverse Australian press coverage

Being away from family and friends

Being the tournament favourites

The English team arrived in Australia two weeks before the first game against Georgia on 11 October 2003. In this way, players had time to acclimatise to the new time zone they were in. The time spent in Australia before the tournament also allowed for players to get used to the different climate.

The England Rugby team also took the following staff with them:

- a video analyst
- two physiotherapists
- a chef
- an awareness coach
- a doctor
- a masseur
- a kitman
- an R.F.U. referee
- seven coaches, including Clive Woodward.

The doctors and coaching staff were on hand to give advice on training and diet, to ensure that each player's body was fully prepared to cope with the change. The chef ensured that players ate the correct food, prepared in a way they liked with no risk of food poisoning, etc.

Players were able to contact their families, and many had their families in Australia with them. The self awareness coach helped players with the psychological aspects of the game, so that they were mentally tough and ready.

Now answer the following questions:

1. In small groups, produce a display which highlights all the various external factors that might have affected the England players while in Australia.
2. Compare your display with other groups, and discuss.
3. What steps did the England management team take to prevent problems which might have affected the performance of the players?
4. Which do you think were the most important problems to deal with?

Medical back-up

Injury can have a disastrous effect on performance levels. Many athletes have suffered injuries at some time in their career. This usually means that training and competition has to stop until the injury heals. This can take many weeks or even months. The effects of sports injuries are taken very seriously today. Top performers have access to doctors, physiotherapists and masseurs to ensure that:

- injuries are avoided, as far as possible, through correct training and exercise
- when injury occurs, it is treated promptly using the best facilities and expertise, to ensure the athlete can return to competition as quickly as possible.

While teams will be able to employ a vast array of staff at a match or tournament, individual players will not. Tournaments in sports like tennis and athletics provide doctors and physiotherapists for the athletes and players competing. The table below shows the different roles in medical back-up.

Medical staff	Function
Physiotherapist	Treats injuries using massage and exercise instead of drugs
Sports therapist	Treatment given is designed to relieve or heal a disorder or injury
Injury consultant	Diagnoses an injury so that the correct treatment can then be administered, using exercise or drugs

At the lower levels of sports performance, access to medical assistance is more difficult. Local G.P.s are able to offer some non-specific treatment and local sports centres may offer access to a physiotherapist, but treatment can be expensive. This cost may prevent a player from receiving the treatment required. Some local semi-professional teams may have a club trainer or physio. Local colleges may also offer sports therapy classes, and so might be able to provide the treatment needed.

Other pressures and demands

Another factor that can affect performance is the conflict between the needs of the sport and the performer's other responsibilities.

Let's do it!

1. Think of some examples of demands that are placed upon you. Identify as many sources as you can. These might come from school, home, friends and family, as well as your sport. List and describe them and try to identify how and why they conflict with each other. An example might be training in the evening and completing homework.
2. Now choose a famous sporting personality and repeat the exercise. What additional demands are faced by top level performers? For example, it might be pressure from a sponsor to undertake an activity, such as promoting their products or services.
3. Compare the conflicts you have identified for yourself and the famous sports personality. What conflicts are common to both of you? Which only apply to one of you?

Factors affecting different sports

In addition to the factors you have considered in this section, there are a number of other factors that can affect the performance of a sport. These are based on the nature of the sport itself.

The sports we play can be divided into two categories:

1. Individual sports – with one person playing another.
2. Team sports – where two teams compete against each other. For example, volley ball is played between two teams with six players on the court at any one time. Rugby Union has teams of 15 players. A badminton doubles team consists of two players and this pair may be of the same gender or a mixed team.

Many factors affecting sports from these different categories are the same. In many events, both individual and team, the competitors are required to produce set routines or to perform combinations of set moves upon which they are judged. Ice skating, where competitors must complete set skills in the routines they perform, is an example of this. However, there are also a variety of different factors that come into play, depending on whether the sport is played as an individual or as a team.

Individual sports

If you play an individual sport, the following factors may affect your performance:

- Personal fitness level – you have to be fitter than your opponent to have a chance of success. In a boxing match, the boxer with greater strength or stamina, or faster reflexes, is likely to prevail, all else being equal.
- Motivation to succeed – you need to be motivated to succeed because there are no team mates to 'keep you going' when things get tough.
- Tactics employed – for example, a swimmer must decide at what pace he or she will swim each length of a race. If the pace is too fast the swimmer may run out of energy too early but if it is too slow, there may be too much distance to catch up.

Team sports

If you play as part of a team, different factors come into play:

- **Team work** – as a team, all members must work together to promote the success of the team and the individuals within it. Jonny Wilkinson's now famous winning drop goal in the 2003 Rugby World Cup is a good example. He was able to perform only because the rest of the team had all played their parts in taking the ball up the field to get him sufficiently 'in range'. A single error by any of the other 14 players, a missed pass or an infringement of the rules, might have meant the chance was lost.

- **The strengths and weaknesses of individual players** – in any team game, each side will have strengths and weaknesses within their players on the field. These may be physical, skills-based or to do with tactics. The way in which a team plays to its strengths, compensates for its weaknesses and exploits the weaknesses of its opponents may have a major effect on the result of the game. For example, in basketball, teams will try to match up their best player with the opponent's weakest player to gain an advantage.
- **Substitutions** – these are allowed by many (although not all) team games. This means that players who are having a poor game, who have sustained an injury, or who are fatigued, can be replaced. This, of course, is not possible in individual sports.
- **Stopping play** – in many team games, the coach is able to stop play to give teams advice on how to play. Basketball and volleyball both allow coaches to call 'time outs' for this purpose.

Disabled sports

Another category within sport which will be affected by different factors is that of disabled sports. This is an exciting and growing area in sport. More facilities and more events are being organised for disabled competitors. Various factors come into play when considering disabled sports:

- **Modifications** – there have to be modifications to any sport before it can be played by disabled people. It may be necessary, for instance, to adapt the rules, the pitch or court, or the equipment used in the sport. For example, in wheelchair basketball, the court dimensions actually remain the same, but the rules covering travelling and so on are modified to take account of the particular needs involved. Similarly, in wheelchair tennis, the ball is allowed to bounce twice, to allow play to take place. Blind sprinters are allowed a partner who runs with them, tethered to them by a short piece of rope.
- **Categories** – there are a wide range of disabilities, and many sports have to be categorised to allow the competition to be fair and ethical. In athletics, categories may be based on the nature or severity of the disability and these categories will produce different levels of performance. It would be unrealistic to expect an amputee to be able to swim as fast as someone with a mild learning disability.
- **Technology** – with the growth of disabled sport has come improved technology in the equipment used by the performers, and this has had an effect on performance. The wheelchairs used in disabled sport, for example, are far removed from the traditional wheelchairs you normally see, and allow a high level of performance to be achieved. The level of performance allowed by the technology also has to be considered by organisers of events, as well as the level of disability of the performer.

Assessment activity 1: Factors that affect performance

In this section, you have looked at a variety of factors which may affect the performance of a sports performer. These factors affect teams and individuals, professionals and amateurs, local players and international stars. The effects can be positive or negative. You have also looked at ways to overcome the effects through providing appropriate support, such as medical back-up or financial assistance.

Using what you have learned from studying this section and carrying out the activities, complete one of the following activities:

P List the factors which can affect performance, using relevant examples from your two chosen sports.

M Describe the factors which can affect sports performance. Apply them to your two chosen sports, using different examples.

D Compare the factors that affect sports performance in two different sports.

Opportunities to train and compete

Training and competition are fundamental to any sport and require:
- facilities – such as pitches and courts
- services – such as doctors and physiotherapists
- funding – such as grants and sponsorship.

As you progress in a sport, you will experience better facilities and support to help you fulfil your sporting potential. In this section, you are going to identify the opportunities in your area to train and compete. You will then look at regional, national and international facilities. You will need to complete this task for three sports of your choice and be able to assess these opportunities in a critical way by commenting on the good and bad points for each.

Local provision of opportunities for training and competition divides into three categories:
1. the public sector
2. the private sector
3. the voluntary sector.

You might decide to use yourself as a case study, and imagine where you could take part in each of the three sports you have chosen locally. This information could then be presented in a numbers of ways, for example:

- as a table.
- as a chart (perhaps one for each provider)
- as a leaflet.

The case study below provides an example.

Case study: Samantha

Samantha Young is a 17-year-old swimmer from Huntingdon. She swims for Huntingdon Piranhas Swim Club and competes in the following events:

- 100 metres freestyle
- 100 metres butterfly
- 100 metres backstroke
- 100 metres breaststroke.

Samantha trains and competes at the local St Peters Pool in Huntingdon, which is a 25-by-12 m, four lane facility.

Samantha learnt to swim when she was 7. She took swimming lessons at her junior school and the local leisure centre. When she was 10, Samantha had a trial at the local swim club, where coaches looked at her strokes and techniques.

The trial was successful, and Samantha joined a training squad. This meant that Samantha was now swimming and training more frequently and at a higher level. The focus was not only on stroke development but also on swimming longer distances to develop stamina and strength. Samantha began to train on Tuesdays, Thursdays, Saturdays and Sundays, at times when the pool was available for club training (usually early mornings and evenings).

Samantha began to swim competitively at the age of 12, competing in local 'open' meetings. As Samantha progressed, she swam in a number of different competitions including open championships, where swimmers enter under their own names rather than the names of clubs, in the Fenland League, in county championships and also abroad in invitation meetings. She now trains five times a week, and completes roughly 2000 metres per session.

The factors which have affected Samantha's progress in swimming include:

- sufficient and suitable local facilities being available
- a supply of qualified teachers and coaches in the area.
- the existence of a club to which she could progress
- the necessary financial assistance to be able to afford to travel
- the necessary personal qualities, such as the motivation and ability needed to compete.

Peterborough has a number of swimming facilities that are available for training and coaching. The main two are summarised in the following chart:

Name of facility	Length	Width	Number of lanes	Deep end/ shallow end	Other features
The Regional Pool and Fitness Centre	25 m	12.5 m	6	1.75 m/0.9 m	Diving pit – 3.8 m Springboard – 3 m; 4 m High board Learner pool – 0.75 m Swimming lessons Base for City of Peterborough Swimming Club
The Jack Hunt pool	20 m	10 m	4	2.0 m/0.75 m	None

Both these facilities provide opportunities for swimmers to learn and train. There is only one 'competing' club in Peterborough. This is the City of Peterborough Swim Club. The club trains at the Peterborough Regional during the early mornings, (sometimes from 5.30 a.m.), or evenings (from 4–6 p.m.) during the week, and 2 p.m. on Saturdays. It caters for swimmers from the age of 7 up to adults. It is involved in swimming at a variety of levels such as county and regional championships, competes abroad and entertains foreign swimming clubs. It provides a route to national and international competition for its members.

The disadvantages of the facilities that Peterborough offers are as follows;
- There is only the one 25 metre pool, which is now 25 years old and in need of refurbishment.
- There is no 50 metre competition pool in the city or area. The nearest is in Cambridge, 40 miles away. There is little public transport, so the pool is inaccessible to swimmers without a car.
- Due to the size and use of the pool, training is only possible at very unsociable hours. Schools and the general public have access to the pool at all other times. For instance, swimming lessons for beginners and improvers need to be offered at times when the children are not at school.
- The city lacks coaches at a number of levels.
- The club lacks facilities within the town for land-based training. There are insufficient funds available at present to correct this.
- There is limited liaison between the swimming teachers employed by the city and the swimming club. As a result, there is a lack of progression from swimming lessons to the competitive side of the sport.
- The lack of facilities limits the chance of competition. The Regional Pool is unable to host regional events because it is too small.

Now answer the following questions:

1. Complete a table, like the one on page 256, showing swimming provision for your local town or area. List all the swimming facilities available.
2. In small groups, use the Internet to fill in the missing details below for national facilities. Add any local facilities you have which you feel are important nationally. This might be because your local college or university has a swimming academy or high level swimming squad.

Name of facility	Length	Width	Number of lanes	Deep end/ shallow end	Other features
Ponds Forge International Swimming Centre					
Manchester Aquatics Centre					
Crystal Palace National Sports Centre					

3. Do any of the disadvantages listed for Peterborough's facilities apply to your local facilities?

Opportunities to train

Sports training at school

As a performer progresses in a particular sport, he or she will train at a variety of levels. Initially, most people start playing sport at an early age at school, where they are introduced to the basic skills in a range of sporting activities. The National Curriculum lists certain things that young people should be able to do in respect of a number of sports. To use swimming as an example, Key Stage 3 requires that pupils use a range of recognised strokes, techniques and personal survival skills with technical proficiency.

Swimming clubs

Once the basic skills have been mastered, you might then progress to a higher level. This could be a local club offering specialist coaching in a particular sport. As you progress and improve, you may then progress from a club swimming squad to a county squad, followed by regional and then national swimming groups.

Sports academies

A number of other opportunities support this progression. These include sports academies, which are usually based in colleges and universities. At a sports academy, the student's time is split between academic studies on an appropriate course and regular high level training under a specialist coaching team.

Let's do it!

Investigate local sports academies in your area.
- Are there any academies in any of your local colleges or universities?
- What sport(s) do they provide for?
- Are they male, female or mixed sex?
- What opportunities do they offer?

Bring your findings back to the class for discussion.

Centres of excellence

Centres of excellence are at a level above sports academies. Many are run by the English Institute of Sport. This organisation provides many services and facilities to elite athletes.

What we do

The English Institute of Sport provides sports medicine, sports science and athlete career and education advice to the nation's elite athletes from a variety of locations, in nine regions throughout the country.

This advert comes from the the E.I.S. website. Visit it at www.heinemann.co.uk/hotlinks to find out more about your area and a particular sport.

The table below shows one way of displaying information about training opportunities in your chosen sport.

Chosen sport – Swimming			
Facility name	**Ability range covered**	**Facilities available for training**	**Other facilities available to the athlete**
Local facilities			
Regional pool Peterborough	All abilities, from beginners to club swimmers	Fitness suite Running track Meeting rooms	Fitness suite Club meeting room
Jack Hunt Pool, Peterborough	Beginners and improving swimmers	20 m × 10 m pool	None
National facilities			
Swimming Academy, Filton College, Bristol			Academic studies
Crystal Palace National Sports Centre			Accommodation for overnight stays, etc.
International facilities			
Ponds Forge International Swimming Centre	All abilities, from lessons to national squad training in diving	50 m pool with moveable floor Diving pit, 6 m deep	
Manchester Aquatics Centre		50 m 8-lane pool Fitness suite Meeting rooms Warm up pool	

The table below shows one way of displaying information about competition opportunities in your chosen sport.

Chosen sport – Football			
Competitions available	**Locally**	**Nationally**	**Internationally**
League Competitions	Local school/college league	National	International e.g. (European Champions League in football)
Cup competitions	Cambridgeshire Cup Under 18	E.S.F.A. Schools Cup	World Club Championship
Friendly matches	Between schools/colleges inside and outside the area	End of season School Tour	Friendly matches with 'twinned' towns, etc.
Tournaments	e.g. Local 5 aside School/Town Championship		Tours abroad organised by Sports Travel Companies

Let's do it!

Fill in a table like the one below showing the competition opportunities in your chosen sport. Think about the various competitions available locally, nationally and internationally. Where possible, give examples, as in the table above.

Chosen sport – Competition venue	Range of levels catered for	Examples of competitions held
Local		
1		
2		
National		
1		
2		
International		
1		
2		

Opportunities to compete

As with training, there are a number of different levels at which you might compete in a particular sport:

- local friendly matches and inter-school matches
- leagues – local and national
- regional fixtures and matches between counties or regions in the country such as the Midlands versus the North
- international matches and fixtures.

These competitions also take place at a variety of levels, which can vary depending on the sport. Usually they are based on age groups, for example, Under 10s, Under 16s, and so on. Ages are usually taken from a set date. For example, if the set date was the end of August, the age you are at that point determines the age group you compete in.

In adult life, you may compete in age groups over a certain age. For instance in swimming, the masters age group is for people over the age of 25.

Let's do it!

Choose a sport and investigate the different age groups it caters for. Are these age groups given names, for example, Junior, Intermediate, Senior, and so on?

Place these different age groups in a pyramid like the one opposite, showing the different competitions they can take part in.

Two examples have been given:

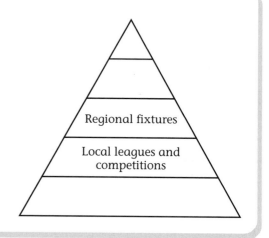

As you progress to a higher level, the number of participants decreases but the level of performance, coaching and necessary facilities and resources increases. The number of opportunities to compete at each level also decreases as the level gets higher. There are many more local netball or football matches than there are internationals, for instance.

Assessment activity 2: Training and competition opportunities

Choose three sports that you either play yourself, or are very interested in.

P Identify the opportunities to train and compete in your three sports locally, nationally and internationally.

M Explain the opportunities to train and compete in your three sports locally, nationally and internationally.

D Critically analyse the opportunities to train and compete in your three sports. Identify areas for future developments. What is good? What is bad?

Think about it

IWhat is good about the opportunities provided for your chosen sport? What could be improved? Look at training and competing at different levels. How do the opportunities in your sport compare with other sports in your area, or the same sport in other areas? Give reasons for your comments. Look at different levels and comment whether provision changes with each level of performance.

Action plan to improve performance

In the previous two sections you have looked at:
- the factors which can affect your sporting performance, looking particularly at two different sports
- how and where you can train and compete locally, nationally and internationally, looking particularly at three different sports.

This next section is designed to help you:
- set goals for improvement and development in a chosen sport
- form a plan to achieve these desired improvements
- record and regularly review your progress.

Key point

Remember that for assessment, you will need to complete this for one chosen sport over a period of one month.

Action plan

Planning your training and competition is vital to success. Without a plan, your training and competitive programme will lack focus and direction. Keeping a record of your progress is also important. It means you can monitor which aspects are going well and which are not, and so identify what further training is required for you to achieve your ultimate goal.

Identifying goals

The Oxford Concise Dictionary defines a goal as 'An aim or desired result'. In performance terms, your first task is to sit down and decide what aim or result you wish to achieve. This might be one of many. Some examples include improving your personal best time or distance in a track and field event, or increasing your maximum lift in power lifting, or qualifying for a particular final or competition. Whatever your aim, you will need to decide and agree upon it with people who can help you, for example your tutor, coach or team mates.

Once you have agreed it, you will need to set it down as one of your performance goals. Goals should be S.M.A.R.T.:

Specific   Measurable   Agreed   Realistic   Timed

(this is covered in detail in Unit 5 pages 202–4)

Let's do it!

- In small groups, talk about the goals the runner in the picture may have set. List them on flip chart paper and be ready to discuss them with the class.
- List the factors that may have affected these goals. Why, for instance, might deadlines have been moved backwards or forwards?
- How might the goals this runner set be measured?
- Discuss the use of S.M.A.R.T. targets for this runner or another athlete from your chosen sport.

Short, medium and long term goals

Goals can be set over different periods of time, as short, medium or long term goals. Short term goals might have a timescale of a day, a week or a month. Medium term goals might have a timescale of six months. Long term goals may be set over a period of several years. Goals set at different periods may run together. For instance, an athlete aiming to make the team for the Olympics may set the following goals:

- short term – this year – win county title; improve personal best to xx
- medium term – within two years – win A.A.A. title; improve personal best to xx
- long term – within four years – qualify for British Olympic Squad; achieve Olympic qualifying standard.

Identifying strengths and weaknesses

When you plan your goals, you will need to decide upon targets to be achieved along the way. These targets may be physical, to improve basic strength, for instance. They could involve setting actual times or distances to be achieved within a certain timescale. They could involve competitions or events to be used as a training or performance guide.

Before this can be done, you will need to analyse your performance and identify your own strengths and weaknesses. You may do this with the help of your coach or tutor. You will need to do this in relation to your chosen event or goal. Make sure that you also consider the range of other factors which might affect your performance, for example:

- **Timescale** – How long will activities be undertaken? When will testing take place? What times of the day/week, etc. are you going to allocate to various parts of your action plan?
- **Planning** – each training session should be planned, so that you know in advance the duration of each session, its content, the type of training you will undertake, and so on.
- **Mental preparation** – you need to think about this in addition to your physical training. How will you try to improve it? When will this take place?
- **Diet** – When you examine your diet, analyse strengths and weaknesses, for instance, do you eat too many fatty foods? Are your meals eaten too close to training and competition?

Once you have all this information, you can begin to design and plan your training.

Think about it

Part of your assessment for this unit is to identify your current strengths and weaknesses in your chosen sport. In pairs, think of how you might do this. What ways could you identify these strengths and weaknesses before planning suitable training.

There are a number of ways you could identify your good and bad points:

Self-evaluation using video analysis

Observation of your performance by a coach or tutor

Comparison of your performance with a better performer in the same event

Objective measurement — of times and distances or via fitness tests, etc.

Discussion with your coach or tutor, playing partner or other player

Let's do it!

1. Complete the following table for analysing your performance in your own sport:

Method used	Advantages	Disadvantages	Comments
Observation by tutor/coach			
Self-evaluation using video analysis			
Objective measurement			
Discussion with coach/tutor			
Comparison with a better performer			

2. Choose two methods of analysing your performance in your chosen sport. The methods you choose may depend on your chosen event, the equipment available or the opportunities for objective measurement (ice dancing, for example, is assessed very much on opinion).

3. Carry out the two methods of analysis, and draw up a chart which identifies your strengths and weaknesses. These might be skill based or fitness based. They might refer to tactical awareness or strategies employed in game situations.

Once you have identified your strengths and weaknesses, you can:

- explain what they are and how they have arisen
- examine how they are affecting your performance
- think about what you need to do about them.

> **1** Identify a weakness through two means, such as an observation by either you or your coach, or through completing an appropriate fitness test
> *e.g. poor stamina*

↓

> **2** Explain the effect this weakness is having on performance
> *e.g. You are often unable to maintain your performance right to the end of a long match*

↓

> **3** Produce an action plan to deal with this weakness and give a timescale for completion
> *e.g. Chance your training programme to include activities to improve your endurance*

↓

> **4** Reassess your progress at agreed times
> *e.g. You might complete the same stamina test you used to identify the weakness in the first place*

↓

> **5** Review your action plan and comment on its effect
> *e.g. Did it improve your stamina? If so, by how much? What effect did this have on your performance?*

If you fail to plan, you plan to fail

 Key point

When you are completing your action plan, remember to consider the factors that affect sports performance (see pages 229–51).

Other sources of help

Apart from your coach and tutor, you may need specialist help on:
- diet
- injury treatment
- mental preparation.

You should aim to include all these factors in your action plan if possible. Before the start of your training period, identify who may be able to offer you specialist support and advice. For example, there may be lecturers or tutors at your school or college in food technology, catering or sports therapy. If your local sports club or leisure centre has a resident physiotherapist, he or she may be able to help you.

Key point

Before you start your programme it is a good idea to spend some time assessing yourself. Put together a profile of yourself – who you are, what you do, details of your height and weight, current fitness levels and so on.

Assessment activity 3: Being SMART

Now you can begin to set out your action plan to improve your performance!

P With the help of your tutor, identify S.M.A.R.T. performance goals and produce an action plan for the next month. Your plan should set out targets, goals and training. It should identify your strengths and weaknesses and show how you are going to improve your performance.

M Identify S.M.A.R.T. performance goals. Explain them and independently produce an action plan. This should set out targets, goals and training. It should explain your strengths and weaknesses and show how you are going to improve your performance in your selected sport over the period of one month.

D Independently produce and review an action plan to improve your performance in your chosen sport over the period of one month. You will need to justify your choice of targets, goals and training, and provide realistic alternatives.

Implementing your action plan

The initial assessment you have carried out should allow you to design and plan a suitable scheme to identify your weaknesses and develop your strengths. If test results indicate a low level in a specific area, then your programme should start off at a relatively low level. Remember that the wider the range of activities you use, the less chance there is of boredom being a problem.

During your four week programme, you should aim to try out a variety of strategies and techniques to improve your personal performance. Find out:

- what works best for you
- what is ineffective
- why certain things work/don't work.

There are a variety of ways that you can carry out and record your action plan, and then review and amend it as necessary. Whichever way you decide, it is important that you record all necessary information and the results of all games and training sessions and matches you are involved in during the period of your action plan. The comments and observations of your tutor and/or coach are also important and need to be recorded.

The most common way to record this information is to keep a training diary or log book. This should record various items of information about each training session or competitive event that you undertake. Any part of the session that has had an effect on the training needs to be recorded. This might be the weather, illness or injury, or problems with facilities. The example below illustrates these points:

Date and time	Tuesday, 25 September, 2003, 2 p.m.
Location	College sports hall and playing field
Details of session	Pre-season fitness and skills session
Conditions	Hot and sunny, slight breeze Pitch very hard – no rain for previous 10 days I felt tired after working unexpectedly last night
Warm up	4 laps of the pitch–10 minutes stretching 4 x 15 metre sprints, gradually increasing speed
Main session	Circuit training – all round body circuit using body weight and partner Ball work – short range passing and movement, two touches Soccer tennis game to finish
Warm down	3 laps of pitch 10 minutes stretching
Observations	Fitness work was poor. I was tired and lethargic after a long night at work. Need the money so could not refuse offer. Ball work was better – I was more interested in this, so motivation was much higher. Lack of water meant I struggled for the last 10 minutes. MUST REMEMBER WATER BOTTLE!
Coach's/tutor's comments	Good ball skills, used both feet frequently. Fitness work was average. John looked tired throughout the session. Needs to get more sleep. Discussed this with John after session. Warned he will be fined if he forgets his water bottle again! Motivation was better when he had a ball at his feet. Fitness work with ball likely to be more effective

Example of a log book page for a training session.

Key points

1. Remember to start your diary with a profile of yourself – who you are, what you do, details of your height and weight, current fitness levels and so on. It would be a good idea to spend some time assessing yourself before starting your programme!
2. Complete a page in your diary after every session or match during the month of your action plan.
3. Keep your comments concise and to the point.
4. Record match results, teacher/coach comments, fitness test results, etc. each time you make an entry into your diary.
5. Comment on a variety of factors – the weather, the facilities, how you were feeling, etc.
6. Aim to review your plan with your tutor or coach at the end of each week. Check whether any changes or alterations are required, for example: Is the training schedule too hard? Are facilities available on a regular basis? Can you cope with the increased demands?

Assessment activity 4: Training diary

P Record your progress in following your action plan in a training diary. Show evidence of your achievements over one month.

M Record your progress in following your action plan, and explain your achievements over one month.

D Record your progress in following your action plan. Evaluate your achievements and highlight areas for further development and training

 Key points

You need to think about:
- **when** your action plan will take place
- **where** you will carry it out, taking into account facilities and transport considerations
- **how** many times per week you will carry out your plan
- **what** it will cost and whether you can afford it
- **what** activities are best suited to achieving your goals (lifting weights will not help a problem caused by your diet!)
- **who** you will need for assistance and guidance (including specialists, such as a dietician or a physiotherapist)
- **how** you will review progress and assess the success of your action plan.

Producing evidence of possible progress

Reviewing your progress

In any training programme, it is important to review progress regularly. You could use various methods to do this:

- Use your training diary or log book, which provides a documentary record of each session, test and so on that you undertake. Looking back at this will enable you to check that you are following your original plan and you will be able to revise it if necessary.
- Assess yourself against the goals you set out at the start of your programme – check whether you are on track to achieve them and revise them if necessary.
- Repeat fitness or skills tests at intervals – if your results improve, your action plan is working, if they don't you may need to revise your plan.
- Keep a video diary, or make video recordings of your performance over a period of time – if a video is unavailable, an audio diary is another option.
- Review your performance with other athletes, coaches or trainers – discussing your action plan with your tutor, coach or trainer is very important. They know you well and have a good insight into your strengths and weaknesses. You could tape record or video these meetings, or ask a friend to keep minutes of what was said.

Evidence of progress

At the end of this unit, you will need to produce evidence that:

- you are aware of the various factors that affect sporting performance
- you have identified your strengths and weaknesses and their causes and effects
- you have designed an action plan to improve some of your weaknesses and develop some of your strengths
- you have recorded your progress using a diary or log book
- at the end of four weeks, you have assessed the effects of your programme on your strengths and weaknesses, and your performance in your chosen sport.

This evidence can come from a variety of sources, including newspapers and match reports as well as your own observations. You should decide which sources you can reliably use and which are most appropriate. Try to use as wide a variety as is practical.

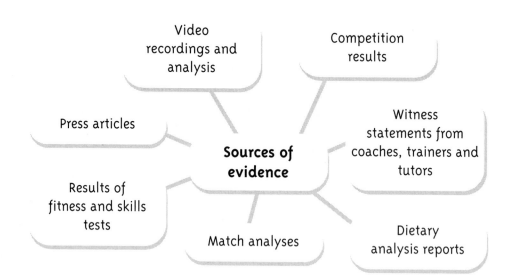

Think about it

In small groups, discuss the different types of evidence you might produce for your assessments.

Assessment activity 5: Recording regular progress

- Describe your progress over the four weeks of your action plan – e.g. the changes in your performance and what you have achieved.
- Explain why this has happened.
- Measure how much change has there been – for instance, your maximum number of press ups might have increased by 10% due to your action plan.
- Comment on the amount of change.
- Ask yourself whether all the changes have been positive.

P With your tutor, complete regular progress reviews and identify areas for future and further development.

M Independently, complete regular progress review and explain areas for future and further development.

D Critically evaluate your progress and justify areas for future and further development.

In summary

In this chapter, you have studied a variety of factors that could have an effect on your performance in sport. These have ranged from internal factors, such as motivation, to external factors, like 'jet lag' and different climates. As a sports performer, it is important that you take steps to deal with these factors to ensure you can play at your best at all times and that the weeks or months of training are not wasted. You need to give yourself enough time to get used to being in a new country or recover from travelling a long way to a tournament or competition.

You should also now be able to identify, for your chosen sports, places and facilities where you can play, train and gain specialist help or advice to aid your performance. By looking at a number of case studies and talking to local sports men and women, you will have gained valuable insight into how real sports stars have carried this out for themselves.

CHECK WHAT YOU KNOW!

Look back through this unit and see if you can answer the following questions:

1 List three factors that can affect sporting performance. Give an example of how each factor can affect performance.
2 For two different sports, consider how two factors could affect players' performance, and how these factors could be dealt with.
3 What are the advantages of training at a centre of excellence?
4 How did having a national league in English rugby help England win the World Cup in 2003?
5 How might a top sports person decide which parts of their performance need to be improved?
6 Why should you carry out an assessment of your performance before drawing up your action plan?
7 Describe the advantages and disadvantages of two ways of monitoring your action plan.
8 What should a training diary include in each entry made?

Practical sport

Introduction

In this unit, you will look at a variety of aspects connected with playing and performing the two sports you have selected to study for your First Diploma qualification. This unit is very practical. It assumes that you play sport a lot! You must have access to coaching and competition, through a club, school or college, for the two sports that you offer for assessment. It will not be enough to 'have a go' for a few weeks.

The range of sports possible cannot be covered in this book. For this reason, three sports will be used as examples to give you guidance on how to collect and present your evidence and information. These sports are:

- a **team** sport – basketball
- a **racket** sport – badminton
- an **individual** sport – swimming.

For each sport, you will be guided through the areas that must be covered in your unit assignment.

The emphasis is on you playing sport! You must develop an understanding of:

- the rules that apply
- the skills required to play
- the tactics and strategies employed
- the roles of match officials.

How you will be assessed

This unit is assessed internally by your tutor. He or she will issue you with an assignment that will give you the opportunity to achieve the highest mark.

Learning outcome 1

In order to achieve success in this learning outcome, you will need to keep a record of your involvement in your chosen sports. This should focus on the playing side. It should demonstrate to your tutor how you have shown the skills needed to play your chosen sports. You also need to demonstrate an awareness of the tactics and strategies needed to play in a range of game situations. You need to develop a knowledge of the rules and regulations relevant to your chosen sports, be able to explain them and be able to look at them in action.

Learning outcomes 2 and 3

You will need to understand the roles and responsibilities of the officials required in your chosen sports and be able to compare these roles. You need to know the basic rules and regulations, the scoring system, and how decisions are made and communicated by officials for each of your two sports.

Learning outcome 4

You need to be able to assess the sporting performance of two athletes from one of your chosen sports. You will need to compare them to each other by highlighting strengths and weaknesses in the skills, tactics and strategies of each athlete.

After completing this unit you should be able to achieve the following learning outcomes:
1. Demonstrate **skills, techniques and tactics** within a range of sports.
2. Examine the **rules, regulations and scoring systems** in selected sports.
3. Investigate the **roles and responsibilities of officials** in selected sports.
4. Examine the **performance of other players** in a selected sport.

Skills, techniques and tactics

All sports require skills, techniques and tactics to succeed. This section will lead you through some definitions of the key terms and allow you to recognise the differences and similarities between them. You will then need to apply this knowledge to your chosen sports.

Keeping a record of your performance

The record you keep of your sports performance can take a number of different forms. The most effective is a simple diary, in which you write down which skills and tactics you employed, why you did so, and what the result was. For example, imagine you have a regular opponent in badminton. You decide that you are going to play in a particular way for one game, to see what happens. Perhaps you will always serve to your opponent's backhand because you have noticed it is a weakness. Or perhaps you will try to engage your opponent in long rallies because you feel your fitness is better and, by tiring your opponent out, you will gain an advantage.

Other ways of keeping a record could include:
- a video diary
- obtaining feedback from observers and coaches who watch you play
- using a simple summary sheet, completed by yourself or a tutor, coach or opponent
- asking someone to watch your performance and then to discuss it with you.

 Key points

Remember, you need to complete this task for **two** different sports over a period of time. Use the feedback you receive from others. Change the skills and tactics you use in the light of the results you obtain during matches.
Remember that your two sports **must** contrast. They cannot be two racket sports, or two events in athletics, for example.

Skills

The Oxford Concise English Dictionary defines skill as, 'The ability to do something well'. In sport, this relates to how various movements and actions in the game are performed.

Skills are **learned.** When you learn a sports skill you pass through various phases, from not being able to perform the skill at all to being able to perform the skill without thinking about it.

 Think about it

In small groups, discuss what you think 'being skilful' means. Try to give examples. Bring your findings back to the class and be ready to present what your group decided.

Generally, a skilful player:

- will make the game look easy – they will often appear to be hardly trying
- will not waste either time or energy – they will always seem to be in the correct position to perform the skill or technique and will not appear to take a great deal of time to perform the skill
- will achieve a desired result with maximum certainty – they will score the point 99 times out of every 100 attempts.

Sport involves individual players and teams performing a variety of skills in order to achieve the best result. Basketball, for example, involves:

- individual skills, including shooting, passing and dribbling
- team skills, including a zone defence, a fast break attack or a set move from a jump ball.

Team skills are as important as individual skills

Skills in sport can be categorised in various ways. The skills used may be:

- **complex** – for example, a tumble routine on the floor mat in gymnastics
- **simple** – catching a ball in netball.

They can also be termed as **closed** or **open**. Closed skills are those that are not affected by the external surroundings, like the weather or other players (a serve in badminton, for example) Open skills are those that are affected by the environment (sailing a yacht, for example, because the sailor needs to react to the force and direction of the wind).

Skills can also be **externally** paced where the performer has no control over when to perform the skill (the start in a 100 metre race, for example, is decided by the starter not the athlete); or **self** paced where the performer decides when the skill is performed (for example, the player decides when to serve in tennis).

Let's do it!

Choose one of the sports you are going to study. Draw a table, like the one below, with three columns headed *Skill/Technique*, *Type of skill* and *Reasons*. Now choose some of the skills and techniques used in your sport and decide what type of skill they are: open or closed; self- or externally paced and so on. Here is an example for a basketball game:

Skill/Technique	Type of skill	Reasons
Chest pass	Open	Opponents try to intercept your pass
Free throw shot	Self paced	You decide when to shoot after receiving the ball from the referee
Tip off jump	Externally paced	You must jump when the referee throws the ball up
Dribbling	Open	You have to react to the movements of team mates and opponents

Techniques

Technique is a word often used in sport. There is confusion between the words 'skill' and 'technique'. A technique is a way of carrying out a task or action. For example, look at the way the current England Rugby fly-half, Jonny Wilkinson, takes a conversion in a game. Then compare this to another international player performing the same task. The end result, a successful kick, may be the same, but the way the task is carried out may be completely different! Each player may be equally skilful, but have vastly different techniques.

Let's do it!

1. In small groups, choose a skill like bowling in cricket or serving in tennis. Look at the skill used by a number of players and discuss the differences in the technique used. Produce a display to highlight these differences.
2. Now repeat this exercise for a skill in one of the sports you are studying. Make notes on the technique of the performer, in other words how he or she carries out the skill. For example, look at the position of the arms, legs and so on. Look at the follow through after the skill.
3. Now, video yourself performing the same skill. Make notes on the differences between your performance and that of the player you have observed. Write these up in a table. Try to use these headings (your tutor can help you with this):
   - early preparation
   - result of the skill
   - body position.
   - footwork
   - follow through

Think about it

The table below looks at the skill of place kicking. It looks at the technique of two players in the final of the 2003 Rugby World Cup.

Component of skill	Jonny Wilkinson (England)	Elton Flatley (Australia)
Position of ball	Very upright	Pointing at the posts Ball at very shallow angle to the ground
Movement from the ball to kicking position	Five steps backwards and to the right	Three steps back followed by two to the left
Body position before kick	Arms held in front with elbows bent and hands together	Arms hanging down beside body
Action before kick	Looks at the ball, then the posts, then at a point high in the stands, then the posts again and finally the ball	Looks once at the posts
Kicks with:	left foot	right foot
Approach to ball when kicking	Four steps to ball	Two steps back and slightly left, then four to the ball
Follow through	Long and across to the right	Long and left

It is clear that each player has a completely different approach to the same skill. In the final, Jonny Wilkinson was much more successful. Does this mean his technique is better?

Tactics and strategies

You will also need to consider tactics in your chosen sport. Tactics are defined by the Oxford Concise English Dictionary as, 'the actions or strategies used to achieve a specific end'.

In sport, the 'specific end' is to win the match or the race. In Formula One racing, for example, tactics will include when to pit for fuel and tyres in the race (two stops or three?). In a 10,000 metre race, for example, a runner like Paula Radcliffe needs to decide at what pace she will run each lap. In football, a Premier League manager will need to consider what formation to play. The decision might be to play a 4-4-2 line up, or perhaps 3-5-2. The opposition the team faces might be the deciding factor. For instance, a football team wishing to add width to their attack while maintaining a strong midfield might employ a five man midfield, with the two 'wing backs' attempting to get forward down the wings to deliver crosses. This means that the opponent's dangerous full back has to help defend this, rather than trying to get himself or herself forward!

Tactics will relate to a number of facets of the game, such as:
- attack and defence – are you in possession or not?
- the situation in the game – are you are winning or losing? How much time is left?
- the style of play you naturally prefer – are you an aggressive player who likes to attack? Or are you more conservative, preferring to wait for your opponent to make errors?
- the opponent you are playing – what are their strengths and weaknesses?

You need to be flexible with tactics, able to change and adapt to respond to the way the game or match is going.

Case study

When the England cricket captain Michael Vaughan selects a team for a Test match, he has to make tactical decisions. All of the decisions he makes will be part of the tactics he employs to obtain the desired result.

Here are some of the questions he might ask himself:
- Am I going to play with a spinner or not?
- How many recognised batsmen are there?
- Do I need to win the match to win the series, or would a draw be sufficient?
- What weaknesses have I spotted in the opponents' batting?
- Do the opponents have bowlers who struggle when bowling to left handed batsmen?
- When on the pitch, in what positions will I place my fielders?
- How will I use my bowlers?
- Will I declare at a particular point, to allow my bowlers time to get their opponents out?

Now answer the following questions:
1. Can you think of other questions that the England captain might ask?
2. How do you think the answers to these questions will influence his tactics?

Think about it

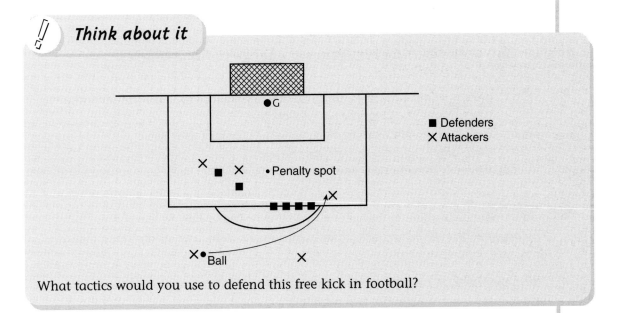

What tactics would you use to defend this free kick in football?

Let's do it!

Many games and sports use special words or terms to signify something. Fill in the table below to define some of these terms:

Term	Sport	Definition
Scrum down		
Double dribble		
"Let"		
Travelling		
Deuce		
Tumble turn		
Offside		
Service over		
Penalty stroke		
Lineout		

Assessment activity 1: Observational checklist for athletes

P In small groups, choose two athletes from any sport that you are familiar with. These athletes might be classmates or players from different teams. With the support of your tutor, draw up an observational checklist that lists:
  - the various skills required to perform the sport
  - each player's strengths and weaknesses in the range of skills you have identified
  - the tactics required by each sport. Look also at the tactics your chosen players uses.

Discuss how best to record and present your results to the rest of the class. Can you draw any conclusions from your results?

M Using the checklist created in **P** compare the performance, strengths, weaknesses and tactical awareness of the two athletes.

D Again using the checklist you have created, further analyse the two athletes by suggesting some 'coaching tips' for improvement or changes to their performance, strengths, weaknesses and tactical awareness.

Rules, regulations and scoring systems

Rules and regulations

All sports have rules and regulations that are written down by the sport's Governing Body and then administered by referees, umpires or judges. These rules and regulations are needed for a number of reasons:

- Rules and regulations decide the format of a game – for example, netball players are not allowed to dribble the ball, whereas in basketball, a very similar game, dribbling is allowed.
- Rules and regulations cover subjects such as the duration of a game, the size of the field of play, the type and nature of equipment that can or must be used, and the number of players and substitutes allowable.
- Rules and regulations are also vitally important to ensure the safety of players and spectators – for example, an ice hockey goalkeeper must wear certain items of protective clothing.

Rules for how to begin a game are also set out

 Key point

All sports are about overcoming a problem within the confines and restrictions of rules. For example, football is about scoring a goal without touching the ball with your hand, with only ten players in the outfield and without straying offside. Rugby football was 'invented' when William Webb Ellis, who was playing football at the time, picked up the ball and ran with it. At the time, this was not against the rules of football and so a rule was invented to make it illegal. However, others liked the idea of running with the ball in the hand, and so the game of rugby was born!

Scoring systems

All sporting activities have scoring systems. A scoring system refers to all the different ways that points can be scored or lost during a sporting activity. In football, the system is very simple: a goal is scored when the entire ball crosses the goal line, between the posts and crossbar of the goal. Goals can be scored from open play or free kicks including a penalty. However in basketball, 'goals' are called baskets and are worth either 1, 2 or 3 points depending on how they are scored and from where.

In badminton, you can only score when you are serving but in tennis you can also score when your opponent is serving. Some systems are *objective* – the winner is determined by who scores the most points, goals, baskets etc. In other sports, the system is *subjective* – the winner is decided by the opinion of judges.

The rules of the particular game will lay down how and when scores can be made and how a winner is decided. In some sports it is decided by who scores the most (football, basketball, netball). In other sports it is decided by who scores the least (golf, motorcycle trials, show jumping). In other sports, there are set ways in which the game must end. For instance, in darts you must finish on a double to win, while in tennis, the fifth set in a men's game does not go into a tiebreak situation.

For this unit, you need to understand the scoring system used in each of your three chosen sports.

Roles and responsibilities of officials

This section will look at the various jobs required in any sport to ensure the rules are observed and safety is maintained. All games have officials – in badminton there are 12 involved in any one game, in football there are three, while at a swimming gala there may be over 20!

 Key points

- A role can be described as 'a function'.
- A responsibility can be defined as 'an obligation'.

For example, a referee in basketball has a variety of roles, which include enforcing the rules or laws of the game. They also have a responsibility to ensure the safety of all the players and to be impartial and fair in all their judgements.

Apart from implementing the rules of the game, referees, umpires and judges are also required to carry out a number of other roles and responsibilities, including:

- maintaining a set appearance by wearing a uniform or certain dress code – they must be clearly distinguishable from the players!
- checking the playing surface, equipment and so on prior to a game or match, to make sure the playing environment is safe and fit to play on
- ensuring fair play at all times
- ensuring that the game is played in the correct spirit
- maintaining the necessary level of personal fitness required to officiate successfully
- ensuring the safety of players and others at all times during the game.

During the game, the responsibilities of the referee, umpire or judge may include all or some of the following:

- to apply the rules
- to keep control of the game
- to record the score
- to keep time
- to perform certain specific tasks, such as watching for a shuttle or ball crossing a particular line on the court or pitch (for example, a line judge in tennis, or an assistant referee in football)
- to scrutinise the performance of a competitor, such as a gymnast, and make a judgement on how good their performance was by looking for errors and then deducting marks.

Communication

Game officials need to communicate with colleagues, players and coaches so that the game is played in the right atmosphere and in the right spirit.

Match officials communicate by

using a whistle, for example to stop play in rugby or basketball

talking, for example to players and coaches

using hand signals, for example many decisions in basketball are communicated in this way

Let's do it!

Look in a basketball rules book or watch a football referee to see how hand signals are used.

In carrying out these tasks the official needs to be confident. He or she needs to be confident when starting the game, when making a decision and in relaying this decision to other people. The official also needs to be confident about using the correct terminology, for example in badminton the score 'zero' is referred to as 'love'.

 Key points

- In football, the game starts when the referee blows a whistle.
- In badminton, the game starts when the umpire calls, 'Play'.
- In swimming, the race is started with a hooter.

Interpreting the rules and making decisions

Referees and umpires need to interpret the rules, and make decisions based on their interpretation. Examples of this kind of decision making in action include:

- a football referee deciding if a player in an offside position was actually interfering with play
- a basketball referee deciding whether a player who was fouled was disadvantaged as a result
- a badminton umpire deciding whether a player's movement during a serve was legal or not.

The more experience a match official has, both as a player and through taking charge of games and matches at a variety of levels, the more informed his or her decision making will be.

Let's do it!

Consider your chosen sports:
- What decisions do match officials often need to make during a game?
- Can you think of any recent decisions that you feel really affected a game?
- Can you think of any recent decisions with which you disagreed?
- Why do you think those decisions were taken?

Assessment activity 2: Observational checklist for officials

P   Using your two chosen sports, draw a chart and list the various roles and responsibilities of the officials, for example:
  - wearing a specific uniform
  - their role during a game or match
  - maintaining a stated minimum fitness level
  - accepted methods of communication used.

Discuss what to include with your tutor.

M   Using your checklist, watch officials from your chosen sports and compare what they do. What actions are the same, and what are different?

D   After watching these officials, analyse each of their performances and make a list of their strengths and weaknesses when officiating. Then give some suggestions on how they could improve. You might recommend, for example, that the official should communicate more clearly or maintain a higher level of fitness. It may help to watch a good referee or umpire on the television or at a game, to give you a model to work from.

Performance of other players

Part of this unit requires you to be able to assess how well other players perform in a particular sport or activity. The following section offers some advice on how this is done.

Studying a player's performance

As a sports studies student, you need to be able to identify strengths and weaknesses in other players. This might be in how they produce various skills and techniques, as well as the tactics and strategies they employ to be successful. There are a number of criteria you could use, including:
  - the starting position for a skill.
  - the follow through used
  - positioning of the body before, during and after the skill.
  - the type of footwork used
  - positioning on the court/field etc.
  - the end result (e.g. did he or she score the goal?)
  - the tactics and strategies employed during a game or match.

There are also a number of ways to examine the performance of another player. These include:

- observing him or her play, in order to identify strengths and weaknesses
- measuring his or her performance using graphs, charts and tables – these could record, for example, the number of passes made or shots on target)
- analysing his or her performance, perhaps by taking a video of a player and then discussing it with him or her, the coach, or even the whole team.

Let's do it!

Choose a player at school, and examine his or her performance using the methods described above.

Compare your player to other players, or even to an elite performer. For instance, compare the top goal scorer in your school or college football team with Michael Owen. Look at the way they each perform a specific skill, for example, taking a penalty.

Recording, displaying and analysing your results

Once you have collected information about a player's performance, it is important that it is presented in a clear and easy-to-understand format. This not only allows you to understand what you have observed, but also to help you make decisions about future action to improve performance.

Tables, charts and graphs

There are various ways in which you could record your observations. You can compare performances by collecting statistics and displaying them as a:

Line graph

Bar graph

25% | 20%
25% | 30%

Pie chart

Sport	Per cent
Ballet	10%
Football	50%
Swimming	20%
Cricket	20%

Simple table

For example, you could record:

- each lap time in a race for two different runners
- how many shots on goal each player made in a game of football
- how many tackles each player made in a game of rugby
- how many assists each player made in a game of basketball.

Your tutor will be able to help you decide which method would be best suited to your chosen sports.

Tables

A table like the one below allows you to look at each player's performance, make observations, and then address any issues raised in training. This will hopefully help to improve your player's performance.

Skill	Taking a penalty	
	Michael Owen	Your star player
1. Approach to the ball	Head still, concentrating on the ball. Relaxed approach	Head too high. Not concentrating on the ball
2. Body position on contact	Still. Looking at the ball. Left foot beside the ball. Head over the ball	Left foot slightly too far back resulting in body leaning away from the ball. Head moving
3. Leg swing	Long swing of the right leg	Good swing but not as far as Michael Owen
4. Follow through	Good follow through	Short follow through
5. Body position	Balanced Relaxed	Stiff Appears nervous and tense
6. Balance	Very good	Good Not leaning to one side or the other
7. End result	Ball struck wide to the keeper's left. Keeper sent the wrong way. Goal scored in bottom right hand corner	Penalty scored but lacked power and placement. Goal would have been saved if keeper had stood still
8. Strategy	Looked once at the goal and then focused on the ball	Kept looking at the goal before taking the penalty

The following table includes a tally chart, and has been completed for two basketball players.

Skill	Player A	Player B	Comments Player A	Comments Player B
Shots on target for 2 points	12	8	Often off balance	Provides for other players
Shots on target for 3 points	2	0	Lacks a 3 point shot	Rarely in 3 point shooting position
Passes made successfully	55	43	Good range used	Lacks a long javelin pass
Passes misplaced	3	2	Occasionally rushes release of the ball	Sound use of the ball
Assists made for team mates	7	18	Tends to 'go' herself rather than pass	Pivotal player for the team
Interceptions made	6	3	Always threatens ball on defence	Not a strong part of game
Defensive rebounds made	2	20	Lacks height	Tallest player on court. Strong rebounder
Offensive rebounds made	1	24	Lacks height	Tallest player on court. Strong rebounder

Charts and graphs

Charts and graphs are useful for the following reasons:

- They show a player's performance in an easy to read way. A chart showing a batsman's score can also be designed to show where he has scored his runs. This might help an opposing captain devise a way of stopping this player scoring so many runs next time.
- They can show times or periods when a player 'disappears' from the game. This might be due to tiredness or loss of concentration.
- They can show tactical flaws in a team's game plan or a player's game strategy, which can then be addressed by the coach. For instance, in basketball, a player may not occupy the correct space when playing a zone defence.

The chart below shows the points scored in a basketball game by one player during each quarter. It also shows how many two and three point shots were scored. Displaying information in this way can help you to look at several aspects of the performance in very visual way.

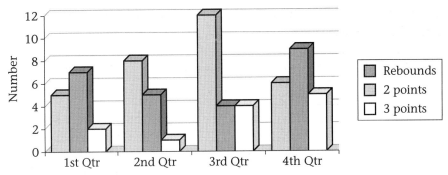

Chart showing points scored by one basketball player during each quarter

Assessment activity 2: Rules, regulations and scoring systems

P M List and explain the main rules of one of your chosen sports to a small group. Produce a handout that each member of the group can take away. Keep it simple and make it easy to understand. Then do the same for the scoring system used. Choose some simple game situations and explain these to a complete beginner.

D Look at how the rules or laws are used in each of your chosen sports. Ask yourself the following questions:

- What is the purpose of each rule? (For example, it might be to ensure safety or to keep the game flowing.)
- Which rules or laws are used most in your sport?
- How is the score relayed to players, spectators and other officials?
- Is the system easy to understand for all involved?

Now repeat the two activities above for your second sport, and complete the following assignments:

P Draw up a poster which lists the basic rules employed in one of your chosen sports. You should include information on player uniforms and any scoring equipment needed.

M Watch a video of your chosen sport with a tutor or classmate, or take a partner to watch it live. Explain the scoring system, giving examples where possible.

D Assess the scoring system of your chosen sport. Is it complicated or easy to understand? Do this by comparing your findings with the scoring system of your second sport. What is the same and what is different?

Looking at three contrasting sports

This book is not a coaching manual for any particular sport. Instead, it is designed to guide you through the assessment criteria for each unit. It does this by giving examples of what you might undertake to achieve each criterion and so complete this unit. You will need to conduct further research of your own, especially if your two chosen sports are not included in this chapter.

We are going to look at an example of a team sport – basketball, a racket sport – badminton and an individual sport – swimming.

Each example will offer suggestions as to how you might approach the study of your chosen sports. Remember that your chosen sports must contrast each other. Do not choose sports that are very similar (e.g. tennis and squash). Your level of personal performance is not assessed but it is recommended that you choose sports that you actually enjoy.

Team sports – Basketball

Basketball is a fast, athletic team game played between teams of ten players, five of whom are on court at any time. The object of the game is to score points by passing a ball through a hoop suspended ten feet from the floor, while at the same time preventing your opponents from doing the same.

Skills, techniques and tactics

The game requires a number of basic skills, including:

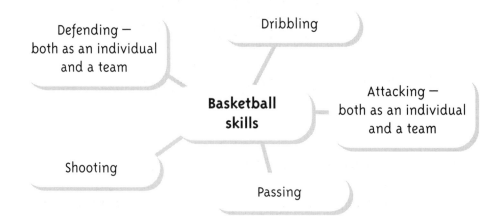

Defending – both as an individual and a team

Dribbling

Basketball skills

Attacking – both as an individual and a team

Shooting

Passing

Before you can assess either yourself or another player's performance, you need to have a 'model' available that shows you what a particular skill looks like when performed. This section will provide models for selected skills. For other skills, you will need to look at specific basketball coaching manuals to find the information you require.

Passing

The main types of pass used in basketball are the:

- chest pass
- bounce pass
- overhead pass
- javelin pass.

The chest pass can be used as an example of a model. The key points to look for in a chest pass are as follows:

1. the ball should be held in two hands with fingers spread apart
2. the ball travels from chest to chest
3. the arms are extended and the fingers point to the target after releasing the ball
4. the player should try to step into the pass.
5. the pass should be flat and fast.

Think about it

Look at the picture. Can you see all of the above points?

Dribbling

When a player dribbles in basketball he or she should:

1. be able to dribble with both the left and right hand.
2. keep his or her fingers spread and the wrist bent to 'push' the ball onto the floor
3. keep his or her knees slightly bent

4. put his or her body between an opponent and the ball for protection
5. keep his or her head up looking for team mates, opponents and so on.

Shooting

Shots in basketball include:
- the jump shot
- the hook shot
- the lay up shot
- the set shot.

We will use the set shot as a model. When performing a set shot:
1. the shooter's eyes should be looking directly at the basket
2. the elbow of his or her shooting arm should be pointing at the target
3. the shooter's feet should be apart so that he or she is balanced
4. the shot should begin with a bending and then straightening of the legs, followed by a straightening of the shooting arm
5. the shooter's hand and fingers should point to the basket after the shot
6. the non-shooting hand should be used to stop the ball going left or right
7. the shooter should aim for the centre of the basket.

Performing a set shot

Let's do it!

1. Investigate the skills of defending and attacking in basketball. Write a short description.
2. Now write about defending and attacking in one of your chosen sports.

Rules, regulations and scoring system

Basketball is governed by 'English Basketball'. This is the National Governing Body, and is responsible for:

- promoting the game
- training coaches and match officials
- developing talent through award schemes and skills awards
- developing initiatives to encourage people to participate in the sport
- choosing representative sides and organising various competitions
- raising finance and generating sponsorship.

The main rules of the game are reproduced on the following pages. These extracts are taken from the *England Basketball Level 1 Coaching Manual*. They are simplified rules, which would allow you to control a game for young players learning the game.

The scoring system

Points are awarded to your team every time the ball goes through your opponent's basket. Two points are awarded when a basket is scored from inside the three point line, and three points are awarded if the basket is scored from outside this line.

When a player is fouled in the act of shooting, then he or she is awarded free throws – either two for a two point shot, or three for a three point shot. Each successful shot is awarded one point. It is important to note that you can score an 'own basket' by scoring in your own net! If you do this, the opposing team will get two points. Points are added together during the game and the team with the most points at the end of time is declared the winner. If the scores are tied, then two periods of extra time are played to determine the winning team.

Assessment activity 4: Rules, regulations and scoring systems

P Make a list of the key rules and scoring system that would enable some beginners to play a basic game of your two chosen sports. Produce this list in the form of a leaflet or handout that you could give to a new player.

M Explain some of the laws of your chosen sports to your partner. Assume they know absolutely nothing about the game. Use practical explanations and demonstrations where possible, by using a court to show how the laws apply.

D Produce a beginner's guide to playing your chosen sports. Tell the reader the main laws and rules to enable them to play a basic game of both singles and doubles. Comment on how rules are used and applied. This can include players' clothing and equipment, how scores are implemented, and what happens if rules or regulations are broken.

Roles and responsibilities of officials

Two officials control a game of basketball on court: a referee and an umpire. During play, they must work together to control the game. In basketball, events can happen very quickly.

During the match, one official is always in front of the ball while the other official remains behind the ball. When possession of the ball changes, these roles are reversed. Officials should always try to ensure there is a line of sight between them. The official behind the ball (the trailing official) watches the player in possession. The other official watches events 'off the ball'.

Off the court, there are table officials who are responsible for carrying out a number of other duties. These include:
- recording and displaying the score
- recording and displaying fouls committed by individual players or teams
- recording the taking of 'time outs' by team coaches
- checking the game clock is properly monitored, started and stopped, to ensure the game is played for the correct amount of time
- completing the score book, which provides a written record of the game.

Key point

Each coach is allowed a number of one minute breaks called 'time outs'. These breaks allow the coach to bring the team together to give fresh instructions on how the game should proceed.

Let's do it!

Look at the table below, which identifies the different roles and responsibilities of officials for the three sports in this chapter:

Role/Responsibility	Basketball referee	Badminton umpire	Swimming judge
To keep game time	No	N/A	Yes
To record the score	No	Yes	N/A
To call fouls	Yes	Yes	Yes
To discipline players	Yes	Yes	N/A
To maintain a certain fitness level	Yes	No	No
To record player bookings/cautions	No	N/A	N/A
To apply the game rules	Yes	Yes	Yes
To check players' uniforms and dress	Yes	Yes	Yes
To carry a whistle	Yes	No	No
To carry other special equipment	No	Pen, scorebook	Stopwatch
To wear a set uniform	Grey shirt, black trousers and shoes	Smart dress generally worn, e.g. shirt and tie for men	White clothing worn

1. What other criteria could have been used in this table?
2. Make a table of your own, contrasting your two chosen sports.

When looking at the performance of other players, it is important that you choose the most appropriate way of carrying this out. As an observer you will need to look for:

- strengths and weaknesses
- use of various skills
- the techniques used to perform these skills
- the tactics they employ as either an individual or team player.

In addition, you will need to choose a method of displaying your results to your tutor, subject or even your class. This might be a graph, chart, video clip or written observation. You will also need to decide on what you are going to look at – for instance in basketball it might be points scored or assists given to team mates, in swimming it might be technique used for breathing, in cricket it might be where a batsman tends to score his or her runs in a match.

Case study: Matthew

This is an extract from a diary kept by a basketball player called Matthew. He plays for a team called Bourne Bullets in the Peterborough under-16 basketball league. This extract refers to a game he played against a team from Spalding.

Date Sunday 21 September 2003
Venue Bourne Leisure Centre
Event Match v. Spalding Sonics

In this game, we were confident of getting the season off to a good start. We had played Spalding in the last game of the season and had won convincingly. In this game we wanted to do the same. I play point guard for the team and am also the captain. I need to set a good example to the rest of the squad, and lead by example. In training, I have been lacking a consistent 2 point shot. Our coach has told me that I do not follow through with my shooting hand when making a shot. I want to concentrate on improving this.

In defence we began with a 2-1-2 zone to allow us to see what our opponents had to offer. In attack, we began with a traditional 'horseshoe', playing two deep, two high from the basket with me acting as the play maker. During the game I demonstrated the following skills:

- dribbling with both hands
- lay ups
- free throws – six in this game, of which I scored four – a 66% completion rate
- set and jump shots for two points – 14 points from a possible 28 – a 50% success rate
- set shots for three points – I scored two – a 66% success rate

In addition, I was involved in five assists and stole the ball from the opposition four times.

At the start of the game, the opposition played a 2-1-2 zone. To play against this, we played an offence with a strong side and a weak side. This means we had more players on the strong side than there were defenders. This allowed us to use 'give and go' moves and 'back doors' to get a player into their zone to score. Later, they switched to a 'man for man' defence in order to pressure us and steal the ball. This meant switching our attack and using screens to free a player to score.

As a result, we won the game 58–49.

I think my strengths against my opposite number were:

- stronger dribbling skills on my weaker hand
- a higher percentage of free shots scored
- better rebounding both on offence and defence.

My weaknesses were:

- a poorer set shot from outside the key
- a weaker overhead pass
- I was often drawn out of position on defence when playing a zone defence.

I need to improve my ability to use a change of pace or a fake to create space for my offence. At present, defenders are often not tricked by my fakes and dummies. My stamina began to go after about four minutes of the last quarter. I need to carry out more training during practice to improve this.

Assessment activity 5: Looking at your own performance

P Using Matthew's diary extract as an example, maintain a dairy or log book of your two chosen sports, over the period of your BTEC First Sport course. In your diary list your own use of practical skills, techniques and tactics.

M In the diary or log book entries you created in **P** compare your performance, use of different skills, techniques and tactics for your two chosen sports.

M Again, using your dairy or log book entries, analyse your strengths and weakness and give suggestions for improvements or changes to your performance in your chosen sports.

Your diaries or log books could be supported by the following:
- comments from the team coach
- video evidence taken from the side of the court
- discussion with the coach
- a copy of the score sheet from the game.

These comments could be countersigned by your coach or teacher to confirm they agree with them and that they were written at the time indicated.

Racket sports – Badminton

Badminton is an indoor racket sport played either between two players (singles) or four players (doubles). When playing doubles, the pairs can be male, female or mixed. When played at the top level, badminton is a fast and dynamic game and requires a number of different skills.

Skills, techniques and tactics

The game requires a number of basic skills, including:

- Forehand strokes
- Serving
- Backhand strokes
- Footwork
- **Badminton skills**
- Team work (when playing doubles)
- A variety of tactics and strategies
- Racket control

In addition, players need a variety of physical qualities, including high levels of stamina, agility, speed and mobility to cope with the demands of the game.

Tactics and strategies

The tactics and strategies for a singles game and a doubles game are different.

Singles

In singles, you try to make your opponent move every time he or she plays a shot. Use the four corners of the court to make your opponent move as much as possible. If you are serving using a long high serve, try to play down the centre line. That way, your next shot requires less movement on your part. If you decide to serve short, again aim for the centre line.

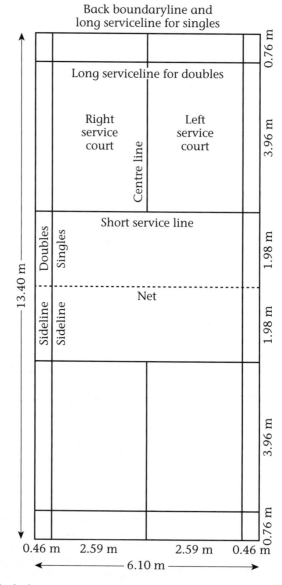

The dimensions of a badminton court

When choosing your tactics, it is important that you consider the following:
- your own strengths and weaknesses
- your opponent's strengths and weaknesses
- previous matches.

There is little to be gained from serving long if your long serve lacks height and distance.

Doubles

In doubles play, the service area is shorter but wider. There is less free space in which to hit the shuttle and so tactics involve moving opponents around to create the free space into which you hit the shuttle. In general, when serving, you should serve short to bring the receiver into the net. If your opponent 'lifts' the shuttle (hits it up), then you and your partner should attack the shuttle (hit it down). You should then adopt positions which put one player in front at the net and the other player behind and in line, covering the rear of the court. This is shown on the diagram below:

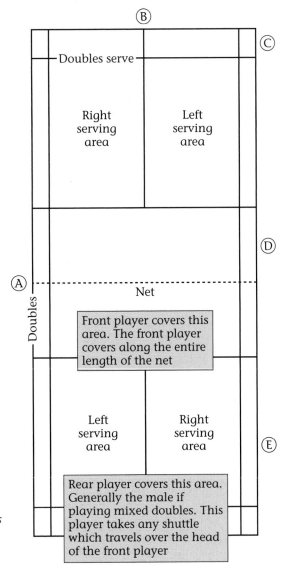

The position of doubles players on a badminton court (front and rear)

If you are forced to 'lift' the shuttle then you are defending and should adopt a side by side formation, as shown below:

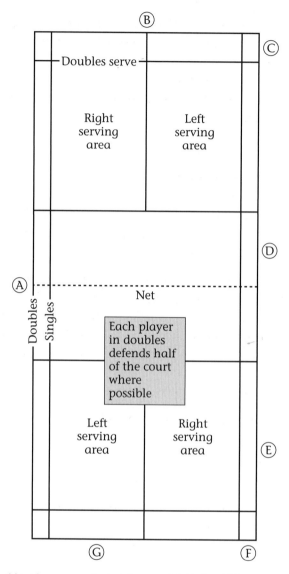

The position of doubles players on a badminton court (side by side)

Doubles tends to be a faster game because the shuttle is being intercepted more frequently.

Rules, regulations and scoring system

The object of the game is to put the shuttle on to the floor on your opponent's side of the net, or to put the shuttle over the net in such a way that your opponent:

- cannot reach the shuttle to return it
- can reach the shuttle but cannot play it back over the net successfully
- hits the shuttle out of the court when trying to return it.

Serving

A badminton court has service areas which are shown in the diagrams on pages 296, 297 and 298.

The badminton court differs for singles and doubles, as shown in the diagrams. The singles service area is often described as 'thin and long', while the doubles service area is described as 'short and fat'.

There are a number of rules attached to serving in badminton, such as:

- the servers feet must not touch any of the lines on the court
- on impact, the shuttle must be below the waist of the server
- on impact, the racket head must be below the hand holding the racket
- the server can only serve when their opponent is ready
- no feinting is allowed
- the receiving player cannot move until the serve is made.

A shuttle landing on a line is deemed to be *in*.

Let's do it!

Visit the World Badminton website at www.heinemann.co.uk/hotlinks to discover more about the rules of the game.

Assessment activity 6: Observational checklist for racket-game athletes

P Choose a variety of shots from your chosen racket game and draw up a table or chart which highlights the key points of each shot. These might include footwork, body position and so on. Discuss your thoughts with your tutor. Watch two sportsmen or women perform these shots and write down your observations using this model. Now look at the same players in a game situation and comment on the tactics and strategies they use. Describe what the players do that is the same and what they do differently in similar game situations. Again, discuss this with your tutor.

M Compare the performances of the two sportspeople by highlighting their strengths and weaknesses, both when playing a variety of shots and in the tactics they use in a game.

D Analyse critically the performances of two players by looking at each player's strengths, weaknesses and tactics. Make a list of things each player performs well or badly, giving your reasons and suggesting how each player might improve his or her play.

Your checklist might look like this:

Shot	Key points	Player observation	Suggestions
The smash	Watch shuttle	Eyes watched shuttle	
	Take shuttle high and early	Racket arm bent on contact	
	Move weight from back to front foot	Little transfer of weight	
	Snap wrist forward on contact	No real follow through	
	Make follow through effective	Stiff wrist throughout shot	
	Hit shuttle sharply down		

The scoring system

Badminton scoring can be confusing! It is important to concentrate on the game, but you also need to remember:
- who is serving
- who won the rally.

The basics are as follows:
- A player can only be awarded a point if they are serving.
- A player receiving the serve, who then wins the rally, can only win back the right to serve – he or she is not awarded a point.
- If you are serving and you win a point, you serve your next point from the adjacent service area – so when your score is an odd number you serve from the left hand service area, and when your score is even, you serve from the right hand service area.
- In a doubles game, both players serve, one after the other, starting with the player in the right hand service area.
- In a doubles game, the pair that serves at the start of the game can only use one player – after this first serve, all players serve.

Roles and responsibilities of officials

Badminton is controlled by an umpire, whose responsibilities include:
- to administer the toss
- to keep and announce the score
- to deal with lets and rule infringements, and any issues concerned with the laws of the game.

A service judge is placed at the net. His or her role is to watch for infringements of the rules of service.

There are various ways of starting the game, for example, a coin may be tossed. Whatever means is used, the winning team has three choices: to choose to serve, to choose to receive (the opposing team serves) or to choose ends.

In badminton, the score zero is referred to as 'love'. When the umpire is ready for the game to begin, he or she calls 'Love all – play'. The umpire always calls the serving player's score first, for instance, 'Five – love'. When one side has finished serving, the umpire calls, 'Service over', followed by the score.

The service judge looks for any infringements of the rules of service (see the rules given under serving on page 299).

In addition to these two officials, there are ten line judges who signal if a shuttle is in or out. The positions of these officials are indicated on the world badminton website at www.heinemann.co.uk/hotlinks.

Line judges are responsible for deciding if a shuttle is 'in' or 'out'. If the shuttle lands on a line, it is regarded as 'in'.

Performance of other players

You can look at a badminton player's performance in various ways, for example:
- movement around the court
- use of, and effectiveness of, forehand and backhand strokes – does she or he score a point?
- rallies won on the player's own serve and his or her opponent's serve.

To help you do this, it is helpful to have a model in your mind of what a particular shot should look like. You can then compare your player's performance against it. Investigate how certain shots should be performed by reading badminton coaching manuals or watching coaching videos.

Key points

You could use a variety of methods to compare players, for example:
- calculating the percentage of serves that win a player points
- timing the length of rallies
- observing the range of shots used
- identifying the tactics and strategies employed.

Let's do it!

Video a match in one of your chosen sports. Draw up a chart and analyse the performance of one player in the game or match, using some of the methods discussed. Produce some charts, tables or other visual displays which allow you to show some analysis of that player's performance.

From this analysis, make some suggestions to the player as to how they could improve. Your chart might look like this:

	No. of forehands	No. of backhands	No. of successful smashes	No. of long serves	No. of short serves	Average length of rally when serving	Basic tactics
Player A	52	35	14	20	10	4	Kept opposing player on back line and then used a drop shot/net shot
Player B	64	15	8	15	15	7	Tried to use opposite corners each time to make opponent move as much as possible

Case study: Badminton log book

This extract is taken from a badminton player's log book. It shows you how you might choose to complete your own.

Date Thursday 8 January 2004
Place school sports hall
Event Match v. Stanground College

During this inter-school match, I was selected to play a singles match over three sets for the school. I had never played my opponent before and so I decided to employ the following tactics:
- serve long to the middle of the court
- engage my opponent in long rallies in an effort to tire my opponent for the second and third sets, since I believe I have a high level of personal fitness.

Match Result I won the match 15-12, 13-15, 15-9

Report

During the first set, I quickly discovered that my opponent had a good smash and net shot. However, his backhand strokes lacked power and distance and his footwork was poor when put under pressure. I decided to change my tactics and varied my serve to make my opponent move as much as possible. This created a number of opportunities to play net shots, as my opponent was unable to control the shuttle sufficiently to keep it low to the net on return. Most of my points came from mistakes made by my opponent.

Match strengths

I returned to the 'T' position well and my serving was reliable and accurate. The distance on my clears was good and my footwork was balanced and sure. My attacking net play was satisfactory but needs to improve in future games. I was stronger on my forehand than my backhand

Match weaknesses

I lacked a strong backhand clear and was unable to cope with shots played onto that side of my game. My short serve was let down by a poor flick serve which hit the net too often. I was unable to keep my opponent moving as much as I wanted. Although this did not cause problems in this game, it may do against other opposition, and needs to be improved.

These comments were written down after talking to my P.E. teacher, who has written a witness statement to go with this diary entry.

Individual sports — Swimming

Swimming is a water-based activity. Other examples of water-based sports are: synchronised swimming, diving (springboard) and water polo. Swimming is controlled by the Amateur Swimming Association (ASA), based in Loughborough.

Skills, techniques and tactics

Swimming is both a team and individual sport. It comprises a variety of disciplines, including the major strokes:
- freestyle (or front crawl)
- backstroke
- breaststroke
- butterfly.

These strokes are swum over a variety of distances. There are also medley relays, where individual swimmers swim each of the four strokes. In addition there are relays of four swimmers, either all swimming freestyle, or each swimming one of the four main strokes. Swimming is not a mixed sport: events are for men or for women.

Skills and techniques

The skills and techniques used in swimming are all designed to allow the swimmer to move through the water as fast as possible and to change direction at the end of each length quickly. At all times, the swimmer is trying to apply as great a force as possible on the water to propel himself or herself forward with the maximum speed. To achieve this, swimmers use specific arm and leg actions designed to allow rapid movement through the water.

The performance of a swimmer can be analysed by breaking the stroke down into:
- the arm action
- the leg action
- the body position
- the breathing sequence
- timing.

Tactics

The techniques used in swimming are less varied than in other sports. Each stroke is governed by a variety of rules, which outline what a swimmer can and cannot do. As a result, the athlete has little opportunity to alter the action used. Similarly, the tactics employed are limited mainly to the pace swum and, in relays, the order the swimmers will swim in. There is no defence and attack to worry about, so there is no concern over defending or attacking formations. Since you swim in your own lane, an important tactic is ensuring that you qualify well from heats to ensure a middle lane draw for swimming finals. This is important, since the middle lanes suffer from less water disturbance during a race.

Another consideration a swimmer must think about is the breathing technique used. If you are in a lane with competitors on both sides then bi-lateral breathing (breathing alternately left and right) is important because it allows you to see where your competitors are. Swimmers may also change when they breathe, for example every stroke, every four strokes, and so on.

Swimming rules and regulations

The basic rules of the sport relate to a number of features, including:
- the start
- turns at the end of each length of the pool
- the stroke itself.

 Key point

> The freestyle swimming stroke is just what is says – the swimmer can swim any stroke they wish as long as it is a recognised stroke. All swimmers swim what we call 'front crawl' because it is the fastest stroke.

The rules vary depending on the stroke concerned. The governing body for swimming in this country is the Amateur Swimming Association and the international Governing Body for world swimming is 'Federation Internationale de Natation'. You can check out both their websites on www.heinemann.co.uk/hotlinks. The rules shown below are set by FINA and apply to competitive swimming from 2003–2005.

THE RACE

SW 10.1   A swimmer swimming over the course alone shall cover the whole distance to qualify.

SW 10.2   A swimmer must finish the race in the same lane in which he or she started.

SW 10.3   In all events, a swimmer when turning shall make physical contact with the end of the pool or course. The turn must be made from the wall, and it is not permitted to take a stride or step from the bottom of the pool.

SW 10.4   Standing on the bottom during freestyle events or during the freestyle portion of medley events shall not disqualify a swimmer, but he or she shall not walk.

SW 10.5   Pulling on the lane rope is not allowed.

SW 10.6	Obstructing another swimmer by swimming across another lane or otherwise interfering shall disqualify the offender. Should the foul be intentional, the referee shall report the matter to the Member promoting the race, and to the Member of the swimmer so offending.
SW 10.7	No swimmer shall be permitted to use or wear any device that may aid his or her speed, buoyancy or endurance during a competition (such as webbed gloves, flippers, fins, etc.). Goggles may be worn.
SW 10.8	Any swimmer not entered in a race, who enters the water in which an event is being conducted before all swimmers therein have completed the race, shall be disqualified from his or her next scheduled race in the meet.
SW 10.9	There shall be four swimmers on each relay team.
SW 10.10	In relay events, the team of a swimmer whose feet lose touch with the starting platform before the preceding team-mate touches the wall shall be disqualified, unless the swimmer in default returns to the original starting point at the wall, but it shall not be necessary to return to the starting platform.
SW 10.11	Any relay team shall be disqualified from a race if a team member, other than the swimmer designated to swim that length, enters the water when the race is being conducted, before all swimmers of all teams have finished the race.
SW 10.12	The members of a relay team and their order of competing must be nominated before the race. Any relay team member may compete in a race only once. The composition of a relay team may be changed between the heats and finals of an event, provided that it is made up from the list of swimmers properly entered by a Member for that event. Failure to swim in the order listed will result in disqualification. Substitutions may be made only in the case of a documented medical emergency.
SW 10.13	Any swimmer having finished his or her race, or his or her distance in a relay event, must leave the pool as soon as possible without obstructing any other swimmer who has not yet finished his or her race. Otherwise the swimmer committing the fault, or his or her relay team, shall be disqualified.
SW 10.14	Should a foul endanger the chance of success of a swimmer, the referee shall have the power to allow him or her to compete in the next heat or, should the foul occur in a final event or in the last heat, he or she may order it to be re-swam.
SW 10.15	No pace-making shall be permitted, nor may any device be used or plan adopted which has that effect.

THE START

The start must comply with the set of rules

SW 4.1	The start in freestyle, breaststroke, butterfly and individual medley races shall be with a dive. On the long whistle (SW 2.1.5) from the referee the swimmers shall step onto the starting platform and remain there. On the starter's command 'take your marks', they shall immediately take up a starting position with at least one foot at the front of the starting platforms. The position of the hands is not relevant. When all swimmers are stationary, the starter shall give the starting signal.
SW 4.2	The start in backstroke and medley relay races shall be from the water. At the referee's first long whistle (SW 2.1.5), the swimmers shall immediately enter the water. At the referee's second long whistle the swimmers shall return without undue delay to the starting position (SW 6.1). When all swimmers have assumed their starting positions, the starter shall give the command 'take your marks'. When all swimmers are stationary, the starter shall give the starting signal.
SW 4.3	In Olympic Games, World Championships and other FINA events the command 'Take your marks' shall be in English and the start shall be by multiple loudspeakers, mounted one at each starting platform.
SW 4.4	Any swimmer starting before the starting signal has been given shall be disqualified. If the starting signal sounds before the disqualification is declared, the race shall continue and the swimmer or swimmers shall be disqualified upon completion of the race. If the disqualification is declared before the starting signal, the signal shall not be given, but the remaining swimmers shall be called back and start again.

Picture	Stroke	Some of the rules
	Freestyle	Freestyle means that the swimmer can swim any style in the race. Some part of the swimmer must touch the wall at the end of each length and when they finish the race.
	Backstroke	Prior to the starting signal, the swimmers shall line up in the water facing the starting end, with both hands holding the starting grips. The feet, including the toes, shall be under the surface of the water. Standing in or on the gutter or bending the toes over the lip of the gutter is prohibited. Upon the finish of the race the swimmer must touch the wall while on the back. The body may be submerged at the touch.
	Breaststroke	All movements of the arms shall be simultaneous and in the same horizontal plane without alternating movement. At each turn and at the finish of the race, the touch shall be made with both hands simultaneously at, above, or below the water level. The head may be submerged after the last arm pull prior to the touch, provided it breaks the surface of the water at some point during the last complete or incomplete cycle preceding the touch.
	Butterfly	Both arms shall be brought forward together over the water and brought backward simultaneously through-out the race. All up and down movements of the legs must be simultaneous. The position of the legs or the feet need not be on the same level, but they shall not alternate in relation to each other. A breaststroke kicking movement is not permitted.

Medley swimming

SW 9.1	In individual medley events, the swimmer covers the four swimming styles in the following order: butterfly, backstroke, breaststroke and freestyle.
SW 9.2	In medley relay events, swimmers will cover the four swimming styles in the following order: backstroke, breaststroke, butterfly and freestyle.
SW 9.3	Each section must be finished in accordance with the rule which applies to the style concerned.

Roles and responsibilities of officials

Swimming competitions take many forms, from club championships to olympic finals. For open meetings, where swimmers enter under their own name, the ASA state that the following is the minimum list of officials required:

- a referee
- a starter
- a check starter
- two placing judges
- two stroke judges
- two turning judges
- a chief timekeeper for each lane
- one timekeeper for each lane
- a male and female competitors steward
- a recorder
- an announcer.

Visit the British Swimming website, at www.heinemann.co.uk/hotlinks, to find out what each offfial does.

Assessment activity 7: Observing officials

Go to the British Swimming website again and find out what the roles and responsiblities of swimming officials are.

P Discuss with a group how the roles and duties of swimming officials and of officials in one of your chosen sports are the same, and how they are different. Record your findings in a chart or table.

M Watch a game of your chosen sport and a swimming competition. Using your chart or table, assess how well the officials did during the game. List the things they did well, and some of the mistakes they made.

D Look at your list of mistakes. How or why do you think they occurred? Here are some possible reasons:

- poor positioning on the court, pitch, etc.
- lack of knowledge of the rules, laws, etc.
- good playing of an advantage, etc.
- different interpretation by officials
- lack of confidence.

Performance of other swimmers

The assessment of a swimmer's performance is relatively simple. You can compare his or her swimming action against an accepted model of a good stroke. A swimming stroke is normally broken down into:

- head position
- arm action
- body position
- breathing
- leg action
- timing of stroke.

Let's do it!

1. The table below provides a general model for an efficient backstroke. Watch someone you know swimming backstroke. In the third column of the table, write your observations of his or her performance. Compare your swimmer's stroke with the model.

Stroke area	Comments	Observation of performer
Head and body position	Almost horizontal, straight and streamlined Back of head in water Head kept still Shoulders roll in a controlled way Chest clear of water Hips and bottom slightly submerged under the water Eyes looking up and forwards slightly	
Feet and legs	In line with body using an alternate kick Feet near to surface but knees under Toes pointed, knees bending slightly Small splash by feet at the surface	
Hands and arms	As hand enters water, elbow is straight, little finger enters first At deepest point, elbow bends and hand presses round and back towards the thigh Thumb leaves water first and arm travels straight and back to the entry point	
Breathing	Regular and naturally in time with the effort made by the arms	
Timing	Should produce a consistent and continuous stroke	

2. Visit the Amateur Swimming Association website at www.heinemann.co.uk/hotlinks to look at the models for the other major strokes.

Recording performance and involvement

If your chosen individual sport is swimming, it is a good idea to ask someone to video you while you swim. You can then replay the video tape and analyse your strengths and weaknesses. Similarly, you can video or observe other swimmers, and assess their performance. It is a good idea to concentrate on one aspect of the stroke at a time, for example, the arm action or leg action. Compare yourself or your subject against a model.

Using statistical information (graphs and charts for example) is sometimes not as easy for individual sports as for team or racket sports. Swimming, for example, is a continuous skill, so the athlete is simply repeating the same action over and over. You might record pace notes for every 25 or 50 metres swum to analyse a performance, or count the number of strokes used to complete each length of the pool. Breathing technique is another area that you could record, for example when and on what side the swimmer breathes.

The type of leg kick used in some strokes can also be analysed. In freestyle, a 'six beat' leg kick is often used (six leg kicks to one left and then right arm pull). In long distance events like the 1500 metre freestyle, the leg kick is almost non existent, as swimmers use their arms and shoulders to do almost all the work. In backstroke and breaststroke, you can analyse the distance travelled under water after each turn, and compare these figures.

Case study: Training diary

This training diary entry records the details of a training session.

Date Sunday 11 January 2004
Location Ponds Forge Swimming Centre
Session Under 16 Advanced Training Session for Front Crawl

Today I did the following training:

Warm up
50m front crawl, 50m backstroke
30 seconds rest followed by:
    25m front crawl – fast
    25m breaststroke – steady
    25m butterfly – fast
    25m backstroke – steady

Main session
20 × 25m front crawl, followed by 25m 'catch up'. In catch up drills, the full stroke is swum but only one arm is working at one time. One arm pulls and 'catches up' the other arm, which then pulls.

Kickboard work
50m kickboard, front crawl.
50m arms only front crawl
10 seconds rest
Repeat for a total distance of 800m

Fin work
400m front crawl (fast) with fins – concentrate on arm action

Warm down
300m front crawl (slow) to warm down
Total distance swum = 2700m

Comment
Felt good throughout the session. Arm action worked well and my coach was happy with the length of my pull. Felt fatigued towards the end of the session but the previous day's weights session was probably to blame. Good advice to keep water on poolside throughout to top up my fluids.

In summary

In this chapter, you have learned the following:

1. Sport requires the performer to make use of a variety of skills and techniques to succeed in particular situations. Skills are learned and require training and practice. There are various types of skills, including individual and team skills.

2. Tactics and strategies are the various ways in which we might play a match or game – they include team formations and individual player positions. It is important to employ a range of tactics and strategies and to be able to change these during a match.

3. You need to be able to assess a player's performance by looking at the skills he or she uses in a game. You can do this using a variety of methods, for example observation, statistical methods such as graphs, or discussion with the coach or player.

4. You need to be able to assess your own performance. This allows you to identify strengths and weaknesses, plan how to improve your performance and play better and more successfully in the future.

CHECK WHAT YOU KNOW!

Look back through this unit to see if you can you answer the following questions:

1 Name four types of skill.
2 Describe and explain one individual skill from a sport of your choice. You should point out the key factors of the skill. Repeat this for a contrasting sport.
3 Describe and explain one team skill from a sport of your choice. Explain the strengths and weaknesses of this team skill. Repeat this for a contrasting sport.
4 Choose a tactic from your chosen sport and explain why it might be employed in a game or match. Explain how an opponent might play against your chosen tactic.
5 Why might you change the tactic employed?
6 Choose three key rules from your chosen sports and explain them to the class.
7 Explain the role of an official from one of your chosen sports.
8 List all the officials required by one of your chosen sports.
9 How might the role of match officials be compared?
10 List five functions of a match official in your chosen sport.

Appendix 1

Health Status Questionnaire

Name _____ **Date**_____

The following questions are designed to ascertain your readiness to participate in the practical physical activities outlined within this chapter. If you answer **YES** to any of the questions outlined below, you should have a thorough medical examination prior to participating in the practical tasks described within the chapter.

1. Have you ever had a heart condition or experienced chest pains or a sensation in your chest associated with exercise?
2. Do you have a family history of heart disease below the age of 55?
3. Have you ever suffered from high or low blood pressure?
4. Are you taking any prescribed medication?
5. Do you suffer from any respiratory problems such as asthma or shortness of breath with minimal exertion?
6. Have you ever had any condition or injury affecting your joints or back that could be aggravated by exercise?
7. Do you suffer from diabetes or epilepsy?
8. Has your GP ever advised you not to participate in exercise?

Now please read the exercise advice below

When undertaking the activities described in this unit start at a slow pace and listen to your body. If you experience any signs of discomfort or stress terminate the activity and seek medical advice as soon as possible.

Index